One in Christ™

# God's Action Plan

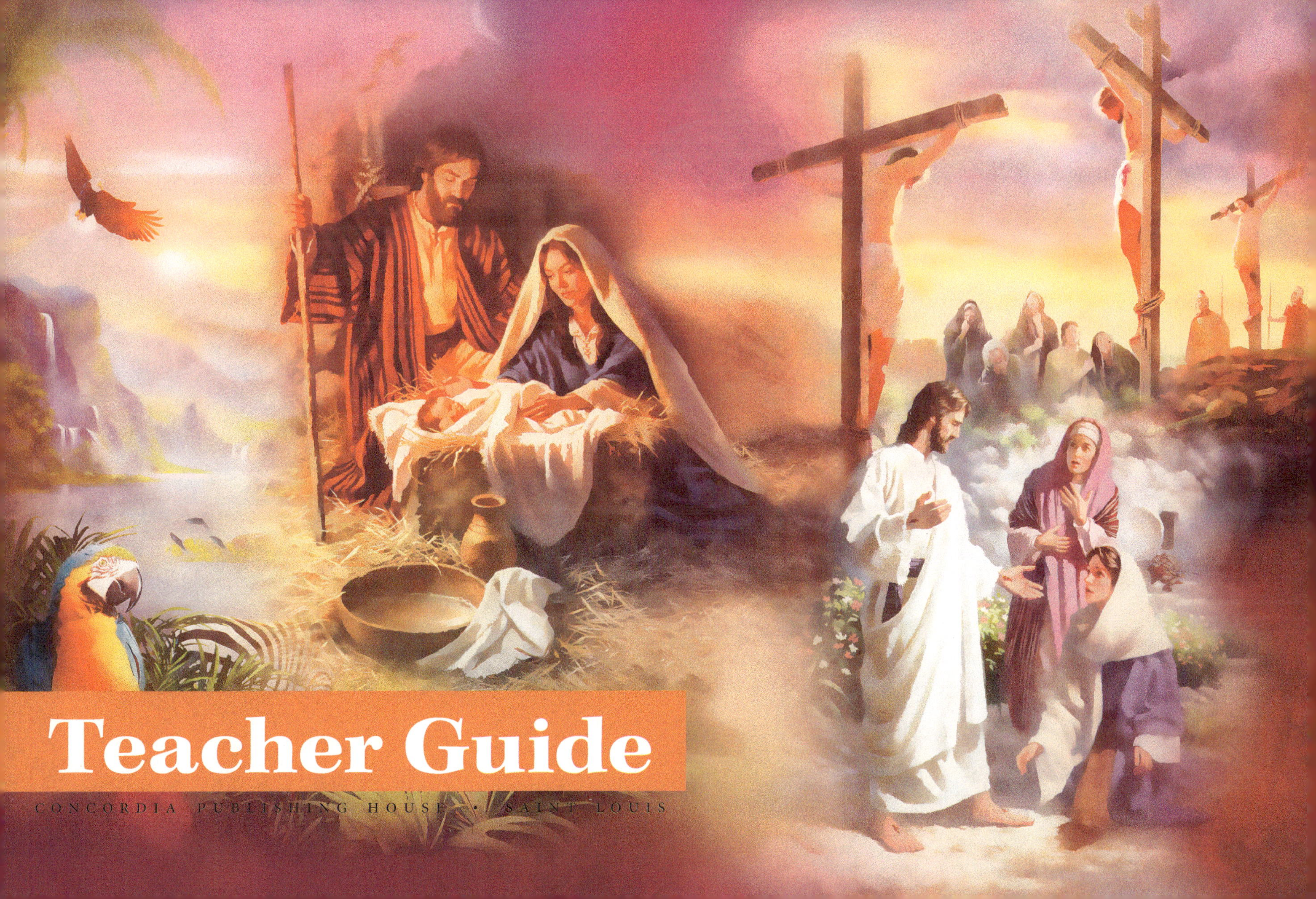

## Teacher Guide

CONCORDIA PUBLISHING HOUSE • SAINT LOUIS

3558 S. Jefferson Ave., St. Louis, MO 63118-3968
1-800-325-3040 • www.cph.org



Writers: Kirstin Genthner, Stephenie Hovland, Julaine Kammrath, Sara Knea, Carrie Kober, Mary Lou Krause, Juanita Krueger, Jill Otte, Karla Roeglin, Annette Skibbe, A. Trevor Sutton, Virginia Terrell, Patricia Thies

Editor: Rodney L. Rathmann

Series editors: Rodney L. Rathmann, Carolyn Bergt, Brenda Trunkhill

Editorial assistant: Amanda G. Lansche



Manufactured in Madison, WI/06576/412183

2 3 4 5 6 7 8 9 10 11 26 25 24 23 22 21 20 19 18 17

# Contents



one God • one Lord • one Savior • one faith • one baptism • one church • one Spirit

Dear Partners in the Faith,

This course contains thirty Bible stories selected from the Old and New Testaments. *God's Action Plan* is revealed in all of Scripture as we read of God at work for the benefit of His people—guiding, preserving, and saving them. As the Old Testament points to the Savior, Jesus Christ, and the New Testament reveals the fulfillment of our salvation in Him, God's action plan continues to unfold according to His grand design.

In 1 Corinthians 1:18, Paul writes, "For the word of the cross is folly to those who are perishing, but to us who are being saved it is the power of God." How wonderful and mysterious are the ways in which God has worked and continues to work in the course of human history.

The greatest marvel of all is the manner in which God chose to save fallen humanity, sending His Son to become one of us so that He might live and die in our place. His resurrection from the dead assures us of the completeness of the victory over sin, death, and all that would lead us to lose saving faith.

In the unfolding of His saving plan for humanity, God has chosen ordinary people—Paul, Augustine, Martin Luther, and contemporary Christians like you and me. As the Holy Spirit works through God's Holy Word, He continues to nurture the saving gift of faith in our hearts and empowers us as we bring the message of forgiveness, new life, and salvation to others.

As a teacher of the Christian faith, you have the unique opportunity to share God's action plan with the young people in your class. God has promised to do wonderful things through you as His Word is witnessed and taught.

You are in our prayers. May God bless your ministry to the young people you teach.

Your partners in ministry,
The Editors

# Introduction

## A Look at Your Role

### You Are a Teacher of the Faith!

God has gifted you with a tremendous privilege. As a teacher of the faith, you have the opportunity to teach the most important truths anyone can ever learn. You can tell the Good News of Jesus, our Savior, who lived, died, and now lives again. He offers us forgiveness for our sins, the chance to begin all over again with the slate wiped clean, and a happy home with Him in heaven. As a teacher of religion, you can show what Jesus means to you in your actions as well as in your words. You can show that you care about each student, genuinely and individually, just as Jesus loves and cares for you. You can handle disappointments and frustrations in ways that show the power of God's Spirit in your life. You can demonstrate what Jesus' forgiveness means to you in your willingness to forgive others.

The challenges of the classroom are many; at times, they may seem overwhelming. We live and teach in a world damaged by sin and its contaminating effects in the lives of our students as well as in our own lives. But the good news is that no one who follows Jesus need ever feel he or she is going it alone. We serve a God "who daily bears us up; God is our salvation" (Psalm 68:19). In His Word, He promises to strengthen and encourage us for the challenges we face. He promises to give our work meaning, our efforts effective outcomes, and our lives joy.

### You Are Part of Something Big!

Before Jesus ascended into heaven, He told His disciples, "Go therefore and make disciples of all nations, baptizing them in the name of the Father and of the Son and of the Holy Spirit, teaching them to observe all that I have commanded you" (Matthew 28:19–20). Christian schools focus on disciple making. They are workshops in Christian living, where discipleship is practiced as lessons are taught, relationships are established, and the issues of everyday life are experienced. This curriculum has been designed to assist those teaching the faith so that through the Word and Spirit of God, people of all ages may

- know the one true God (Father, Son, and Holy Spirit) and the forgiveness and salvation offered through Jesus' death and resurrection;
- come to faith and grow into Christian maturity;
- identify ourselves as members of the Body of Christ, the Church;
- live in joy, contentment, and harmony with God, ourselves, and all others;
- express faith in the worship of God and in the service of God and others;
- value all of God's creation and care for it wisely and well;
- witness their faith in Jesus, their personal Savior and the Savior of all people;
- live in the Christian hope of a new and eternal life in Christ Jesus.

With an emphasis on these goals, the *God's Action Plan* curriculum focuses on Christ. It seeks to assist teachers in providing students with optimal opportunities for growing in their faith and Christian life. By God's grace, those teaching in Lutheran schools join in one voice with the writers, editors, marketers, and others who helped prepare this curriculum in the sentiment of 1 John 1:3: "that which we have seen and heard we proclaim also to you, so that you too may have fellowship with us; and indeed our fellowship is with the Father and with His Son Jesus Christ."

## A Look at Your Students

### You Are a Teacher of Students in the Seventh or Eighth Grade!

What are seventh- and eighth-graders like? Consider the common physical, social, psychological, intellectual, and faith-development characteristics of children between the ages of 13 and 14 listed as follows.

## Physical/Social/ Psychological Characteristics

### Your students will

- know much about the world;
- feel concerned about what other people think of them—especially their peers;
- seek ways to make friends and get along with family and friends;
- desire increasing independence from family;
- demonstrate interest in the opposite sex;
- have anxiety about their personal appearance;
- be preoccupied with self;
- wonder or worry about their bodies' physical changes or lack of physical changes;
- shift moods rapidly;
- be physically awkward at times (especially boys);
- embarrass easily;
- be self-conscious.

## Intellectual Characteristics

### Your students will

- show concern about complex social issues such as world hunger or nuclear war;
- imagine themselves in the place or circumstances of others;
- develop problem-solving strategies;
- think through possible solutions to a problem before reaching a conclusion;
- respect a teacher who says "I don't know" more than a teacher who tries to fake an answer;
- commit themselves to a worthwhile cause in order to experience a sense of self-worth;

- act indifferent to conversations initiated by a teacher because of fear of peer rejection, although they enjoy the teacher's attention;
- enjoy working in small groups and have the skills necessary to do so successfully;
- learn best when the teacher uses a variety of methods.

# Faith-Development Characteristics

## Your students will

- think in the present, not the future (How can I apply this biblical information to my life right now?);
- question their faith;
- make decisions concerning the importance of a faith relationship with God;
- question ideas learned in childhood;
- have difficulty comprehending God's unchanging love for them, which is not dependent on how good or how bad they are;
- show interest in discussing social issues (drugs, divorce, suicide, etc.);
- recognize and point out inconsistencies in the lifestyles and values of people, especially adults;
- need assurance that they are significant to Christ and His Church;
- respond positively to adults who genuinely care for them, try to understand their feelings, and accept them as valuable persons.

No child will display all the characteristics listed. Your students are growing in different areas at different rates. A person who is exceptionally gifted in social skills may have difficulty with intellectual skills. Others may seem intellectually gifted but may lack in spiritual maturity. On certain days, you may observe behaviors that make you question whether any of the attention you have given to your students' spiritual nurturing is making any difference. On these days especially, remember that growing faith and producing the words, actions, and attitudes that evidence the presence of faith are the work of the Holy Spirit. Trust in God's mighty power to work faith and spiritual maturity in the lives of all for whom Jesus died. Hold up your students in prayer, encourage them in the faith, and trust in God to work the results.

*A note about Baptism:* Typically, you will have a number of students in your class who have not been baptized. Perhaps some of your students' parents have questions and concerns about what your church body teaches about Baptism and when, how, and under what circumstances this blessing from God is to be received. In your approach, take care not to leave unbaptized children with feelings of inadequacy or guilt. As Scripture tells, we are saved through faith, and we are brought to faith through God's Word; do not imply that unbaptized children are excluded from the community of faith. However, do not react by simply avoiding Baptism, especially when the topic flows naturally from lesson discussions. Instead, stress the clear teachings of God's Word that Baptism welcomes sinners into the family of God, where they receive Jesus' gifts of forgiveness, life, and salvation; that God desires Baptism for all people; and that Baptism applies the words and promises of God together with water, which connects with the recipient by faith. Also, prayerfully look for opportunities to talk with parents of unbaptized children about Baptism. Many children and their families receive the blessings of Holy Baptism each year through the ministry of Lutheran teachers. Speak readily of the joy of being a baptized Christian and of the joy that those in faith have as they look forward to someday being baptized.

# A Look at *God's Action Plan*

## You Are Teaching a Thirty-Session Survey of the Bible

God's Word reminds us that our faith unites us with Christ just as it unites us with other Christians. Our faith in Jesus makes the Christian classroom a unique and wonderful place, different from any other classroom. Jesus Himself has promised, "For where two or three are gathered in My name, there am I among them" (Matthew 18:20). Classrooms dedicated to Jesus look, feel, and sound unlike all other classrooms. The lessons in *God's Action Plan* do not merely guide and equip the teacher for helping students learn God's Word. They also provide practical, engaging ideas and suggestions for rooting and connecting all that takes place in and extends from the classroom, reaching into the other areas of the curriculum as well as onto the playground, to the playing field, into the home and neighborhood, and ultimately around the world.

Each lesson has been planned and developed so that it may be taught in approximately thirty-five to forty-five minutes. In order to plan and teach these lessons, you will need the ESV Bible (English Standard Version), a Teacher Guide, and Student Books. You will also want to have *Luther's Small Catechism with Explanation* available for quick and easy reference.

These materials have been developed to emphasize biblical stories and themes presented in a chronological sequence. The goal of the materials is to help students grow in their knowledge and understanding of God's Word and to recognize it as a Means of Grace as well as the norm and source for Christian teaching and the source of power and guidance for living the Christian life.

# A Look at the Teacher Guide

## Unit Organization

The lessons included in *God's Action Plan* have been organized into four units. Two of these units contain lessons on stories found in the Old Testament, and two contain lessons dealing with stories from the New Testament.

Music suggestions in the curriculum refer to *Lutheran Service Book (LSB)* and particularly to those hymns recorded in the two sets of CDs called *Hymns of the Month (HOM)* and *Hymns of the Season (HOS).* This will provide an organized and progressing hymnody curriculum. Suggestions are also made for *All God's People Sing! (AGPS),* particularly from the list of fifty songs recorded on the accompanying CD set called *Jesus' People Sing.* Of course, be sure to include other hymns and songs that appropriately fit the lesson theme and give glory to God alone!

## Unit Introduction Pages

The following Teachers Guide features, provided in each two-page unit overview, will assist you in your planning.

**Contents:** This list of the lesson titles in the unit provides the teacher with at-a-glance information about the scope and content of the unit. At the close of the unit, you may want to use some of these titles to assess student learning, asking students to write two or three sentences in answer to several of these questions.

**Theme:** This summarizes the main theme of the unit, while also providing helpful suggestions for emphasizing, applying, and extending unit concepts.

**Worship:** This section provides suggestions for relating your opening devotions with the unit theme.

**Extending Unit Concepts and Integrating the Faith throughout the Curriculum:** These activities will help students apply and extend lesson concepts in their lives. Activities may be selected according to student interest, readiness, and the availability of time and resources.

**Test:** Unit multiple choice and short answer questions are provided at the back of this guide.

# A Look at Teaching the Lesson

## Lesson Overview

The first page of every lesson in the Teachers Guide begins with a section called "Background." This provides additional information for the teacher's own growth and development, while also giving high interest facts that may be helpful in presenting and discussing the lesson.

A special feature is the classroom devotion, which can be read to the class. The life application stories always have a direct relation to the day's theme and can be used as introductions to the lesson itself.

A long sidebar always lists key information for your preparations for the lesson, including the "Central Truth," which is a statement that provides the main theme of the lesson. Each lesson also has three "Objectives." As you review these statements, keep in mind the importance of including Law (God's expectations of us, which remind us of our sinfulness), Gospel (what God has done for us in Christ Jesus to restore us to Himself), and our response (how we respond to the Gospel in the new life God empowers us to live). You may choose to read these statements to students at the beginning of the lesson or refer to them at the lesson's conclusion. Research suggests that students are more likely to achieve lesson objectives if the objectives are clearly identified for them.

There is also a "Materials" list, noting items needed to teach the lesson. "The Basics" (used in each lesson) include the Student Book, an ESV Bible, and a pencil. The "Bible Prep" list is very important. It includes the Bible references students will need throughout the lesson. Post them on the board in advance so students can bookmark these verses before school. This will make the lesson flow more efficiently and it will also "level the playing field" so as not to single out students unfamiliar with using the Bible.

## The Lesson Plan

*God's Action Plan* lessons make use of various technologies to achieve lesson objectives. Included on the second and third pages of each Teacher Guide is a reduction of the two Student Pages and the Reproducible sheet, each with answers included. You will find a lot of the questions and directions given in the Teacher Guide rather than in the Student Book because this series has an emphasis on group discussion and group work. Please note the **red print** as it appears in the Teacher Guide as a reminder to make sure students receive a clear presentation of the Gospel in the teaching of the lesson. The Student Book is not meant to be a workbook where you assign pages; instead, students will use these pages to respond to and to record group interactions.

All lessons follow the same easy-to-teach format of three distinct parts: "Into the Lesson," "Into the Word," and "Into Our Lives." The "Into the Lesson" section is designed to capture students' interest and to delve into the lesson concepts. The "Into the Word" section provides the Bible story or Bible study that supports the theme of the lesson. Finally, the "Into Our Lives" section encourages students to react, or respond to and apply, the concepts they have learned. One reproducible page has been designed for each lesson and is included as the fourth page of each lesson. A copy of each lesson's reproducible with answers provided is also included with each lesson.

These materials have been prepared with the goal of replacing academic activities with more of a focus on reflection, discussion, and application. By God's grace and through the working of His Spirit, your students will experience the oneness in Christ that occurs when God's people gather around His Word in times of study, reflection, and prayer. The goal of those who have prepared these lessons is to help make the portion of the day devoted to the study of God's Word unique and distinctive—the students' favorite time of the school day.

## Student Book

Two facing pages of the Student Book have been dedicated to each lesson. These pages are also reproduced in this Teacher Guide with answers provided for easy teacher reference. The emphasis of these materials on God's Word and discipleship is readily apparent upon a quick review of these pages. All studies of God's Word, life-related activities, and memory verses have been chosen and included with the overall goal of helping students learn more about God's love for them in Jesus Christ.

# A Couple of Special Resources

## The *Faith Alive Bible*

Designed especially for young people, and recently revised for use with One in Christ materials, this ESV Bible is full of features to help readers discover the wonderful messages and promises in God's Word.

- Every word in the Bible is loaded with meaning for everyone, but these 4U boxes will help you understand what certain passages mean FOR YOU personally. Check out the "4U" sections and discover God's Word FOR YOU!
- Cross Connection icons mark verses that point the reader to Jesus' death on the cross and to the forgiveness, life, and salvation Jesus earned for us there.
- Boxes containing Who, What, Where, When, and Why facts about God's Word and the story of our salvation from sin, death, and the devil can be found throughout this Bible to help readers understand and appreciate the real people, places, and life in Bible times!

- Colorful pages throughout the Bible, between testaments, and between books or chapters of the Bible will help and encourage Bible students in their application of God's Word in their lives.
- Information is also provided about the books in each section of the Bible. Each Bible book also has an introduction page to give readers the big picture on the contents of that book: author, date, main themes, and events.
- The back of the *Faith Alive Bible* includes a handy glossary. These pages will help readers learn the meanings of words they may not know in the Bible.
- Timelines and maps will enrich and inform students' study. The events recorded in God's Word are real. Timelines provide a visual history of God's unfolding plan of salvation. Colorful maps help readers pinpoint where these events took place and where those locations are found in the world today.

## *Concordia's Complete Bible Handbook for Students*

Developed as a companion book to the *Faith Alive Bible*, this handy, insightful, and interesting resource will help both new and experienced Bible students grow in their understand of the purpose, history, and contents of the Bible. Colorful sidebars will inform those looking for background information, while deepening their understanding about life and conditions in Bible times. More important, this handbook will help Bible students connect the central theme of God's plan to save all people through the sending of His Son to those living in any period of human history with the ultimate goal of helping students apply God's Word to the joys and challenges of their daily lives.

# Unit 1—God's Grace to His People in Ancient Times

## Theme

The first unit of *God's Action Plan* deals with God and the relationship He established with the earliest people. Beginning with the account of creation and the fall into sin; continuing with the great flood; and extending through Abraham to the call of Moses, the exodus, and the giving the Law, we will see how God shows Himself always about the business of rescuing and providing for His people. Throughout our reading and discussing of these earliest sections of God's Word, we will see God first giving and then later reinforcing and setting the stage for the fulfillment of His promise to provide a Savior to pay for human sin.

As you begin this school year, let the theme of unit 1 set the tone for your classroom and for the relationships you build with your students. Through the words you speak, the things you do, and the attitudes you project, help your students to know and become curious about the God you serve and the Savior to whom your school is dedicated. We have a mighty God who never ceases to love and provide for us and for all people. He demonstrated the extent of His love when He sent His Son to save us from our sins and to earn, for us all, an eternal home in heaven. Help your students to satisfy their curiosity and desire to know more about their God and Savior by encouraging them in their study of God's Word in establishing and maintaining an active devotional life.

### Unit 1

1. Creation and Fall
2. The Great Flood
3. God's Promise to Abram
4. The Offering of Isaac
5. The Call of Moses
6. The Exodus
7. The Ten Commandments
8. The Serpent on the Pole

## Worship

Each lesson in this curriculum has a classroom devotion that teachers may read to students during the opening of your day. (The devotion always has a direct connection to the day's Bible lesson. If you already have an established plan for opening devotions, you can still use the one suggested in the Teacher Guide as an introduction to the lesson.) It is suggested that your devotions this month close with the words of Martin Luther's Morning Prayer. (It can be found in *Lutheran Service Book* [*LSB*], the *Faith Alive* Bible, *Luther's Small Catechism with Explanation*, and several other sources.) You will probably notice that, through frequent use, most students will know the prayer by memory by the end of the month. (Putting the prayer to use is a much more effective means for memorization than as an assignment.) Though you can feel free to choose a variety of hymns and songs, suggestions will be made mostly from the *LSB* hymnal and the songbook *All God's People Sing! (AGPS)*. It will always be noted if the hymns are on the recorded set of *Hymns of the Month* (*HOM*) or *Hymns of the Season* (*HOS*), available from Concordia Publishing House (CPH), which will give students a good background in Christian hymnody and will also help them to more readily participate in church worship services. Note that the CPH recording *Jesus' People Sing! (JPS)* consists of fifty songs, all from *AGPS*.

# Extending Unit Concepts

## Community Building

*Whose Favorites?:* Have each student compose a list of their favorites, including (but not limited to) season, fruit, vegetable, animal, bird, fish (all God's creations). Collect the papers, mix them up, and read them one at a time. Let students guess to whom each list belongs. Comment on the individuality of each of God's children.

*Zoo!:* Divide students into two teams, one with tags of some sort, one without. Each team should have an elected "keeper." Players on each team are divided equally as cows, chickens, pigs, and donkeys. Establish the goal or similar area at the end of each court as each team's "pen." Have animals run randomly about the play area. At the sound of a whistle, all students must stop and remain where they are but begin to make the sound of their animal. The "keepers" are now instructed to locate their animals and lead them, one at a time, back to the pen. The "animal" remains silent once in the pen. The first team to be collected and silent in the pen wins. (Now we know what it might have been like for Noah.) All animals and keepers should relax with a treat.

*Dominoes:* Give students at least twenty dominoes each and instruct them to create a design by standing them close together on end. After observing the designs, have them gently push one of the end dominoes so that they all collapse. Discuss examples of how one sin leads to another in the lives of God's Old Testament people as well as in our own lives.

## Tools for Witness

- *Room-Size Solar System:* Cover the ceiling with black plastic. Divide students into three groups: planets, moons, and stars. Have students make and hang models of planets, moons, and stars. Use materials such as beach balls, balloons, tennis balls, and aluminum foil. Cut and hang a star shape for each student. Read Psalm 8. Have students each give a reason why each student is a "star."
- Have each student create a collage depicting an emotion or feeling that might have been experienced by Adam and Eve, Noah, Moses, Aaron, God, Joshua and Caleb, or others from this unit. Hold up each finished collage and have the class identify the emotion portrayed. Have artists tell when and by whom they think this emotion might have been felt.
- Have students make clay models of the two tables of the Law, the ark of the covenant, or the tabernacle and its furnishings.

## Service Projects

- *Keep God's World Beautiful:* Encourage students to become involved in environmental cleanup projects. Collect and recycle aluminum cans and other items. Money raised can be used to buy and plant trees or for other environmental projects.

## Reaching Every Individual

- *Learning Groups:* Provide opportunities for students to work in groups not only to learn together but also to support and encourage one another in prayer and fellowship.
- *Remembering Prominent Characters:* Prepare a poster for each of the major Bible characters discussed in this unit. On each poster, include pertinent information about the individual's life.
- Equip students to lead one another; train students for and implement a peer tutoring program.
- Write out and post each of the Ten Commandments. Throughout this unit, discuss biblical narratives relating to each.
- The "Father Abraham" action songs target physical and musical modalities. Students could be invited to compose additional or enriched versions of such songs. Schedule an opportunity to teach these songs to younger children.

# Integrating the Faith throughout the Curriculum

## Social Studies

- Study the tropical climate ecological system, and research its flora and fauna.
- Explore why the Garden of Eden had a tropical climate.
- Look through the newspaper and list the different crimes reported. Match each with the command(s) broken. Discuss crime and consequences in class.

## Science

- Observe and record the kinds of birds that frequent a bird feeder.
- Create a nature trail, making labels identifying varieties of trees and plants.
- Investigate the challenges of desert nomads in Bible times.
- Report on poisonous snakes common in the Middle East today.

## Mathematics

- Watch a program on TV. Count the number of offenses against one of the commandments. Combine class findings and graph the collective data.
- Calculate the approximate number of miles from Egypt to the land of Canaan.
- List leading teen temptations. Vote on the most common, most difficult to defeat, and so on. Poll the class and graph the findings.

## Technology

- Create group videos, slide shows, or photo displays on the topic of God's creation.
- Use the Internet to research an animal or other topic from nature and tell how it illustrates divine creation.
- Conduct an Internet investigation of the Sinai Desert.

## Fine Arts

- Create a diorama or wall mural of a tropical rain forest or the Garden of Eden.
- Prepare and share a tropical fruit salad or drink.
- List and describe common road signs. Use the same shapes, colors, and wording to create new signs that provide directions as we travel our road with Jesus (e.g., DO NOT ENTER into sin).

## Language Arts

- Read a variety of "creation stories" common in various cultures. Although these may not be true to the biblical account, they all testify to a belief in creation. See also the Babylonian and Assyrian epics of creation.
- Write a poem in celebration of God's creation.
- Write a list of personal sins of rebellion. Compose a repentance prayer. Ask for God's forgiveness and help in overcoming these temptations. Tear up the sin list and throw it away.

## Bringing It Home

- Ask students to interview their parents, grandparents, or relatives to find out how God led them to become Christians and members of God's family tree. Based on the interview findings, have the students write prayers of thanksgiving for God's guidance and grace or prayers of petition for God to bring unbelieving relatives into His family.

# Creation and Fall

## GENESIS 1–3

## Background

Christianity is being attacked at every angle, but it seems that many who oppose belief in the triune God begin their argument with a rebuke of the creation account. Atheists and evolutionists spend much time and energy ridiculing those who believe in creation and the existence of God. Some regard God as an outdated notion, a fable, or myth for childhood, like Santa Claus. Those who believe in God and trust in Him for salvation are pigeonholed as uneducated, ignorant, misguided, or all three.

Second-century Stoic philosopher and Roman emperor Marcus Aurelius summed up the perspective of many living today when he said: "Live a good life. If there are gods and they are just, then they will not care how devout you have been, but will welcome you based on the virtues you have lived by. If there are gods, but unjust, then you should not want to worship them. If there are no gods, then you will be gone, but will have lived a noble life that will live on in the memories of your loved ones."

In this kind of world, youth may be tempted to doubt some aspects of Scripture, which gives clear information about the person and work of almighty God, of the natural human condition, and of the only way to salvation—by grace through faith in Jesus. As they yield to the power of the Holy Spirit, we pray that all assembled in your classroom this year *will* believe the Word of God—passages such as John 1:3: "All things were made through Him (God), and without Him was not any thing made that was made."

## Central Truth

God, the giver of life and all things, shows that He wants only what is best for us by re-creating us in Jesus.

## Objectives

- Acknowledge our triune God as the maker and preserver of the universe and all it contains.
- Explain the history of human sin from Adam and Eve to the world of today and, confessing our sins, express confident trust in Jesus and rejoice in the forgiveness He came to provide.
- Express a desire to resist temptation by the power of the Spirit and to honor God in wise management of all He has given us.

## Materials

- The Basics
- Reproducible 1

## Bible Prep

Post in advance so students can bookmark references before class time.

- Genesis 1–3
- James 1:15
- Romans 7:15–20
- 1 John 1:8
- John 3:18

## Devotion

"Steve go to church? I don't think so!" joked Denny.

"Hey, I am a dedicated Christian," Steve defended himself. "I have even read through the Bible twice."

"Really?" James exclaimed.

"I don't think I could read through the whole Bible. The Old Testament is just too boring," Denny added.

"Actually, the Old Testament is really interesting if you just keep with it. It tells of some pretty amazing stuff," Steve said.

Jenny joined into the conversation. "I actually love reading the Old Testament. God did some wonderful things in the lives of people back then."

"The Old Testament just scares me, because it's full of God's laws and wrath," said James.

Steve answered, "That is what most people think, but if you really let yourself read it, you will see God's forgiveness and grace throughout the whole Old Testament."

"Just in the first few chapters of Genesis, God gives us the gift of creation. Man messes it up, and then God gives us a way out through the promise of a Savior. That pretty much sums up the way God deals with us on an everyday basis," said Jenny.

At times, we may feel like James and Denny when we think about the Old Testament, which does contain many facts and details, laws, and accounts of God's wrath. But by God's grace, we can also see the Old Testament as Steve and Jenny do: as God's very Word that reveals His majesty, His unchanging ways, and the way He deals with His people using both Law and Grace—the Old Testament that shows sinners and saints; and the Old Testament that points the way to our Savior, Jesus Christ.

**PRAY: Dear Lord, we praise You for Your Word. We ask that You would be with us as we study Your Word today. Help us to see You and Your plan for our salvation clearly. In Jesus' name we pray. Amen.**

Read 2 Timothy 3:16–17. Sing together "Open Our Eyes" (*AGPS* 195; *JPS* CD 2, track 10).

# INTO the lesson

## In the Dark

Read the introduction together. Discuss the false viewpoints of the secular world. Under the "Bad News" heading, have students write specific problems and dangers involved with each belief. Below is some additional information for each topic.

*Evolution*: Evolution is presented in two different ways—small, observable changes (natural selection, speciation, adaptation) and large, unobservable changes (molecules-to-man evolution). Since evidence supports some aspects of natural selection, many scientists conclude that the second type of evolution took place as well.

Bad News: Say, **"Evolution and other attempts to explain life apart from faith have led to horrible, murderous, and even genocidal practices. Modern theories of eugenics and racial superiority—based on evolutionary ideas—contributed in shocking ways to the debasement and destruction of human life in the nineteenth and twentieth centuries"** (*The Lutheran Study Bible*, p. 10)**.**

*Sinlessness*: Postmodernism thinking in today's culture does not accept absolute truth. ("What is right for you may not be right for me.") This even sneaks into some Christians' mind-sets when talking about big issues such as abortion or gay unions. ("I do not think it is right, but I cannot tell someone they should not do it.")

Bad News: Say, **If someone does not believe in sin or believes they have the power to be sin-free, they see no need for Jesus as their Savior. Making up a personal code of right and wrong brings chaos and confusion to the world. With this way of thinking, basic laws soon will be abolished, including those related to life issues of abortion and euthanasia.** Look up the following Bible verses: James 1:15; Romans 7:15–20; and 1 John 1:8.

*Earning heaven*: Many even say heaven and hell do not exist. Those who do believe in heaven may not believe God would let anyone go to hell. All religions, other than true Christianity, believe you must do something to earn your own salvation.

Bad News: Say, **The ultimate bad news for those in the dark is eternal damnation. All that the devil and the world want us to believe ultimately lead us away from our faith in Christ and the salvation He brings.** See John 3:18.

## Review

Match the words to their definitions.

1 Genesis 1–3

### Creation and Fall

**In the Dark**

If someone does not have a clue, or if people do not seem to know anything on a subject, then we say they are "in the dark." Conversely, if someone suddenly gets it, sees the truth, or finds an answer, we say "a light comes on." We find many people who are in the dark when it comes to creation, the fall into sin, and God's redemptive plan. Investigate the following false ideas and theories.

**Darkness**

Evolution—the widely held belief that through "natural selection" organisms became more complex and enhanced. Finally, man evolved from an apelike creature. Although introduced as a theory, many scientists teach evolution as a fact.

BAD NEWS: **Answers will vary.**

Sinlessness—belief that we are born innocent. If there is sin, we learn it from others. Or something is wrong only if it hurts someone else. Or, we can make decisions by what feels right or is in line with what society thinks.

BAD NEWS: **Answers will vary.**

Earning heaven—belief that if you work hard to do good and are basically a good person, you will go to heaven. Or, as long as you believe in *something*, you will go to heaven after you die.

BAD NEWS: **Answers will vary.**

**Review**

Match each word to the phrase that best describes it.

Redemption — c
Evolution — b
Natural Selection — a

a. theory that states weaker species die out while stronger species evolve into stronger, more complex species

b. theory that states all living things evolved from a single organism

c. deliverance from sin, salvation

4

# INTO the Word

## In the Light

Read through the creation account in Genesis 1. *Option:* Divide students into six groups. They are to show what happened on the day that is assigned to the group. This can be done through drawing a sketch, acting out the scene, or finding objects to represent the creation. Fill in the information under the subheadings. Under "Good News," have students write what good news there is for those who believe in creation, sin, and salvation.

## Creation

Discuss the importance of creation being six literal days. Doubters try to say this did not happen because they cannot believe in a God this great. To say it could not happen in a week is to discredit God and His power.

Have students tell what God created on each day: Day 1—light. Day 2—expanse between sky and earth. Day 3—land, oceans, vegetation. Day 4—sun, moon, and stars. Day 5—water animals; birds. Day 6—land animals; man.

Discuss the importance of God creating through speaking. We should not think of God's abilities as we think of our own. His ways are beyond our understanding. His power is so great that all He has to do is speak, and it is done.

Good News*:* Say, **The creation account shows that the world and ev-**

### In the Light

We have heard the lies Satan puts in our path. We now turn on the light and read God's Word. Shed some light on the false beliefs of the world.

**Light**

CREATION

1. God created the world in six days. He set the seventh day aside to rest. As you look at the things God created on each day, which day's creation amazes you most? ________ Why? **Answers will vary.**
2. God uses repetition to show how He created everything. How did God create? "And God **said**." Genesis 1:3, 6, 9, 11, 14, 20, 24, 26. "And it was **so**." Why is this also important? **God only had to speak and it was done. There was no need for animals, plants, or man to evolve from other organisms. God is powerful enough to create by His word.**

GOOD NEWS: **Answers will vary.**

THE FALL

1. Read Genesis 2:15–17. What was the command God gave Adam and Eve? **Do not eat of the tree of the knowledge of good and evil.**

   What would happen if they disobeyed? **You shall surely die.**
2. Read Genesis 3:1–5. Satan used God as the enemy in his temptation. He convinced Eve that God was holding back something good from her. According to Satan, what would happen if Eve ate of the fruit from the tree of the knowledge of good and evil? **Her eyes would be opened and she would be like God.**

GOOD NEWS: **Answers will vary.**

REDEMPTION

1. Read Genesis 3:8–13. How did the relationship between man and God change? **They were afraid of Him.**
2. Read Genesis 3:14–15. God shows how He is going to defeat sin, death, and Satan in these verses. Who is the offspring that will be in conflict with Satan? **Jesus** What will He do to Satan? **Bruise his head**
3. Read Genesis 3:16–19. What are some of the consequences of the first sin? **Pain in childbearing, husband rules over his wife, pain and toil in living, physical death—returning to the dust of the earth**
4. Read Genesis 3:20–24. God shows His continued care and provision for man after the fall. How did God take care of Adam and Eve after they sinned? **Made clothes for them, protected them from the tree of life by sending them out of the garden**

GOOD NEWS: **God promises a Savior who would earn eternal life for us.**

**REMEMBER**

The people dwelling in darkness have seen a great light.

Matthew 4:16

5

**erything in it belongs to God. He is the Maker, Ruler, and Judge. When we acknowledge this fact, then we live our lives for Him. It changes the way we use our bodies, because they are His. It changes the way we use our time, because it is His. It changes the way we use our resources, because they are His. Think about the comfort we have because we know that such a powerful God is in control of everything.**

## The Fall

**1.** God sets up the Law and also gives the consequence for breaking the Law. Discuss the good news of believing in sin: We realize that we cannot save ourselves; we need a Savior.

### Sin: From the Garden to Today

Sin is devastating. Sin brings death, sadness, conflict, and many other negative results. Its devastation was first felt in the Garden of Eden, and we continue to feel it today. Read and discuss the following stories to see how sin affects everyday life. Decide if the sin in the following situations is by **others, self,** or the **natural consequences of sin** (not specifically brought on by an individual's actions, but happens just because there is sin in the world). Then look up the Bible references to identify an example of the kinds of help God provides.

1) Nolan wishes he could get control of his temper. It just seems like everything makes him angry. It seems like every interaction with a friend or family member ends up with him getting mad. Now he feels all alone. Not too many people want to be around him.

Sin by **self**

God provides **power to change his lifestyle** (Ephesians 4:31–32, Galatians 5:22–23).

2) Ava does not want to go to school tomorrow. Everyone stares at her and is whispering about her. She thought Morgan was her friend. Why did Morgan spread rumors about her to everyone?

Sin by **others**

God provides **guidance for a Christian lifestyle** (Proverbs 12:18–22).

3) Jack has a four-day suspension and has been kicked off Student Council for pulling a prank in P.E. class. He is in even more trouble at home.

Sin by **self**

God provides **forgiveness for repentant sinners** (Psalm 51:10–12).

4) Mary cannot stop crying, her best friend, Jenny, was in an accident this weekend. She did not survive. It is not fair. Jenny had her whole life ahead of her.

Sin by **natural consequences**

God provides **comfort** (Matthew 5:4, Revelation 21:4).

5) Luke has cerebral palsy. He has to use a wheelchair. He often is depressed because he can't play basketball and baseball, his two favorite sports.

Sin by **natural consequences**

God provides **power to endure difficult circumstances** (Psalm 139:13–16, James 1:2).

Although at times it does not feel like it, God is always present in our lives. He is ready to help us fight the temptation of sin, forgive us when we mess up, and give comfort and healing to us as we experience the effects of sin. How can God help each person in the situations above? Ultimately, His plan of salvation is the final cure for the tragedy of sin.



**2.** Ask students to read Genesis 3:6–7. **What were the three reasons Eve decided to eat the fruit?** (It was good for food, a delight to the eyes, and was desired to make one wise.) **What happened after Adam and Eve ate the fruit?** (Their eyes were opened; they knew they were naked.) Distribute copies of **Reproducible 1** to explore further the concept of sin and its consequences.

Say, **We often think we know what is best for us by our own feelings, logic, or reasoning.**

Good News: Say, **What good news can there be about sin? The good news is that when we acknowledge our sin and confess that sin, then we are forgiven. If we know we are sinners, then we know that we are in need of a Savior.**

## Redemption

**1.** Because of sin, our relationship with God is broken. After the fall, Adam and Eve became ashamed because of their sin.

**2.** God gives the promise of Jesus here. Christ would come to restore the broken relationship that sin has caused.

**3.** Although we have the promise of eternal life through Christ, we continue to suffer the natural consequences of sin each day.

**4.** God shows that He not only cares about our eternal salvation, but He also cares deeply about our lives here on earth.

Good News: Say, **God lays out the plan of our salvation. He gives us the promise of a Savior. Because we believe in Jesus Christ as our Savior, we will have eternal life. What wonderful news it is to know that God has done all the work. Our salvation is fulfilled in Christ.**

# INTO our lives

## Living in the Light

Discuss how evolution is being taught in public schools and colleges. Science centers and displays often show evolution in their presentations. Media messages are full of false teachings about sin and redemption. Brainstorm. God's Word and prayer are the most powerful weapons. Talk about ways we can help one another remain faithful. Be creative. Think of individual ways or a class project that shows the truth to others.

# Sin: From the Garden to Today

Sin is devastating. Sin brings death, sadness, conflict, and many other negative results. Its devastation was first felt in the Garden of Eden, and we continue to feel it today. Read and discuss the following stories to see how sin affects everyday life. Decide if the sin in the following situations is by **others, self**, or the **natural consequences of sin** (not specifically brought on by an individual's actions, but that happens just because there is sin in the world). Then look up the Bible references to identify an example of the kinds of help God provides.

1. Nolan wishes he could get control of his temper. It just seems like everything makes him angry. It seems like every interaction with a friend or family member ends up with him getting mad. Now he feels all alone. Not too many people want to be around him.

   Sin by ______________________________

   God provides ______________________________________________ (Ephesians 4:31–32; Galatians 5:22–23).

2. Ava does not want to go to school tomorrow. Everyone stares at her and is whispering about her. She thought Morgan was her friend. Why did Morgan spread rumors about her to everyone?

   Sin by ______________________________

   God provides ______________________________________________ (Proverbs 12:18–22).

3. Jack has a four-day suspension and has been kicked off Student Council for pulling a prank in P.E. class. He is in even more trouble at home.

   Sin by ______________________________

   God provides ______________________________________________ (Psalm 51:10–12).

4. Mary cannot stop crying. Her best friend, Jenny, was in an accident this weekend. She did not survive. It is not fair. Jenny had her whole life ahead of her.

   Sin by ______________________________

   God provides ______________________________________________ (Matthew 5:4; Revelation 21:4).

5. Luke has cerebral palsy. He has to use a wheelchair. He often is depressed because he can't play basketball and baseball, his two favorite sports.

   Sin by ______________________________

   God provides ______________________________________________ (Psalm 139:13–16; James 1:2).

Although at times it does not feel like it, God is always present in our lives. He is ready to help us fight the temptation of sin, forgive us when we mess up, and give comfort and healing to us as we experience the effects of sin. How can God help each person in the situations above? Ultimately, His plan of salvation is the final cure for the tragedy of sin.

# The Great Flood

## GENESIS 6–9

## Background

The great flood is a favorite biblical account for atheists to attack. How could something of this magnitude really happen?

Through faith, we believe in this biblical account showing God's power, presence, wisdom, and mercy. There is also scientific support for the flood. One piece of evidence is polystrate fossils. These fossils have been found all over the world. A polystrate fossil is a fossil tree that is buried upright. Very few of them have roots. This suggests that it did not grow where it was buried, but rather was uprooted and redeposited. More convincing evidence is the discovery of whale fossils in the middle of a continent. One was found in Michigan; one near Lampo, California; and another was found in the Montreal-Quebec area. Other marine fossils have been found in mountains all over the world.

Geologists have also found animals of all kinds buried together at the same depth, which suggests that they were buried by the same catastrophe at the same time. Other evidence of a worldwide flood includes massive sedimentation, random order of fossils, massive volcanism, and significant past global changes in temperature.

Geology points to the reality of a global flood, but skeptics abound. And only through the Holy Spirit and through the eyes of faith can a person believe. The rich man being tormented in hell said, "'Father Abraham, but if someone goes to them (his family) from the dead, they will repent.' He (Jesus) said to him, 'If they do not hear Moses and the Prophets, neither will they be convinced if someone should rise from the dead'" (Luke 16:27–31).

## Central Truth

Because God is holy, He cannot tolerate sin; because He is loving and faithful, He saves His people.

## Objectives

- Recount the events leading up to, during, and following the flood.
- Repent of their sins and express gratitude for the salvation that is theirs in Jesus.
- Relate the flood to Baptism.

## Materials

- The Basics
- Reproducible 2

## Bible Prep

Post in advance so students can bookmark references before class time.

- Genesis 6–9
- Ephesians 4:29–32
- Psalm 101:7
- Colossians 3:12–14

## Devotion

"I finally am going to just tell everybody," Chris said.

"Tell everybody what?" asked Jenna.

"I've talked to a lot of people. I've gone to Web sites. I even talked to a minister at a counseling center," continued Chris.

"About what?"

"It's just who I am. I was born this way. People should not condemn me. It's now accepted."

"Can you just tell me what you are talking about?"

"I am gay, and it's okay," Chris finally said.

"Oh, Chris, but it is not okay. God's Word definitely says it is not okay. I know it is very difficult for you, but we are supposed to fight against sin and temptation. The world and Satan want you to take the easy way out and just give in," Jenna tried to explain.

"I am just so confused. When I listen to TV and popular stars, I feel like I should just go ahead with this choice, but then there is always this knot in my stomach. I thought if I just told everyone, I'd feel better." Chris looked sad.

"The reason you have that uneasy feeling is because you know in your heart that this is a sinful lifestyle. You need to start looking for godly answers. Have you talked to Pastor Rick? He would understand and give you great advice," said Jenna.

"Thanks, Jenna, maybe I will do that."

"I will be praying for you!" Jenna walked over and gave Chris a hug. "Now go see if Pastor Rick is in his office!"

Just like Chris, you may be struggling with some tough sins. Satan wants you to believe the lie that they are not sins. If we listen to the world, we might make decisions that feel good at the time. The truth about sin is that it never is the best thing for you. The end result is always damaging. When we listen to God and His Word, we live in the truth. God gives us forgiveness of sins and help in times of temptation. No one said that fighting against sin would be easy. By God's grace through Christ's death on the cross, we are able to be renewed each day to try once again.

**PRAY: Lord, there are so many messages out there. Sometimes it's hard to know what to do. Show me Your truth. Help me walk in Your ways. Forgive me when I mess up. In Jesus' name. Amen.**

Read 1 Corinthians 10:13. Sing "Forgive Our Sins as We Forgive" (*AGPS* 96).

# INTO the lesson

Say, **When we hear about Noah and the ark, images of cute animals getting on a large boat may come to mind. It is one of the favorite stories of preschool children. Today we are going to look deeper into the story of the flood.**

## This Is Serious . . .

Discuss the listed sins. Depending on experience, the sins could fall into any of the three categories. How are some of the sins portrayed in movies, TV, and other media? How does the class view each sin?

Say, **The worldview around us affects our way of thinking, whether we realize it or not. It is important always to go back to God's Word when making judgments about sin. He clearly shows us how we are to live our lives.**

## What Does God Think?

God shows us many times in the Bible how serious sin is. He does not just sit back and let it slide. He fully hates sin and its damaging effects. We are separated from God because of our sin. If time permits, read and discuss the verses.

Matthew 18:6—God holds us accountable for guiding others down the wrong path.

Matthew 18:8–9—God tells us that it would be better to lose a body part than to sin.

John 8:24—The final result of sin is death.

Isaiah 59:2—Sin has separated us from God. **It is only through Christ that this barrier of separation between God and us is removed.**

Hebrews 13:4—God often mentions the sin of sexual immorality. He will judge this sin harshly. Read together Genesis 6:1–17. As you review the questions, stress that all mankind, with the exception of Noah, fully embraced sin and were unrepentant. God did not take this lightly.

1. What was happening before the flood? (Believers were marrying godless unbelievers, wickedness prevailed, man's heart was evil, and violence and corruption existed.)
2. How did the Lord feel about what was going on? (He was sorry He made man.)
3. What action did God take? (He destroyed man, animals, creeping things, and birds; He brought a flood to destroy all flesh.)

Say, **If we realize how very serious and extreme sin is, then we can better see how very serious and extreme God's forgiveness is.** Distribute **Reproducible 2.**

## Review

Find synonyms for the words *sin* and *covenant.*

2 Genesis 6–9

### The Great Flood

**This Is Serious . . .**

Sin. Transgressions. Iniquities. It is some serious business when we do not measure up to God's Law. But if we stop and think about it, sin is often downplayed. Into which category do the following sins fall?

SIN

| Who thinks it is wrong? | Almost Everyone | Some People | Almost Nobody |
|---|---|---|---|
| Thoughts, Words, or Actions | | | |

| | | | |
|---|---|---|---|
| Murder | Robbing a bank | Gossiping | Gambling |
| Abortion | Taking illegal substances | Lying | Overspending |
| Euthanasia | Overdrinking | Telling a white lie | Hatred |
| Taking a few supplies from work | Overeating | Living together before marriage | Pride |
| Taking a dollar from a family member | Texting OMG | Homosexuality | Jealousy |
| | Cursing | Pornography | Envy |

**What Does God Think?**

Read Genesis 6:1–17. Describe God's attitude toward sin as evidenced in the account of the flood.

**Review**

Write three synonyms for the word *sin.*

For example: transgressions, iniquities, wrongs, mess-ups, evil, corruption

Write one synonym for the word *covenant.*

For example: promise, agreement

6

# INTO the Word

## Some Serious Forgiveness . . .

Read through the account of the flood in Genesis 6–9.

*Option*: Before reading the account of the flood, have students write the flood account in their own words. Share some of these writings. Compare them to the biblical account. Were they accurate? What was left out? Why is it important to reread the biblical account even when we think we know the story well? Remind students that every time we read God's Word, we can learn something new.

Encourage students: **Look for ways God showed mercy throughout the story. Stop after each chapter. Find examples of God's grace. Put what you find under Noah, Ark, Animals, Olive Leaf, Bow in the Clouds. Keep adding to each category as you read.**

Say, **The flood was really an act of salvation and deliverance. God knew how far mankind had strayed from faith, repentance, and salvation. He wanted to save creation and protect Noah and his family from this evil. Noah was righteous—not because he was without sin, but because he knew God and trusted God. God restored creation by wiping out the evil and corruption that was taking over the earth.**

### Some Serious Forgiveness . . .

The Great Flood is not just about sin and its consequences. God shows His incredible grace, mercy, and forgiveness at every turn. Read about the flood in Genesis 6–9. Tell how God showed grace through each of the following:

**NOAH**
God saved Noah and his family from the flood and the evil of the time.

**ARK**
God provided protection, shelter, food, and water to the people and animals.

**BOW IN THE CLOUDS**
God made a promise to never send a flood to wipe out all of mankind again.

**ANIMALS**
God saved the animals for the preservation of creation. Through them, man would have food and clothing.

**OLIVE LEAF**
God dried the land.

All of the promises of God are complete in the blood of Christ. Write the name of Jesus beneath the cross and rainbow at the upper right.

### Are You Serious?

God commands that we take both sin and forgiveness seriously. When it comes to sin, we often want to take the easy way out. Often it seems easier to just go along with a sin. When it comes to forgiveness, we often let pride get in the way. We often find it hard to grant forgiveness. Read the following situations. What would be the easy thing to say or do? What is the response based on God's Word?

1. A friend is telling you some juicy gossip about another friend. It is all very negative and could be very damaging to his reputation.
   You COULD **Answers will vary**. You SHOULD **tell him not to gossip** (Ephesians 4:29).
2. A classmate is bragging that the teacher believed her about the forged permission slip she brought in today.
   You COULD **Answers will vary**. You SHOULD **tell her not to lie** (Psalm 101:7).
3. You did not get invited to a friend's party. She has been ignoring you at school. You are hurt and upset. She calls one night to apologize and ask for your help with a project.
   You COULD **Answers will vary**. You SHOULD **be kind; forgive** (Colossians 3:12–14).

**REMEMBER**
By faith Noah, being warned by God concerning events as yet unseen, in reverent fear constructed an ark for the saving of his household.
Hebrews 11:7

7

### The Numbers Game

What is the correct number? You may use a number more than once. Use Genesis 6–7 to help find the answers.

**Answers: 2, 7, 8, 30, 40, 50, 150, 300, 377, 600**

1. Length of the ark: **300 cubits**
2. Width of the ark: **50 cubits**
3. Height of the ark: **30 cubits**
4. Number of animals of every sort/unclean animals: **2 animals**
5. Number of pairs of all clean animals: **7 pairs**
6. Number of pairs of birds of the heavens: **7 pairs**
7. Number of days until God would send the rain after giving Noah directions to gather the animals: **7 days**
8. Number of days and nights the rain would come down: **40 days and nights**
9. How old Noah was when the flood came: **600 years old**
10. Number of people on the ark: **8 people**
11. Number of days the water prevailed on the earth: **150 days**
12. Number of days it took for the earth to be dry enough for occupation: **377 days**



*Option*: Read the verses about God's continued grace. Divide the class into five groups. Have each group read one of the five sets of verses. The group should find one word that demonstrates God's grace and mercy in the verses. Have the groups share their findings.

1. Baptism (Acts 22:16; Acts 2:38–39): The flood wiped out the sin and evil of Noah's time. Baptism wipes out the sin and evil in each one of our hearts. The old Adam dies daily through our Baptism. We are made a new creation through Christ our Lord.
2. Forgiveness (1 John 1:9; Jeremiah 31:34): God richly and daily grants us forgiveness. Through repentance, we can live as forgiven people.
3. Love (Psalm 106:1; Romans 8:39): God's love for us is so great that we can never fully comprehend it.
4. Comfort (Matthew 5:4; Psalm 23:4): God promises to comfort His people through the trials and heartache sin causes.
5. Mercy (Psalm 103:4; 1 Corinthians 7:25): God's mercies are new to us every morning. He has had mercy on us poor miserable sinners.

Say, **Just as no rainbow is complete without the color red, God's promises are not complete without the saving blood of Jesus Christ. His suffering, death, and resurrection fulfilled all of the promises and covenants of old. God grants us faith in the waters of Baptism, forgiveness, love, comfort, and mercy because of what Christ did for us on the cross. When you see a rainbow, remember all of the great promises God has given us. Let the color red remind you of the greatest promise of all, salvation through Jesus.**

## INTO our lives

### Are You Serious?

We often find ourselves being wimpy Christians. We are wimpy in pointing out sin as a sin. We are wimpy in granting true forgiveness. Talk about each situation. Discuss the wimpy approach we may be tempted to take. What should be done to show how serious sin is, or how should we show some serious forgiveness?

After reading through examples 1 and 2, say, **It can be very hard to stand up and say something is wrong because of risked popularity, a possible conflict, and being viewed as a "goody two shoes." Ask God to give you the words and the power to be true to His Word.**

After reading through example 3, say, **It is very hard to forgive in situations where you are afraid of being hurt again. God's power is behind your forgiveness. His power is complete in our weakness. We can forgive because of the forgiveness He grants us.** Students may want to share personal experiences where it has been hard to point out a sin or grant forgiveness.

### Remember

Talk about faith as it was seen in the life of Noah. How is faith evidenced in the lives of God's people today?

# The Numbers Game

What is the correct number? You may use a number more than once. Use Genesis 6–7 to help find the answers.

1. Length of the ark: ________________
2. Width of the ark: ________________
3. Height of the ark: ________________
4. Number of animals of every sort/unclean animals: ________________
5. Number of pairs of all clean animals: ________________
6. Number of pairs of birds of the heavens: ________________
7. Number of days until God would send the rain after giving Noah directions to gather the animals: ________________
8. Number of days and nights the rain would come down: ____________________
9. How old Noah was when the flood came: ________________
10. Number of people on the ark: ________________
11. Number of days the water prevailed on the earth: ________________
12. Number of days it took for the earth to be dry enough for occupation: ________________

# God's Promise to Abram

## GENESIS 12; 15

## Background

The story of Abraham is a story of God's grace and steadfast love! God called Abraham out of a family in which idolatry was practiced (Joshua 24:2). God called Abraham out of pagan surroundings to live by the promise of His grace!

Terah, Abraham's father, led the family from Ur of the Chaldeans north to Haran. Haran was a commercial city and a center for worship of the moon god Sin, similar to the idol worship found in Ur. It was at Haran that Abram first received the divine call to go to Canaan. This meant leaving his country, his family, and his father's house.

The revelations of God consisted of promises. They called forth faith in response to the promises. God gave Abram such a faith that trusted in that which was invisible and far in the future. Loneliness, uncertainty, already living in Canaan, Sarah's barrenness, or age did not keep him from believing God's Word. Abram cheerfully followed God's Word exactly and promptly. At each junction in the journey, he paused to build an altar to worship God, who was his heavenly Father, Guide, and Redeemer! Today we are in the family of God, heirs of the promise, and we can trust the Lord to direct our future and bring us safely to the promised land, eternal life in heaven.

## Devotion

"O Lord, call me, choose me, fill me, use me, wherever You need me, I will go . . ." The words of the song rang in their ears and touched their hearts.

For some time, Ed and Wilma, a couple in their sixties, had considered helping with Bible translation in Nigeria, West Africa. This time the call seemed loud and clear. It would mean leaving their children and grandchildren and their comfortable home in America. It would mean living in a remote bush village, learning an unfamiliar language, understanding a different culture, and buying food at an open marketplace.

Yes, they answered the call. They would go, trusting in the Lord to lead them and bless them. They arrived in Nigeria and prepared for village life. Then came the lorry (truck) accident only months after their arrival. Again they trusted God. God spared their lives in this terrible accident, and many Nigerians saw the power and love of God to save them in time of great danger. They continued their work. They trusted God to lead them as they traveled to remote areas with washed-out roads and bridges. Everywhere they shared the Good News of Jesus and His free gift of forgiveness and an eternal home with Him in heaven. Ed and Wilma helped people learn to read so they could read the Bible for themselves. God remained faithful at all times as they followed His leading. Daily they thanked God for His faithfulness and continued to sing, "I'm holding on to Your promises . . . Wherever You need me, I will go!"

**PRAY: Heavenly Father, You have made me Your child through faith in Jesus. Help me to follow Your leading throughout my life. I pray in Jesus' name. Amen.**

## Central Truth

As God credits us with righteousness through the merit of Christ, He gives direction and meaning to the new life that is ours in Him.

## Objectives

- List and explain each part of God's promises to Abram.
- Recognize righteousness as God's gift to us through Christ Jesus, our Savior.
- Identify themselves as children of Abram by God's grace through the working of the Holy Spirit.

## Materials

- The Basics
- Reproducible 3
- Materials for Promise Booklets: paper, markers, cardstock, spiral binders, desktop publishing options
- PowerPoint
- Self-adhesive felt or other material and markers for "Faith Patches" (optional)

## Bible Prep

Post in advance so students can bookmark references before class time.

- Genesis 12
- Genesis 15
- Galatians 3
- John 10:27–29
- Joshua 1:9
- Psalm 50:15

Sing: "Go, My Children, with My Blessing" (*AGPS* 102) or "Oh, that the Lord Would Guide My Ways" (*AGPS* 191).

# INTO the lesson

## Moving Day

In our mobile society, many students can identify with the unsettling aspects of relocation. Ask, **If you were going to relocate, what things would you like to know about your new home before you move?** Student comments are likely to reflect that we like to know exactly where we are going, even what our bedroom will look like, and who our friends will be. Transitions are not easy.

Help students understand the enormity of Abram's call. Abram didn't have a clue about where he was going or what life would be like in that strange place. He only knew that God was leading him and that he could depend on God to get him to the Promised Land.

# INTO the Word

## God's Call

God's call is clear and definite. Abram is asked to leave his country, his kindred (or people), and his father's house. This was a huge request for someone in a biblical culture that valued family heritage and communal customs as a way of life.

The Lord in His grace is separating Abram from evil, rebellious, idolatrous peoples of the post-Babel era. God manifested Himself to Abram as the author of salvation and the guide to true life. Abram was to go to a land that God would show him. Though Abram did not know where he was going, he followed God's direction.

## God's Promise

God's promise to Abram has five important components: (1) I will make you a great nation; (2) I will bless you; (3) I will make your name great; (4) I will bless those who bless you and curse those who dishonor you; and (5) in you, all the families of the earth will be blessed.

Abram was to receive wonderful blessings from God. More than that, God's blessings to Abram were also to be a blessing to all nations. From Abram's offspring, the Savior was to be born. **Jesus would come to bring forgiveness of sins, new life, and eternal salvation to all people.**

---

**3** Genesis 12, 15

### God's Promise to Abram

**Moving Day**

Read Genesis 12 and 15. Find out what Abram knew before he answered God's call and moved.

**God's Call**

(Genesis 12:1) Go from **your country**, **your kindred**, and **your father's house**.

Go to **the land I will show you**.

**God's Promise**

(Genesis 12:2) I will **make of you a great nation**.

I will **bless you** and **make your name great**.

I will **bless those who bless you and him who dishonors you I will curse**

and in you **all the families of the earth will be blessed**.

More promises to Abram: Genesis 15:4 **Your son will be your heir.**

Genesis 15:5 **Your offspring will be as numerous as the stars.**

What was Abram's response to God's Word? Genesis 15:6 **Abram believed.**

**Review**

Use the story of Abram to describe the relationship between these words: *covenant, heir, offspring.*

**God made a covenant promise to Abram that he would have an heir, and all nations would be blessed from his offspring. (Answers will vary.)**

8

---

## Review

Students are asked to reference the Abram story as they describe the relationship between the following words: *covenant*, *heir*, and *offspring*. Comment that Abram is the father of all the faithful. So the stars Abram gazed upon in the sky represented, in a sense, all believers, including those alive today.

### Where You Belong

Define Abram's family (Galatians 3:7–9): Those with faith in Jesus

How do you fit into Abram's family (Galatians 3:27–29)? We belong to Christ; therefore, we are heirs of the promise.

Personalize the Family Tree. Put yourself, Abram, and others in God's Family Tree.

### Promises You Can Count On

Check out these promises from God. In the stars, tell how each is important in your life.

Faith: the assurance of things hoped for, the conviction of things not seen. Hebrews 11:1

How did Abram show faith in God?

**Remember**

By faith Abraham obeyed when he was called to go out to a place that he was to receive as an inheritance. And he went out, not knowing where he was going. By faith he went to live in the land of promise, as in a foreign land, living in tents with Isaac and Jacob, heirs with him of the same promise.

Hebrews 11:8–9

9

# INTO our lives

## Where You Belong

God's Family Tree diagram shows God at the foundation with those who had faith in God as branches on the tree. Instruct students to add their own names as well as family members and patriarchs such as Abram. Students should recognize that we are recipients of God's promise to Abram to bless all families of the earth through his offspring, our Savior Jesus.

## Promises You Can Count On

God's Word is full of promises to His dear children. You may want to design a bulletin board with favorite promises of God posted by the students. Let them share testimonials telling when the promise was especially meaningful.

Students should summarize each of the promise references listed in the stars and add other favorites, writing them in the margin of the page.

Remind students of the definition of faith found in Hebrews 11:1. Faith is demonstrated in Abram's life as he (1) goes to a foreign land; (2) leaves his people and his country; and (3) believes God can give him a son. Working through God's Word, the Holy Spirit brings contemporary believers that same kind of bold, dynamic faith. Distribute copies of **Reproducible 3** for students to complete to underscore the blessings God always provides to His people, to Abram as well as to contemporary believers.

## Personal Bible Promise Booklet

Have students create their own personal Bible Promise Booklet. God's Word is full of promises to encourage and empower us on life's journey. Have students work individually or with a partner to search God's Word for significant promises they would especially like to remember. (*Hint*: The Book of Psalms might be a good place to begin searching since it is filled with God's promises. Also, suggest students use their catechism and Bible concordance and that they also consider Bible verses they have memorized.) Have students collect the references and type the verses on pages so they can be collated into a book. Students may wish to add designs or symbols to each page to enhance its meaning.

The Promise Booklet will be a blessing to the students as well as to others who use it. Decide what type of production works best in your class: individual, group, or whole-class edition. This project is designed to be a faith-strengthening as well as a faith-sharing project. Exercise many talents as this booklet is being constructed: artists, researchers, editors, designers, printers, and even photographers!

Motivation will be especially high if the class has decided to produce this booklet(s) as a gift of encouragement for others (e.g., those who are sick, in the service, or in nursing homes). If resources permit, add a cardstock cover with a spiral binding to the pages designed by the students. Take time to pray with the class that the construction and distribution of the Promise Booklet may be a blessing to many.

## Remember

Hebrews 11:8–10 comes from the great faith chapter and documents Abram's faith-filled responses to God's Word. Hebrews 11:6 emphasizes that "without faith it is impossible to please Him (God)." Those who are led by the Spirit of Christ *can* do good works. Thank God for the Holy Spirit, who strengthens us to respond in faith to God's leadership in our lives.

# The Path of Father Abram

Read about Abram in Genesis 12 and 15. Use the Word Bank at the bottom to complete the sayings on each section of The Path of Father Abram, father of all the faithful.

**Word Bank**

| | |
|---|---|
| praise | leading |
| Believe | unseen |
| Obey | Word |

# The Offering of Isaac

## GENESIS 21:1–8; 22:1–19

## Background

The birth of Isaac to Abraham, who was one hundred years old, and to his wife, Sarah, who was ninety years old and was known to be barren, was indeed a miraculous blessing from the Lord. It had been twenty-five years since God first promised that Abraham would be blessed with offspring (Genesis 12:2), and Abraham's faith required patience and reassurance from God as he waited for the fulfillment of the promise.

The name *Isaac* means "he laughs." It was the name given by God in Genesis 17:19. Isaac's name recalls Sarah's laughter at the announcement of his coming birth (Genesis 18:9–15) and also the incredible joy this son brought as a gift of God's grace.

The joy, wonder, and celebration of Isaac's birth stands in stark contrast to the account of the offering of Isaac by his father, Abraham. The Word of the Lord came to Abraham, asking him to offer up his own dear son, the heir of the promise, for a burnt offering on one of the mountains that would be shown to him. God desires complete surrender to His will. Abraham does not question God's Word, but obeys by faith in God (Hebrews 11:17–19), believing that God had power even over death.

As Abraham was about to slay his son, the Lord called for him to stop. God saw that Abraham's obedience of faith extended even to the sacrifice of his own beloved son. The site of this offering was Mount Moriah near Jerusalem. The offering of Isaac served as a prototype of the sacrifice for the sins of the whole world, when God would not spare His own Son but offer Him up to death on the cross, that we might have eternal life through Jesus.

## Devotion

Think of what is dearest to you . . . what you love the most. It may be a person, a family heirloom, or an electronic gadget. What if you were suddenly asked to give up that person or thing?

That's what happened to Abraham. God did a "heart check" to see what Abraham's real priorities were. He asked Abraham to sacrifice his own dear son. Abraham faced a tough decision. He could have refused. He could have argued. He could have stalled. Instead, he followed God's Word exactly down to the last detail.

God gave Abraham faith to trust and obey Him even in times of trial and testing. God's wonderful promise to bless all nations through Abraham was fulfilled when Jesus, the Savior of the world, was born as an offspring of Abraham's family. If you are baptized, you are in God's family today. Rejoice in God's awesome love for you. May the Holy Spirit be working in your heart, helping you to obey God's Word in all circumstances.

PRAY: Ask students to suggest blessings they have received as a result of being in God's family. List them on the board. Use the listed blessings to form a praise litany in which the teacher reads the blessing and the students respond to each blessing with the words "We praise You, O God!"

Sing: "The Lamb" (*LSB* 547) or "Salvation unto Us Has Come" (*LSB* 555), especially stanzas 1, 6, 7, 9, and 10.

## Central Truth

God gives His people faith to follow Him and receive His blessings in their lives.

## Objectives

- Desire to obey God's Word, even in challenging circumstances.
- Ask God for strong, unwavering faith in times of testing.
- Rejoice in the family heritage of the Promised One, Jesus, the Savior.

## Materials

- The Basics
- Large drawing paper
- Reproducible 4

## Bible Prep

Post in advance so students can bookmark references before class time.

- Genesis 21:1–8
- Genesis 22:1–19
- Genesis 11:30
- Genesis 17:21
- Galatians 3:14, 26–29

# INTO the lesson

Ask your students to tell about important decisions they have had to make recently. What made the decision hard? How did they decide what to do? More big decisions loom in their immediate future, decisions that will affect how they live their lives and how they use the time God is giving them.

Talk about things people do before they make a decision. Perhaps they talk to others about the decision, evaluate the pros and cons of the decision, think about how friends will react to the decision, and so on. How big a role does prayer play in this process?

In today's lesson, we will see how Abraham listened carefully to God's Word. Through faith, Abraham consistently followed God's Word and obeyed His instructions. Abraham looked to God for answers and trusted in God to lead him. His own reason and logic were subject to the commands of God's Word. May Abraham's faith-filled obedience and response to God's commands be an example for our decision making in all circumstances.

4

Genesis 21:1–8; 22:1–19

## The Offering of Isaac

**A Journey of Faith . . .**

How do you decide what to do when you face hard choices?

Read Genesis 21:1–8 and Genesis 22:1–19 to learn how Abraham faced a test.

Write or draw the steps in Abraham's journey.

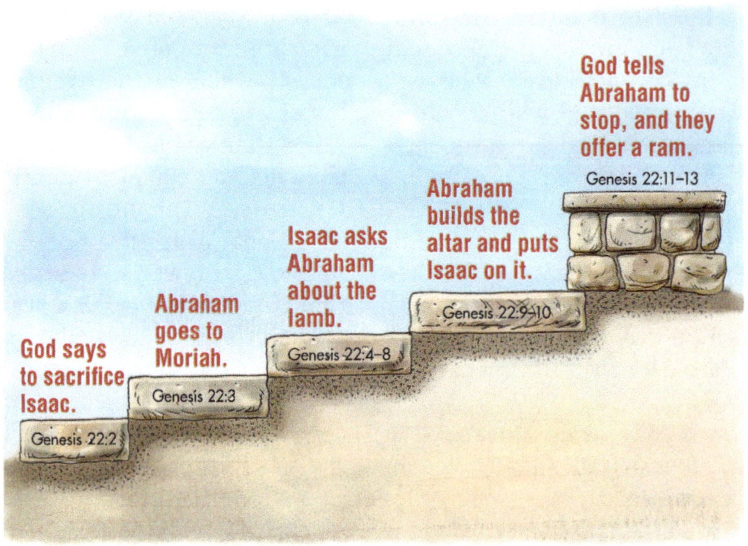


**Review**

| | |
|---|---|
| prototype— | something or someone that provides a picture of a later type |
| foreshadow— | to prefigure or indicate beforehand |
| sacrifice— | to give up for a cause |
| only-begotten son— | sole biological son |

10

# INTO the Word

## A Journey of Faith . . .

Isaac was truly a treasured and precious son. Abraham was about to face a highly emotional challenge and test from God. Ask, **What made Isaac an especially treasured and precious son?** (He was born in Abraham's old age [Genesis 21:2]. His birth was miraculous [Genesis 11:30]. His mother, Sarah, was considered barren. God promised to establish a covenant with Isaac [Genesis 17:21].)

Be sure students read the story from the Bible prior to this summary review. This emotionally touching story foreshadows in human terms the great sacrifice of God the Father, who gave His only-begotten Son as a sacrifice on the cross to atone for the sins of the whole world.

Let students write or draw Abraham's journey of faith in this story. If you prefer, let students draw the story steps on large drawing paper to post in the hallways or share with other classes. As students retell the story, be sure to note Abraham's exacting obedience to God's commands every step of the way.

## Review

Allow time for students to define these words. Explore with students comparisons between the events associated with Mount Moriah and those associated with Mount Calvary. Have students use the review words as they describe the analogy. Point out, for example, that Isaac carried the wood for the altar on which he was to be sacrificed just as Jesus carried His cross to the mount of crucifixion..

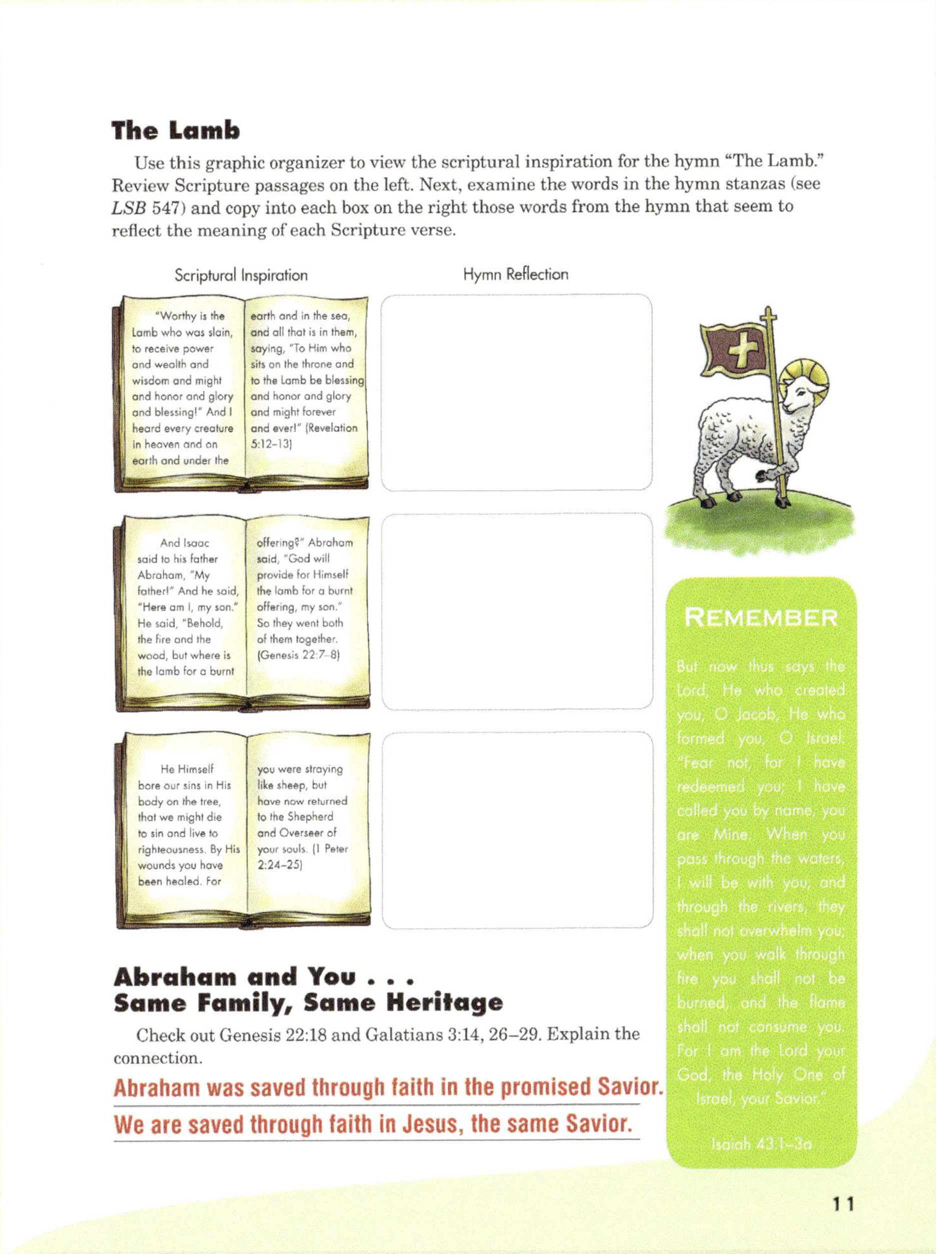

### The Lamb

Use this graphic organizer to view the scriptural inspiration for the hymn "The Lamb." Review Scripture passages on the left. Next, examine the words in the hymn stanzas (see *LSB* 547) and copy into each box on the right those words from the hymn that seem to reflect the meaning of each Scripture verse.

| Scriptural Inspiration | Hymn Reflection |
|---|---|
| "Worthy is the Lamb who was slain, to receive power and wealth and wisdom and might and honor and glory and blessing!" And I heard every creature in heaven and on earth and under the earth and in the sea, and all that is in them, saying, "To Him who sits on the throne and to the Lamb be blessing and honor and glory and might forever and ever!" (Revelation 5:12–13) | |
| And Isaac said to his father Abraham, "My father!" And he said, "Here am I, my son." He said, "Behold, the fire and the wood, but where is the lamb for a burnt offering?" Abraham said, "God will provide for Himself the lamb for a burnt offering, my son." So they went both of them together. (Genesis 22:7–8) | |
| He Himself bore our sins in His body on the tree, that we might die to sin and live to righteousness. By His wounds you have been healed. For you were straying like sheep, but have now returned to the Shepherd and Overseer of your souls. (1 Peter 2:24–25) | |

**REMEMBER**

But now thus says the Lord, He who created you, O Jacob, He who formed you, O Israel: "Fear not, for I have redeemed you; I have called you by name, you are Mine. When you pass through the waters, I will be with you; and through the rivers, they shall not overwhelm you; when you walk through fire you shall not be burned, and the flame shall not consume you. For I am the Lord your God, the Holy One of Israel, your Savior."

Isaiah 43:1–3a

### Abraham and You . . . Same Family, Same Heritage

Check out Genesis 22:18 and Galatians 3:14, 26–29. Explain the connection.

Abraham was saved through faith in the promised Savior.

We are saved through faith in Jesus, the same Savior.

11

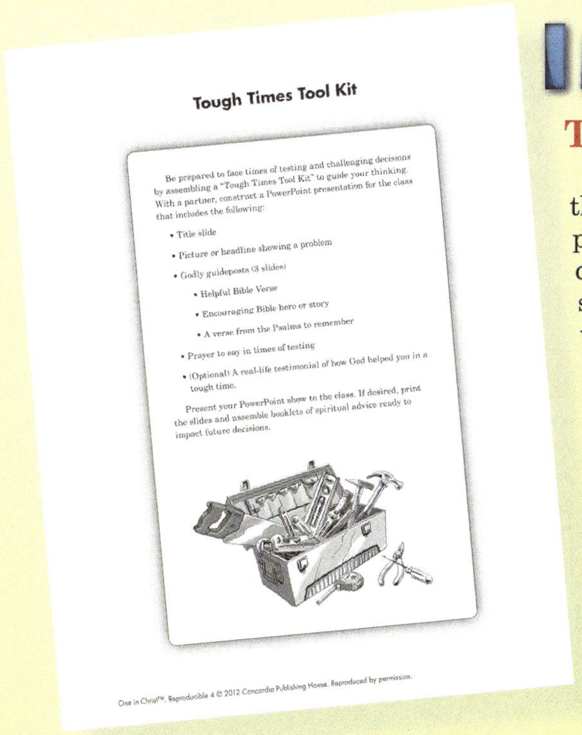

### Tough Times Tool Kit

Be prepared to face times of testing and challenging decisions by assembling a "Tough Times Tool Kit" to guide your thinking. With a partner, construct a PowerPoint presentation for the class that includes the following:

- Title slide
- Picture or headline showing a problem
- Godly guideposts (3 slides)
    - Helpful Bible Verse
    - Encouraging Bible hero or story
    - A verse from the Psalms to remember
- Prayer to say in times of testing
- (Optional) A real-life testimonial of how God helped you in a tough time.

Present your PowerPoint show to the class. If desired, print the slides and assemble booklets of spiritual advice ready to impact future decisions.



# INTO our lives

## The Lamb

Continue your discussion of how the account of the sacrifice of Isaac prefigures the account of Jesus' crucifixion on Mount Calvary. Although sections from the hymn stanzas will vary somewhat, the words of this beloved hymn link well the two events. **Jesus willingly became the lamb God provided as a worthy sacrifice for our sins and the sins of all people.**

If you choose to do so at this time, follow up with the project described on **Reproducible 4**. This project is designed to give students an opportunity to prepare for godly decision making. Review the specific outline of expectations for this presentation. Plan for a quick choice of partners or small groups, so time for creating the presentation is maximized. Some possible problems involving decision making could be the following: choice of friends, which movies to watch, doing drugs or not, which video games to buy/play, type of posting on Facebook, or worship habits.

Be sure the class is aware of the time parameters you are allowing for completion of this project, so that time on task is productive. The headline showing a problem could simply be typed on a PowerPoint slide, or students could do a Google search and import a picture or newspaper article using a program such as Grab. If some students are unfamiliar with PowerPoint, try to pair them with students who are comfortable with it. Students without access to PowerPoint can design "slides" using paper and markers to depict each item of the Tool Kit. Schedule a time to share the presentations. You may want to share the presentations remotely with another class using applications such as Skype, GoToMeeting, or iChat. The interaction between classes offers another avenue for witness to the Word of God active in our lives and impacting our decisions.

*Option:* For a less ambitious alternative, have students work in pairs or small groups to prepare oral presentations (possibly including handmade visuals). Encourage them to tell how to prepare for times of testing or for making challenging decisions.

## Abraham and You . . . Same Family, Same Heritage

This section brings Abraham up close and personal. He is no longer just an ancient, faraway patriarch, but a fellow member with us in God's family of believers: all those who are saved through the sacrifice of Jesus, our Savior. The Holy Spirit, who helped Abraham obey God, is also at work in our lives, strengthening us and blessing us as we follow God's commands. We are counted in the numbers Abraham saw by faith when God blessed him in Genesis 22:18.

## Remember

The wonderful words of Isaiah 43:1–3a seem to wrap the Lord's loving, saving hands securely around each of His children no matter what troubles or challenges they encounter. Let the students know that each of them is precious to the Lord, called by name! This is the Lord and Savior who called and led Abraham throughout his journey. His steadfast love will carry us to the promised land of heaven. Students may be inspired to produce artwork that depicts God's promises in these verses.

# Tough Times Tool Kit

Be prepared to face times of testing and challenging decisions by assembling a "Tough Times Tool Kit" to guide your thinking. With a partner, construct a PowerPoint presentation for the class that includes the following:

- Title slide
- Picture or headline showing a problem
- Godly guideposts (3 slides)
    - Helpful Bible verse
    - Encouraging Bible hero or story
    - A verse from the Psalms to remember
- Prayer to say in times of testing
- (Optional) A real-life testimonial of how God helped you in a tough time

Present your PowerPoint show to the class. If desired, print the slides and assemble booklets of spiritual advice ready to impact future decisions.

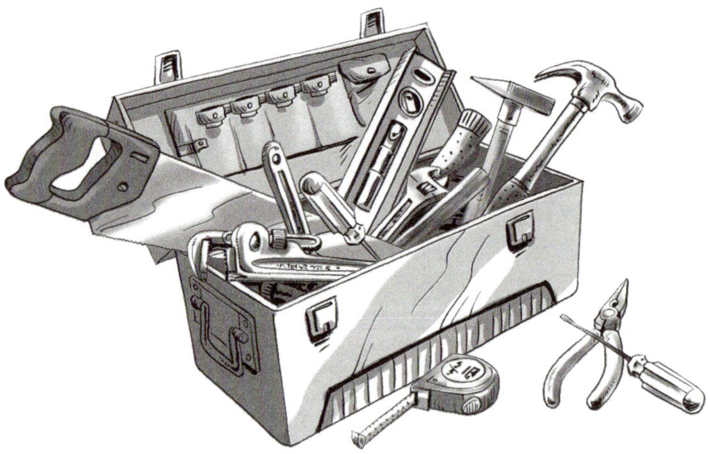

# The Call of Moses

## EXODUS 3–4

## Background

Teachers and students sometimes relegate biblical study to recalling facts. When the Holy Spirit breaks through, God's people come to see beyond the facts into the living witness of Jesus acting right here, right now. Such was Moses' experience herding sheep on a routine day. What he knew about God from His parents was about to change drastically with a personal encounter. It all began when he stopped to pay attention.

Jesus tells us in John 5:17 that God is always at work. The question is do we pay attention?

What's going on around you that is unusual? For Moses, a bush burned too long, and shortly he found himself barefoot before a live fire. For one teacher, a handicapped student's issues left her contemplating God's lesson plans instead of her own. For one eighth grader, an inner-city field trip broke through his "you deserve a break" self-focus to join God's focus.

God is always at work. When we pay attention, He may choose to reveal Himself and call us to join His work. Then what? What did Moses do? "Here I am" (Exodus 3:4). If God is indeed calling you or a student to join Him, He will reveal Himself and His plans. Bible words in a regular devotion will stand out. Someone will say something that resonates. Circumstances will put the issue right at your feet. Asking God to increase your desire does, in fact, make you more passionate. Moses found out God's plan to save His enslaved people and to demonstrate His power in such a way that Jews for all generations would remember. Christians would get the deep connection between the Passover Seder and the Lord's Supper. God calls you and your students to take your eyes off the daily to-do list. Take this opportunity to stop and pay attention!

## Central Truth

Just as God sent Moses to rescue His Old Testament people from slavery in Egypt, He sent Jesus to save all people from their sins.

## Objectives

- Tell how God prepared Moses to lead and save God's people.
- Look for God at work around you and for His possible call to join Him.
- Praise God for the rescuing, leading power and presence of Jesus.

## Materials

- The Basics
- Sticky notes marked with the verses in Bible Prep
- Reproducible 5

## Bible Prep

Post in advance so students can bookmark references before class time.

- Exodus 3:4
- Exodus 3:11
- Exodus 3:13
- Exodus 4:1
- Exodus 4:10
- Exodus 4:13
- Exodus 4:18–20

## Devotion

"Warning! This class is under construction," the sign read. Mojan grinned to himself. Mrs. Rogers, his English teacher, put up unusual signs. After four years in America, Mojan's English had improved, but some things still surprised him—including Mrs. Rogers inviting him to join the school paper staff. Mojan just ducked his head and looked down. He thought, Why is she asking me? I'm not one of the popular kids. When she got distracted, he slipped away.

Mrs. Rogers was an amazing teacher. She never gave up on any student, because she knew that Jesus, her Savior, never gave up on her. A week later, Mrs. Rogers approached Mojan in the hall. "Listen, I've been coaching students as editor for more than twenty years. I've seen your writing. I really believe you can do this." Mojan smiled politely but shook his head and blended into the passing crowd. I wonder if she really can do what she says and turn writers into journalists? he thought.

Doggedly, Mrs. Rogers snagged Mojan another day. This time, Mojan spoke: "Why would anyone give me an interview? Nobody knows me." Mrs. Rogers smiled. "But they know me! If you use my name, they'll listen to you." She put her hand on his arm. "Come on! Join us! I'd like to know you better—see what we can do." Mojan was almost convinced, but a sudden negative crowded in. "I can't really talk to other kids," he mumbled. Mrs. Rogers patted his arm. "You'd be surprised. Most of them are really okay."

Once again, Mojan hesitated. Then he backed away. "Sorry, Mrs. Rogers. I think you'd be better off with someone else." Mrs. Rogers stared after his retreating back. "Well, Mr. Mojan, you're a stubborn one. But I'm more tenacious than you can imagine. I'll give you a breather, but only for a little. Then I'm asking again."

Read aloud the first stanza of "Wake Us, O Lord, to Human Need" (*AGPS* 250). Together paraphrase that stanza into a class prayer. Then sing all four stanzas.

# INTO the lesson

## Rescue

Direct students to write a response beside each drawing to finish each sentence: **What probably would have happened to the injured person if the rescue team had not answered the call?** (Serious disability or death) **to the isolated eighth grader if the girl had not joined her for lunch?** (Continued estrangement and distance)

Now ask, **What would have happened to the slaves if Moses had not answered God's call?** (Continued slavery) **to you and me if Jesus had not followed God's plan?** (Push for personal responses such as "I would live with no hope," "I could not ask for help," "I would be completely on my own against Satan," or "I would spend eternity in hell.") Stress that **Jesus is our great rescuer.**

## Review

Ask students to define and then to draw symbols representing *tenacious* and *called*. Then have them share their artwork with a partner.

**5** Exodus 3–4

### THE CALL OF MOSES

**Rescue**

Directions: As your teacher directs, write beside each picture what would happen if . . .

**God Is Tenacious to Save**

Moses had all kinds of excuses for not leading the people out of Egypt. How did God respond to those excuses?

**1st Excuse** Exodus 3:12 God said that He would be with Moses.

**2nd Excuse** Exodus 3:16–20 God told Moses to go to Egypt and tell the people, "The God of our fathers has appeared to me and said He has seen our suffering, and He promises to bring us out of Egypt to a land of milk and honey."

**3rd Excuse** Exodus 4:3–9 God gave Moses three miraculous signs to perform.

**4th Excuse** Exodus 4:12 God said He would be with Moses' mouth and teach him what to say.

**5th Excuse** Exodus 4:14–15 God said that Aaron would join Moses, and God would be with both of their mouths.

**REVIEW**

Illustrate each word:

*tenacious*

*called*

*tenacious*—persistent, tending to hold fast, cling

*called*—to invite or summon with a view to service

12

# INTO the Word

## God Is Tenacious to Save

Read Exodus 3 and 4. As you do, have students highlight any references to God, Lord, He, as well as the verb or verb form with it. They should note units such as these: Lord appeared (3:2), Lord saw (3:4), God called (3:4), He said (3:6), I am (3:6), I have seen (3:7), I have heard (3:7), I know (3:7), and I have come to deliver (3:8). If you have an interactive whiteboard, put the text up and highlight it with the students.

Ask, **What do these highlights cause you to conclude?** (God does not passively observe; He actively responds by revealing Himself to the person He invites to work with Him.)

Allow time for students to review the text to identify the excuses Moses offered in response to God's call to serve Him. Possibilities include the following:

*Moses said he was not a leader, but just an ordinary person (3:11).

*Moses thought the people wouldn't believe him when he said God was sending him (3:13).

*Moses thought the people would not believe him (4:1).

*Moses said he could not lead because he was not a good speaker (4:10).

*Moses thought he was the wrong person. God should send someone else (4:13).

Ask, **If you had to convince Moses each time to join you in leading Israel out of slavery, how would you do it?** Accept their answers. Then divide the class into pairs or threesomes. Using their Student Books, have them fill in under the verses listed how God actually did respond to Moses to convince him to join God's work.

Challenge the class to think of five ways God had already prepared the way for Moses to lead. (God saved Moses' life right at the start; God caused Moses to understand Egyptian administration; God placed Moses in the very desert where Israel would travel; God gave Moses signs to perform; God sent Aaron ahead to meet Moses.)

Conclude, **God was tenacious. He took five noes before He got a yes. Moses had to leave his comfort zone at Jethro's home and head into work he wasn't sure he could do. But the most amazing thing happened right from the start of God's plan for deliverance. Exodus 4:31 says, "And the people believed**

**Check In**

God is always working and

- ☐ I find myself sometimes aware of His presence.
- ☐ I pretty much focus on my activities, my life.
- ☐ I sometimes sense a tug in my spirit to do something God wants.
- ☐ I sometimes sense a tug in my spirit to act, but I figure someone else will take care of it.
- ☐ I read a Bible verse, and certain phrases sometimes seem to stand out.
- ☐ I don't actually read the Bible much.
- ☐ I hear a song, and it seems to direct me, or I hear a sermon/chapel talk, and something stirs inside.
- ☐ I mostly daydream during church.
- ☐ When I wonder if God wants me to join His work, I ask God to confirm this. I pay attention for anything that God might use to respond to my prayer, like an open door in circumstances or an increased passion for action.
- ☐ I check to be sure my feelings are in line with what I know from the Bible.
- ☐ I stay mostly in my comfort zone because, really, I've got to admit, my life is mostly about me.

**REMEMBER**

For consider your **calling**, brothers: not many of you were wise according to worldly standards, not many were powerful, not many were of noble birth. But **God** **chose** what is foolish in the world to shame the wise; God chose what is weak in the world to shame the strong.

1 Corinthians 1:26–27

13

and when they heard that the LORD had visited the people of Israel and that He had seen their affliction, they bowed their heads and worshiped." Moses' involvement in God's saving plan brought people into a deeper connection to God.

**Flow Chart**

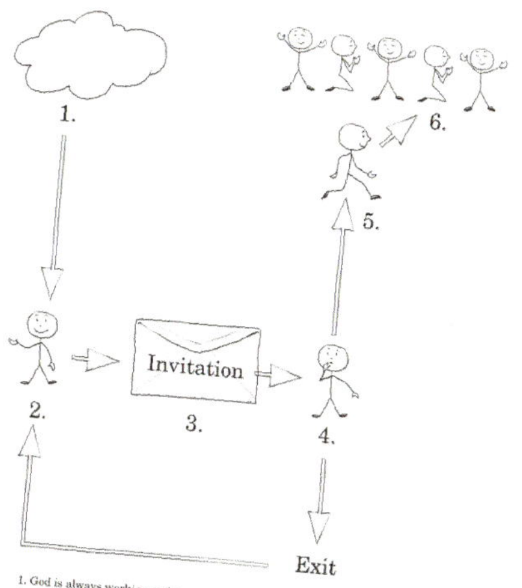


1. God is always working and prepares me.
2. God reveals Himself, and I stop to pay attention.
3. God calls me to join His work.
4. I face a tough challenge to trust Him.
5. I move out of my routine and into the challenge.
6. Working with God deepens my faith and leads people to worship.

EXIT: I ignore God, but God continues to call me tenaciously.



# INTO our lives

Direct students' attention to the flowchart on **Reproducible 5**.

*Or, in advance, make a transparency for the overhead, or draw it on the board. Enlarge the word text as fly-ins for a PowerPoint or for use on word text cards.*

Put up the flowchart. Explain each action as you add the word text:

1. **God is always working and prepares me.**
2. **God reveals Himself, and I stop to pay attention.**
3. **God calls me to join His work.**
4. **I face a tough challenge to trust Him.**
5. **I move out of my routine and into the challenge.**
6. **Working with God deepens my faith and leads people to worship.**

**EXIT: I ignore God, but God continues to call me tenaciously.**

Remove the word text cards, mix them, and challenge volunteers to place them correctly. Then pair students to practice explaining the flowchart to someone else. Consider the homework option below.

## Check In

Direct students to the Student Book "Check In" section. After each person checks the boxes privately, use this to launch a discussion. **What is God doing around us right here, right now? How would we know He was calling us? What would we do next?**

## Remember

Sometimes, students think God doesn't call adolescents, but in fact, God does! This verse talks about God calling the ordinary, the weak-appearing people like them, rather than the wise adults. God does this so that people are drawn to God. That's the whole point of being here—to join God's work of drawing people to Himself. Earth is not meant to be heaven. It is a place to see God's revelation with sinners.

# Flow Chart

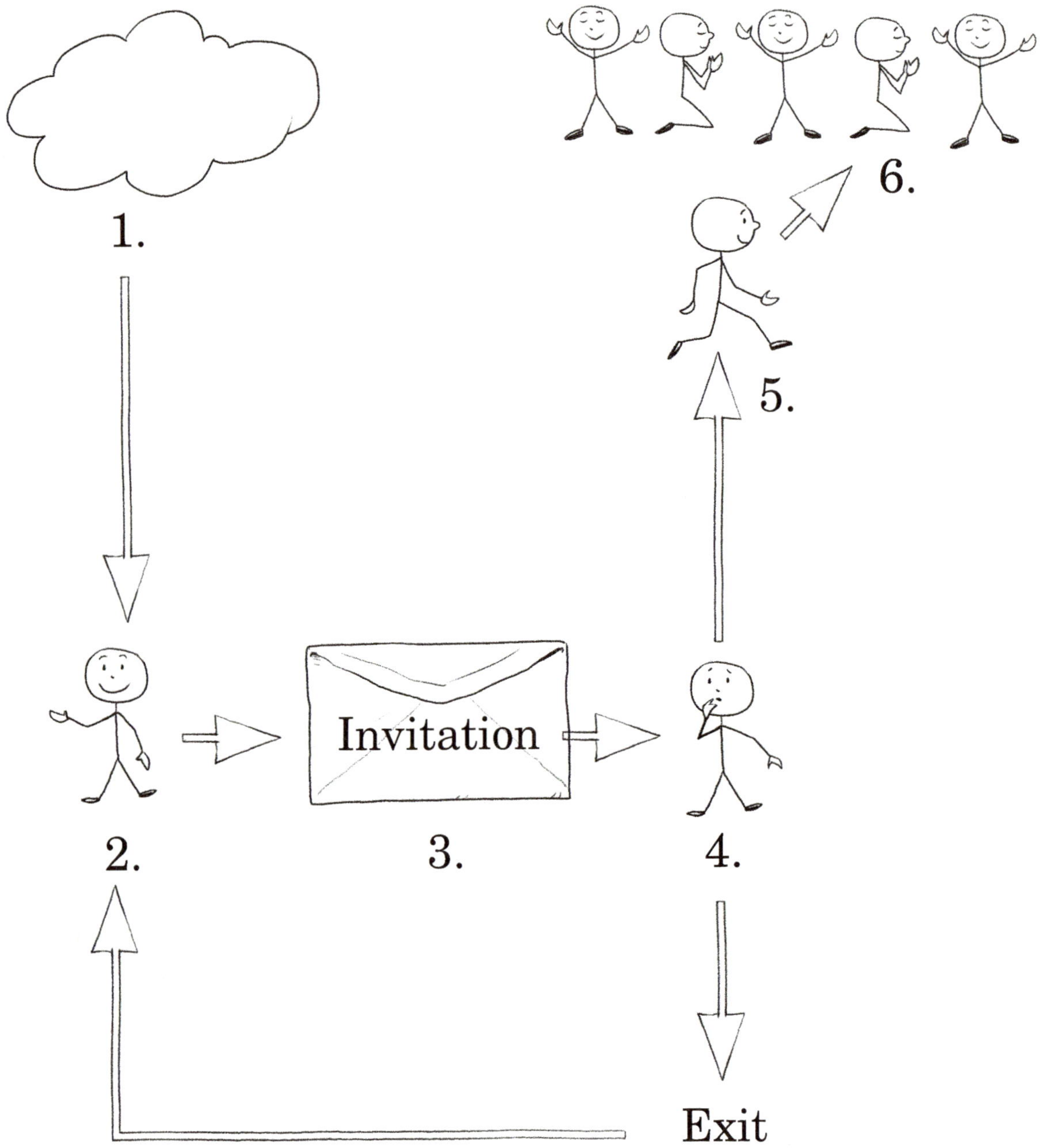


1. God is always working and prepares me.
2. God reveals Himself, and I stop to pay attention.
3. God calls me to join His work.
4. I face a tough challenge to trust Him.
5. I move out of my routine and into the challenge.
6. Working with God deepens my faith and leads people to worship.

EXIT: I ignore God, but God continues to call me tenaciously.

# The Exodus

## EXODUS 13:17–15:21

## Background

Crossing the Red Sea was a foundational event for the children of Israel in the establishment of their national and religious identity. This common experience shared by these former slaves would cement them together as they experienced firsthand the awesome power of God. So important was this event that it is commemorated in the modern Jewish celebration of the Passover. In a part of the Passover Seder called the *b'chol*, modern Jews are encouraged to think of themselves as having crossed the Red Sea. The crossing of the Red Sea is more than something that happened to their ancestors. It is something in which they participate—an event that grounds them in their identity as Jews.

In 1 Corinthians 10:2, St. Paul writes that this event was a kind of baptism for his forefathers. It was a foreshadowing of our own Baptism experience. Just as this miracle in water formed the foundation for Israel's national and religious identity, so, too, the miracle of water and the Word in Holy Baptism forms the foundation of our identity as children of God.

It is little wonder that the song of Moses found in Exodus 15 is used as the Old Testament Reading on Easter. Just as God defeated Israel's enemies by drowning them in the Red Sea, so, too, did God defeat our greater enemies of sin, death, and the devil in Jesus' cross and empty tomb, the salvation in which we participate through the waters of Holy Baptism (Romans 6:3–4).

## Devotion

"Mom, why do we have to have peas again tonight?"

"Can't you put my clothes away? It is just too much work for me."

Jenny's mom decided she had had enough of the complaining and grumbling. One night, Jenny's mom "forgot" to make supper for Jenny. Jenny had to do the job on her own.

Finally, Jenny was getting the idea that something was different in her house when her clothes hamper was buried in dirty clothes. Her mom simply didn't do Jenny's laundry, and Jenny wanted her favorite jeans for the dance on Friday. Jenny had taken her mother's care for granted. And Jenny's mom was showing Jenny how much she depended on her.

Something similar happened with the Israelites immediately after they left the Promised Land. Only recently, God had delivered them from Egypt after ten plagues that dramatically demonstrated His desire to care for and save His people. But when Pharaoh came after them with his mighty army riding on horses and chariots, the people quickly began to grumble and complain.

How often do we forget about all that God has done and continues to do for us just as the people of Israel did? Thankfully, God never stops loving and caring for those who belong to Him. And God continued to provide for His people Israel. He parted the Red Sea so His people could cross over on dry land, and then He drowned the approaching enemy. He provides for us too. He sent Jesus to rescue us from our greatest enemies—sin, death, and Satan's power. Thank You, God, for Your love and care!

**PRAY: Dear Lord, thank You for caring for us. Thank You for reminding us of our need for You in the events that come into our lives. Lead us by Your Holy Spirit to place our trust in You. We pray in the name of Jesus, our Savior and Lord. Amen.**

Sing: "Now Thank We All Our God" (*LSB* 895).

## Central Truth

Just as God saved His people from Pharaoh and his army, God in Christ has saved us from sin, death, and Satan's power.

## Objectives

- Recall the facts of how God rescued His people at the exodus.
- Explain that like Pharaoh and his army, sin, death, and Satan's power constantly seek to bring those Christ has freed back under their control.
- Compare the exodus deliverance with the rescue Jesus has provided for us and for all people through His life, death, and resurrection.

## Materials

- The Basics
- Reproducible 6

## Bible Prep

Post in advance so students can bookmark references before class time.

- Genesis 47:13
- Exodus 1:9
- Exodus 3:7–12
- Exodus 13:17–14:30
- 1 Peter 5:8
- Genesis 4:7
- 2 Corinthians 5:16–21
- Ephesians 6:11–20

# INTO the lesson

Begin the class period with a review of the children of Israel and what has happened to them thus far. Start with Joseph and review the narrative of Pharaoh and the ten plagues leading up to Passover. This lesson begins with Moses leading the children of Israel out of Egypt as they head toward the Red Sea. Use the following questions/answers to review the history of God's people and their need for deliverance. Stress in your discussion that God worked in the lives of Joseph and Moses so that He might preserve His people—the people from whom the **Savior of the world would come to pay the penalty of all sins and earn eternal life for all people.** Ask, **Why were the people of Israel in Egypt** (Genesis 47:13)**?** (There was a famine in the land. The children of Israel went to Egypt for food and were helped by Joseph.) **Why did Pharaoh fear the people of Israel** (Exodus 1:9)**?** (Many years later, the children of Israel had grown in number, so Pharaoh feared they had become too strong. He feared they would take over. So he first enslaved them and then ordered the murder of all baby boys born to Hebrew women. Moses' mother, Jochebed, placed Moses in a basket to be rescued from certain death.) **Because of his fear, Pharaoh enslaved the people of Israel. But God chose one man to lead the people of Israel. Who was that man** (Exodus 3:11–12)**?** (Moses. After being discovered by Pharaoh's daughter, Moses is rescued and raised in her court. He grows to be a powerful leader, used by God to rescue His people.) **What did God promise to give the people of Israel** (Exodus 3:7–10)**?** (God promised to rescue them from the Egyptians and bring them to a land flowing with milk and honey.) Comment that in today's lesson we will reflect on how God remains true to His promises.

6 Exodus 13:17–15:21

THE EXODUS

**Follow My Lead**

True to His promise, God brought the people of Israel out of Egypt (Exodus 12:50). But they still had a long journey. Review the account of Moses and the people of Israel crossing the Red Sea in Exodus 13:17–14:30. Fill in each footstep below with highlights from Israel's journey. Use the verses to guide your reading.



REVIEW

pillar— an upright shaft or column

exodus— leaving or departing

14

# INTO the Word

## Follow My Lead

Remind students that the children of Israel lived in Egypt for four hundred years. As a result, they were exposed to many different gods (such as Ra, Isis, or Hapy). Even though the children of Israel had witnessed the power of the one true God as He sent the Egyptians disease, darkness, and other plagues, they began to question and doubt God's desire to care and provide for them. As we journey with the children of Israel, watch as they doubt the power of God. The following exercise shows the beginning of those doubts.

Encourage the students to follow the footsteps as the people of Israel travel in Exodus 13–14.

Exodus 13:18 states that the children of Israel were prepared for battle. When they left Egypt, they departed, carrying Joseph's bones with them (Exodus 13:19).

Emphasize that the pillar of fire and cloud (Exodus 13:21–22) remained with God's people night and day. The Lord remained constant with His people, guiding and protecting them.

When the people saw the powerful army following them (Exodus 14:10–14), they began to doubt the power of God and became afraid. But Moses met their cries with strong faith and confidence that God would save them, true to His promise.

### Trouble along the Way

Reread the footsteps again. Most show God's great power and love for His people, but one shows sin creeping into the hearts of the people of Israel. Shade in that footstep to remove it from the path.

Even though God's people have witnessed great miracles like the plagues on the Egyptians and are led by a man in direct communication with God, sin still lurks in their hearts. Satan plants the seed of doubt as the people of Israel see Pharaoh's large army coming after them.

Satan works overtime to make us doubt God's power and love. How do the following verses describe Satan's power and human sin?

*Be sober-minded; be watchful. Your adversary the devil prowls around like a roaring lion, seeking someone to devour* (1 Peter 5:8).

Satan is like a prowling, roaring lion looking for someone to devour.

*If you do well, will you not be accepted? And if you do not do well, sin is crouching at the door. Its desire is for you, but you must rule over it* (Genesis 4:7).

Sin crouches at the door; it desires to have us, but we must master it.

How do you picture Satan using his power?

Answers will vary.

Satan is sneaky and tricky. He fills us with doubt or fear when we least expect it. In the Bible, there were times when God's "heroes," even Moses himself, sinned and did not see the power of God working in their lives.

### The Power of God Is on Our Side

Though we want to trust God fully and follow only Him, God knows that is impossible for us to do on our own. We can try and try, but only Jesus kept the Law perfectly.

How do we benefit from what Christ has done for us (2 Corinthians 5:16–21)?

Christ took on our sin, and in exchange, He gave us His perfect life. We are fully forgiven in Him.

Read Ephesians 6:11–20. How do we put on the "full armor of God"?

Learn the truth about God, spread the Gospel, rely on faith in your salvation and the Holy Spirit's power, and pray.

**Remember**

You have led in Your steadfast love the people whom You have redeemed; You have guided them by Your strength to Your holy abode.

Exodus 15:13

15

This section concludes with the miraculous parting of the Red Sea and with Moses' Song of Deliverance.

## Review

Allow time for students to look up and record the meaning to these words. Comment that just as a pillar offers support to buildings, in this case the pillar of cloud and the pillar of fire reminded God's people of His presence and care. Remind students of the common root of the words *exodus* and *exit*.

### Bringing It Home

Interview someone from among your family and friends. Ask them to tell you about a "Red Sea" moment—a time when they felt they had to put their whole trust in God and God alone, a time when they felt cornered and unable to move except by the grace of God.

Let the following questions guide your interview.

1. Tell about a time when circumstances forced you to rely solely on God.
2. Why did you feel you needed to fully rely on God? Had you tried to do it on your own and failed?
3. What lessons did you learn from this experience?
4. When did you finally feel comfort?
5. How did you approach God for help?



# INTO our lives

## Trouble along the Way

Students should recognize that Exodus 14:10–11 shows sin creeping into the hearts of the Israelites.

Start a discussion about sin. What evidence of sin do you see in Exodus 14:10–11? Why might Israel have doubted God's power? How are their fears addressed?

Ask students if they ever doubted the power of God. When that happens, who do you want in control of your life? How can you recognize doubt? What can you do to rid yourself of doubt?

Brainstorm why Satan uses doubt in our lives. Underscore how sneaky Satan is. He can trick us into believing that God has abandoned us and that we need to fend for ourselves.

Encourage students to pray for strength when they are feeling weak. Pray that the Lord would continue to work through our doubts to make us confident in who we are and what we were created to do.

## The Power of God Is on Our Side

Remind students that only Christ has kept the Law perfectly, and His death and resurrection was an exchange for us. Through His death and resurrection, our imperfections are exchanged for Christ's righteousness. We become the redeemed children of God; Jesus' victory over our enemies is our victory!

Just as the children of Israel and even Moses doubted God's power, we may have doubts. But it is important to remember that we are forgiven only through the reconciliation found in Jesus Christ.

God prepares us for battling Satan. He has blessed us with the full armor of God in Ephesians 6. If you have access to presentation software, illustrate a warrior going into battle. Putting on the armor of God involves Bible study, prayer, and worship. This armor equips us to battle Satan, especially when we are armed with the Word of God.

## Remember

In the memory verses, the people of Israel are just realizing how much they need the Lord's help as they leave Egypt. We can make these verses a prayer too. We are sinful and need Jesus to rescue us from our sin. We are safe and victorious over our enemies because of Christ and what He has done for us. We rejoice in the power of God, glorify His name, and thank Him for His power in our lives.

Distribute copies of **Reproducible 6** for students to complete.

# Bringing It Home

Interview someone from among your family and friends. Ask them to tell you about a "Red Sea" moment—a time when they felt they had to put their whole trust in God and God alone, a time when they felt cornered and unable to move except by the grace of God.

Let the following questions guide your interview.

1. Tell about a time when circumstances forced you to rely solely on God.

2. Why did you feel you needed to fully rely on God? Had you tried to do it on your own and failed?

3. What lessons did you learn from this experience?

4. When did you finally feel comfort?

5. How did you approach God for help?

# The Ten Commandments

## EXODUS 20

## Background

The Ten Commandments are part of the old covenant, which bears striking similarities to a Hittite suzerainty (or vassal) covenant. In such a treaty, a more powerful king would initiate a six-part covenant with a less powerful king.

The greater king would remind the lesser king of who he was and what he had done for that king in the past. He would outline what he expected the lesser king to do in response and call on the gods to bear witness to the covenant. The final part detailed blessings and curses.

All six parts are present in the old covenant, the Ten Commandments, recorded in Exodus 20. First, God reminds His people who He is (Exodus 20:2a) and what He has done for them (Exodus 20:2b). Then, He explains that He expects them (Exodus 20:3–17) to keep the Commandments, not to earn God's favor, but because they already had it through His grace.

The same is true today. We are no longer under the old covenant but the new covenant (Jeremiah 31:31–34), which shares a similar structure. God initiates our relationship with Him through His Son's death and resurrection, not because we deserve it or have kept the Commandments well enough but because of His grace.

## Devotion

Mrs. Meyers cringed as she heard a screech followed by tears. Once again, some of her preschoolers didn't follow the rules and someone got hurt. As she walked over to the scene, she repeated in her head, "Stay calm, stay calm." It seemed like she had been going through boxes of bandages like crazy this week.

She knew not to ask what happened because those words always resulted in yelling and more tears. As she spied a tricycle tipped over, front wheel still spinning and the little girl clutching her knee, she said, "It looks like someone crossed in front of a moving tricycle, and the tricycle did not stop."

As the two children opened their mouths to argue back, the teacher held up her finger. "Seems like you both did wrong, correct?"

The kids looked at the teacher and at the situation and just hung their heads.

"Now, let's take a look at that knee, Madison."

Madison removed her hand to show a small scrape on her knee.

"Good, no blood. I don't think we'll be needing a bandage, do you?"

Madison shook her head, stood up with a slight limp, and held her hand out to James, the tricycle rider. He reached out and grabbed her hand. When they were up, the two children hugged. They said, "I'm sorry," and began to pick up the tricycle together. Off they went to play together again, seemingly having forgotten the incident altogether.

Wouldn't it be neat to have a cure-all bandage or someone to pick us up when we fall down? How about someone who forgets when we wrong them? We may not have a physical person to do all those things, but we do have a spiritual Father who will offer us love and forgiveness, even when we break the rules again and again.

In a way, God is like a teacher who oversees our situations and assesses and helps us on a daily basis. Our God saw our need for a Savior and sent His only Son to solve that need. What more can He do for us?

**PRAY: Dear heavenly Father, thank You for giving us rules to live by in our lives. Thank You for offering us help when we break those rules. Help us to live the way You want us to live on a daily basis and to forgive others as You forgive us. This we ask in Jesus' name. Amen.**

Sing: "Lord, Keep Us Steadfast in Your Word" (*LSB* 655).

## Central Truth

Through Moses, God provided His people with the Law; through Jesus, God provided the one who achieved total and complete obedience to the Law in our place.

## Objectives

- Explain God's purpose in giving the Ten Commandments.
- Identify the Ten Commandments and the various ways we sin against God.
- Acknowledge that through Jesus we receive the forgiveness of sins and are declared holy and righteous before God.

## Materials

- The Basics
- Reproducible 7

## Bible Prep

Post in advance so students can bookmark references before class time.

- Exodus 20
- Colossians 1:13–14
- Romans 10:4
- Psalm 119:9

# INTO the lesson

Say, **Think about the rules you have to follow in your daily life. What would God think of these rules? How do the rules benefit your life?** Discuss rules that currently affect students. Evaluate if the rules are godly—do they help students live a godly, safer, or better life?

Follow up with, **After the children of Israel were freed from slavery and began their journey, God gave them rules to follow. These rules established a trust between God and His people. God continued to provide for His people, though they tested Him. When the people of Israel reached the wilderness of Sinai, God spoke to Moses. He gave them the promise "You shall be to me a kingdom of priests and a holy nation"** (Exodus 19:5–6), **and the people agreed to keep His covenant. So Moses climbed Mount Sinai to receive the Commandments.**

# INTO the Word

## A Gift of Good Living

As you move into this section, remind students of the purpose of rules. In the previous lesson, the children of Israel were given rules about the manna. Review those rules. **How were these rules helpful?** The rules about the gathering and use of manna reminded the people to trust and obey God and to observe the Sabbath Day. Now, in Exodus 19–20, God will offer them a promise in return for their obedience.

Read or paraphrase the paragraphs in this section. Stress that God's Commandments are for our good—they are a gift that outlines the best, meaning the most healthy and rewarding, way to live. Allow time for students to match each book title to the commandment to which it most closely relates. Encourage students to use their catechisms if you choose. If you choose to do so, distribute **Reproducible 7** and allow time for students to complete it.

*Note*: Some denominations have a different numbering system for the Ten Commandments. The important thing to remember is that all the content of the Commandments is represented.

7 Exodus 20

## The Ten Commandments

### A Gift of Good Living

The Commandments were to guide the people of Israel in how they were to live and also as a reminder of what God had done for His people. The Commandments also serve these functions in the lives of God's people today.

Imagine that you are looking at books in the library or bookstore when you discover a shelf labeled The Good Life. Upon closer examination of the titles, you discover that the shelf contains ten books, one for each of the Commandments. Write the number of each of the Ten Commandments in the blank on the spine of the book to which it most closely relates.

**Review**

honor— to highly regard in thought, speech, and action

covet— a wrong and unhealthy desire to be, or possess the things of, another

testimony— authorization given of something as a fact

16

## Review

Ask students to define these words relating to the Ten Commandments. *Honor* is the word used in connection with the Fourth Commandment and the regard we are to have for parents and others in authority over us. *Coveting* is the sin identified in the Ninth and Tenth Commandments. *False testimony* is the sin against the Eighth Commandment.

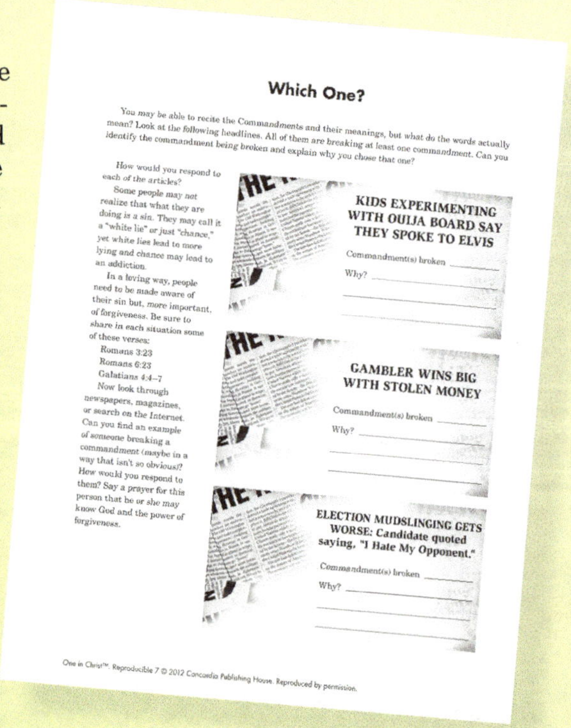

**Which One?**

You may be able to recite the Commandments and their meanings, but what do the words actually mean? Look at the following headlines. All of them are breaking at least one commandment. Can you identify the commandment being broken and explain why you chose that one?

How would you respond to each of the articles?

Some people may not realize that what they are doing is a sin. They may call it a "white lie" or just "chance," yet white lies lead to more lying and chance may lead to an addiction.

In a loving way, people need to be made aware of their sin but, more important, of forgiveness. Be sure to share in each situation some of these verses:

Romans 3:23
Romans 6:23
Galatians 4:4–7

Now look through newspapers, magazines, or search on the Internet. Can you find an example of someone breaking a commandment (maybe in a way that isn't so obvious)? How would you respond to them? Say a prayer for this person that he or she may know God and the power of forgiveness.

KIDS EXPERIMENTING WITH OUIJA BOARD SAY THEY SPOKE TO ELVIS

Commandment(s) broken ______

Why? ______

GAMBLER WINS BIG WITH STOLEN MONEY

Commandment(s) broken ______

Why? ______

ELECTION MUDSLINGING GETS WORSE: Candidate quoted saying, "I Hate My Opponent."

Commandment(s) broken ______

Why? ______

### Why We Need God's Law

God's Word teaches that we need God's Law to do three things for us:

| Curb | Mirror | Guide |
|---|---|---|
| | | |

Sin came into the world through Adam, and a consequence of sin is death. Because we were born sinful, we cannot keep God's Commandments and live the good life He intended. The Commandments help to show us our sin. Although we try to keep them, our sinful nature ultimately leads us to disobey.

### What Can We Do about Sin?

What do the following verses remind us about our need for a Savior?

Colossians 1:13–14— We are rescued from sin through Christ, who has given us forgiveness of sins.

Romans 10:4— Those who believe are made righteous through Christ.

So what can we do about it? Nothing! Christ has done it all for us. We were born sinful, are baptized into the redeeming waters of Baptism, and are made free again. Christ took on the sins of the world and redeemed us.

What does God's Law provide for those who believe in Jesus and are rescued from sin?

Psalm 119:9— God's Word shows us how to live our lives for Jesus.

**REMEMBER**

Christ redeemed __us__ from the __curse__ of the __law__ by becoming a __curse__ for us—for it is __written__, "Cursed is __everyone__ who is hanged on a tree."

Galatians 3:13

17

# INTO our lives

## Why We Need God's Law

Review Exodus 20:1–17 with your students. Point out that the Ten Commandments are a list of laws referring to how we treat God and others. They can be divided into two sections. Commandments 1–3 refer to God and can be summarized with "Love the Lord your God with all your heart and with all your soul and with all your mind" (Matthew 22:37; Deuteronomy 6:5). Commandments 4–10 make reference to how we treat others: "Love your neighbor as yourself" (Matthew 22:39; Leviticus 19:18).

The Law has three uses. It acts as a mirror, curb, and guide. Have the students illustrate each object in the box and below it write a small description as to why each object was chosen. Discuss these illustrations.

Mirror: **Why do we use them? What do we see when we look into a mirror?** (As the Law shows us our sin, the mirror shows us our spiritual condition.)

Curb: **Where do you see curbs? What are their purpose?** (As the curb stops cars from jumping onto a sidewalk and hurting someone, the Law helps keep order in the world.)

Guide: **What is a guidebook? How is it helpful?** (As directions guide an activity, the Law tells Christians how to lead a God-pleasing life.)

Ask, **What do we know about human beings and sin? Where did sin come from? What was the consequence of our sin?** ([Genesis 3:14–19] Since the fall into sin, all of humanity has become totally corrupt [Psalm 51:5; Romans 5:12; James 4:17].) Ask, **Since we didn't cause Adam and Eve to sin, why do we need a Savior?** (We are all born into sin. Because we are born sinful, we need a Savior. Nothing we can do alone can stop us from sinning. Romans 5 reminds us that one consequence of sin was death, and since we sin, we will all eventually die, unless Christ returns before we die.)

Ask, **What about this situation? You are on the playground watching a group of students bully a younger student. They are calling him names, maybe shoving him around. You are there, watching but not participating or laughing. Is this is a sin?** (The answer is yes. According to James 4:17, if we know what is right and don't do it, that is sin too. It is called a sin of omission. We allowed something to happen even though it was wrong.)

## What Can We Do about Sin?

On our own, we cannot gain forgiveness. We may feel sorry and right the wrong with the other person, but we cannot do it alone. The only way is through Jesus.

Together read and discuss the verses. Stress the message of all of these verses—**Christ conquered sin and overcame death for us.**

## Remember

As you assign and review your students' memorization of this verse, underscore its significance by having students create a poster drawing attention to Christ and His overcoming of sin for us. It could picture the cross, a loving hand, or a "battle." Under the box, have them explain why they chose that illustration.

# Which One?

You may be able to recite the Commandments and their meanings, but what do the words actually mean? Look at the following headlines. All of them are breaking at least one commandment. Can you identify the commandment being broken and explain why you chose that one?

How would you respond to each of the articles?

Some people may not realize that what they are doing is a sin. They may call it a "white lie" or just "chance," yet white lies lead to more lying and chance may lead to an addiction.

In a loving way, people need to be made aware of their sin but, more important, of forgiveness. Be sure to share in each situation some of these verses:

Romans 3:23
Romans 6:23
Galatians 4:4–7

Now look through newspapers, magazines, or search on the Internet. Can you find an example of someone breaking a commandment (maybe in a way that isn't so obvious)? How would you respond to them? Say a prayer for this person that he or she may know God and the power of forgiveness.

**KIDS EXPERIMENTING WITH OUIJA BOARD SAY THEY SPOKE TO ELVIS**

Commandment(s) broken ____________

Why? ______________________________

__________________________________

__________________________________

**GAMBLER WINS BIG WITH STOLEN MONEY**

Commandment(s) broken ____________

Why? ______________________________

__________________________________

__________________________________

**ELECTION MUDSLINGING GETS WORSE: Candidate quoted saying, "I Hate My Opponent."**

Commandment(s) broken ____________

Why? ______________________________

__________________________________

__________________________________

# The Serpent on the Pole

## NUMBERS 21:4–9

## Background

They are at it again. More grumbling. More complaining. This time it is a new generation. A new generation stands ready to go to the Promised Land, but they are repeating the sins of their parents. Numbers 20 records the death of Miriam and the story of Moses striking the rock instead of speaking to it so that water would come forth. Because of that disobedience, Moses and Aaron will not enter the Promised Land. Chapter 20 also records the death of Aaron. So now, without his siblings, Moses continues to lead the people to the Promised Land.

Things are changing for Moses, but one thing remains the same. God, in His steadfast love, continues to care for the grumbling Israelites. This time, the Israelites are complaining because they are traveling away from the Promised Land instead of toward it. This change in direction takes place because the king of Edom refused to allow the Israelites to travel through his land. So they have to go around. That is what has brought on the complaining this time, along with boredom with manna and the lack of water.

## Central Truth

Though we often grumble and complain, God continues to forgive, restore, and provide for us as His people through Jesus, our Lord.

## Objectives

- Recognize that in the hardship that befell His people, God was calling them to repentance.
- Draw parallels between the serpent on the pole and Jesus on the cross.
- Express the intent to "look to the cross" always.

## Materials

- The Basics
- Reproducible 8

## Bible Prep

Post in advance so students can bookmark references before class time.

- Numbers 21:4–9
- Romans 3:23
- Romans 6:23
- John 3:14–17

## Devotion

"Good night. Sleep tight. Don't let the bedbugs bite." This used to be a common saying of many parents when they tucked their children into bed. Bedbugs are small nocturnal insects that love to live in bedding material and bite people while they are sleeping. Bedbugs were a common pest in our country in the 1930s and 1940s. Over time, the pests were exterminated and were no longer a concern of many people. However, in 2010, the pests made a comeback, and many hotels and homes again saw the presence of bedbugs. Yuck!! These pesky insects changed the habits of many people staying in hotels and caused a huge inconvenience for people affected by them.

The sin of grumbling can be compared to bedbugs. Left unchecked grumbling can return again and again to bring us down and keep us from focusing on our Savior and His goodness to us. Thank God, Jesus took our grumbling and all other sins to the cross. He has earned forgiveness for our grumbling.

A trained professional must be called to exterminate bedbugs from a home or hotel. Home remedies just don't work. When we, on our own, try to get rid of the grumble bug, we often fail, falling back into the same old grumbling as before. We need to call on Jesus, the only way of salvation, for help.

The Israelites were part of an infestation of grumbling. They continued to do it over and over, even when they knew of God's blessings. Our story today will help us to "look to Jesus," the founder and perfecter of our faith (Hebrews 12:2). Jesus is our only source of salvation and the exterminator of our grumble bugs.

**PRAY: Lord, forgive our sin of grumbling. Help us to appreciate with thankfulness all of the many blessings we continue to receive from You. Help us to look to You and Your cross when we go through times that disappoint and challenge us. Help us to use all we are and have in service to You. In Your name we pray. Amen.**

Sing: "Lord, Be Glorified" (*AGPS* 165).

# INTO the lesson

Point out that habitual complaining or a culture of complaining can be very difficult to break away from. Talk with the class about things that disappoint and discourage them. In your discussion, draw special attention to those things that happen to derail or detract from events they were especially looking forward to. Comment that in today's lesson we will see the people of Israel falling back into their habit of grumbling and complaining when they faced an unexpected disappointment.

# INTO the Word

## The Serpent and Our Savior

As you read through today's text with your class, allow time for them to complete the chart. Read Numbers 21:4–5. Explain that the Israelites have experienced major disappointments in the last few chapters of Numbers. Moses and Aaron disobeyed God by striking the rock to bring forth water instead of speaking to it. Miriam died. Aaron died. And now the king of Edom refuses to let the Israelites pass through his country. Show students on a map where the land of Edom is. The Israelites are now heading back toward the Red Sea, away from the Promised Land. Together with some new complaints, the same old grumblings about food and water arise again.

We are going the wrong way!
We are impatient!
This land has no food or water!
We are tired of manna!

Read Numbers 21:6–7. A new consequence for sin is recorded this time. This one points back to the Garden of Eden, where Satan, in the form of a serpent, tricked Eve. It also points back to the plagues in Egypt because there were so many of them. The Israelites sound like Pharaoh, talking to Moses and asking him to pray to the Lord to take the serpents away.

Read Numbers 21:8–9. Healing and relief came simply from looking at the bronze serpent that Moses made and put up on the pole. The people did not have to do anything to receive healing—simply look to the source of the healing. Looking up at the snake would direct their eyes upward toward God.

8 Numbers 21:4-9

### THE SERPENT ON THE POLE

**The Serpent and Our Savior**

| | People in the Wilderness | People Today |
|---|---|---|
| Who sinned? | Numbers 21:5<br>The people | Romans 3:23<br>**All people** |
| What was the consequence of the sin? | Numbers 21:6<br>The people died | Romans 6:23<br>**Death** |
| What was the plan for saving the people? | Numbers 21:8<br>Moses made a bronze serpent<br>Put it on a pole<br>People look at it in faith and live | John 3:16<br>**God sent His only Son to die on the cross**<br>**People look and believe and live** |
| What was lifted up? | Numbers 21:9<br>Bronze Serpent | John 3:14<br>**Jesus, Son of Man** |
| What needed to happen in order that the people would live? | Numbers 21:9<br>Look and believe | John 3:15<br>**Believe in Jesus** |

**REVIEW**

Draw lines to connect the meanings with three words that describe the life of the Israelites.

rebellion — being led to realize sin and confess it
repentance — turning away from God and His blessings
restoration — being brought back to a trust and belief in God

18

Jesus referred to Moses and the bronze serpent during His ministry. Nicodemus, one of the Pharisees, came to speak to Jesus. He came at night, under the cover of darkness, most likely because he did not want his fellow Pharisees to know that he was having a faith conversation with Jesus. He did not understand all of Jesus' teachings and miracles but was interested enough to ask more questions. We know that the Holy Spirit worked in the heart of Nicodemus through that conversation with Jesus. John 19:39 records that Nicodemus was present at the burial of Jesus, bringing seventy-five pounds of spices to anoint His body. That seems to be a large amount, but was not uncommon for royal burials (see note in *TLSB*, p. 1824).

Nicodemus looked to the Lord for help with questions regarding matters of faith. Nicodemus came to the right place. Like the serpent in the wilderness, **Jesus was lifted up on a piece of wood for the forgiveness of Nicodemus and all people, including you and me.** Have students complete the chart using the Bible references given.

## Review

Have students draw lines to connect the words with the meanings.

**Look to the Cross**

God wants only the best for us. Read John 3:17. For ___God___ did not ___send___ His Son into the ___world___ to ___condemn___ the world, but in ___order___ that the ___world___ might be ___saved___ through Him.

God rescues those who belong to Him. He forgives our sin for Jesus' sake. He works things for our good.

God used the fiery serpents to call His people back to trusting in Him. God used the death of His Son to reconcile the world to Himself.

How can God work in your life to bring good to you? Discuss the following with your class: how could God bless and grow you as His child as you contend with each?

A bad grade

A sickness or injury

The death of a loved one

An argument with a friend

A rainstorm

A car running out of gas

Running late

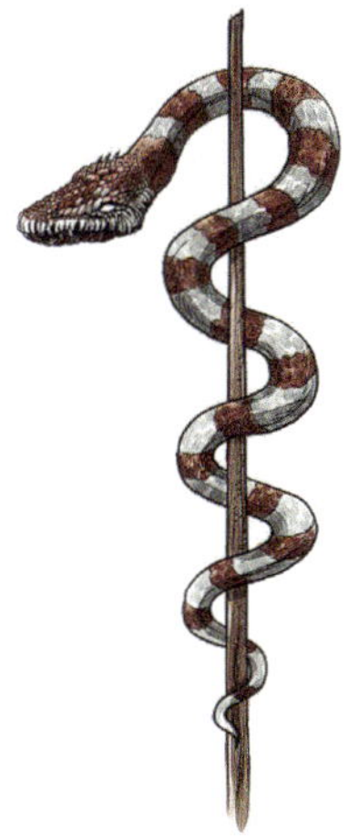

Sometimes, God allows us to see the good that comes out of a situation. Other times, it is difficult to see anything good. Of what can we remind ourselves when it is difficult to see the good?

Answers will vary, but will point to God's unending love for us through Christ Jesus.

**REMEMBER**

And as Moses lifted up the serpent in the wilderness, so must the Son of Man be lifted up, that whoever believes in Him may have eternal life.

John 3:14–15

19

# INTO our lives

## Look to the Cross

The words of John 3:17 remind us of God's reason for sending Jesus into the world. God does have an amazing plan for each one of us, including each of your students. One of the best blessings for Christians is to see the good that comes out of every situation. Our lives can be full of joy and peace when we see ways that God turns tough situations, some of which we bring on ourselves, into blessings for us. Read Romans 8:28 with the students. Have them underline the words *all things* in their books and in their Bibles. God works for the good in all things, not just "some" or a "few" things.

Discuss how God can use each of the situations given to bring His good blessings to His people.

A bad grade—can encourage us to ask for help or put forth more effort in studying

A sickness or injury—can give us time to slow down, reflect on how God heals our body

The death of a loved one—that person is relieved from pain and sickness; he or she has received the goal of salvation

An argument with a friend—can be a chance to gain understanding of the other person's perspective, a chance to show forgiveness and compassion

Distribute copies of **Reproducible 8** for students to complete

A rainstorm—might ruin our outdoor plans, but it waters the earth; gives us an opportunity to do something different and maybe even better

A car running out of gas—could offer protection from an accident

Running late—could put you in a place where someone needs help or could avoid some kind of problem for you

Remind students that God may be using those bad things to draw us closer to Him and call us to repentance as He did the Israelites with the fiery serpents.

Encourage students to be prayerful about seeing the blessings in our hardships. It is certainly not an easy thing to do. The devil wants us to believe that the troubles come because we are bad and that we have caused those bad things to happen. He wants us to believe that a loving God would not allow such things to happen to us. He wants to use troubles to turn us inward and put the focus on ourselves.

However, God's plans are always best. Through prayer and study of His Word, we are reminded about His constant blessings and presence in our lives.

## Remember

As you assign and reflect on the meaning of this verse with your students, stress that God remains in control of all things. He sees our trials and difficulties. He promises ultimately to work all things for good.

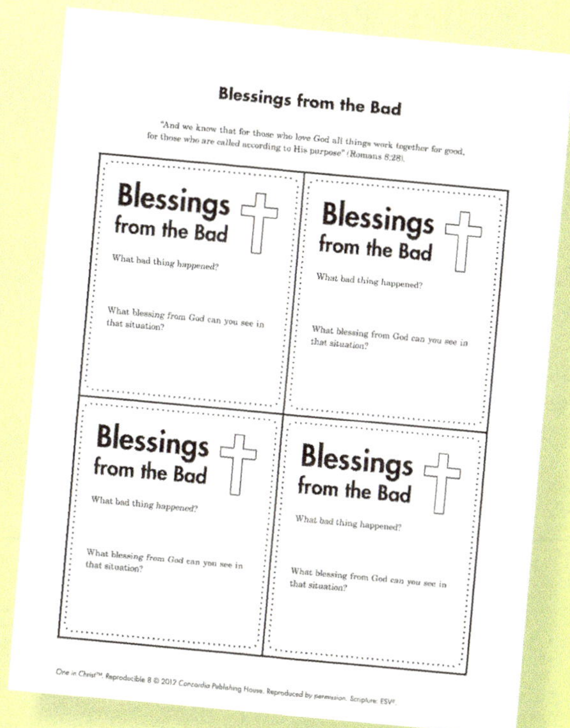

## Blessings from the Bad

"And we know that for those who love God all things work together for good, for those who are called according to His purpose" (Romans 8:28).

| | |
|---|---|
| **Blessings from the Bad**<br>What bad thing happened?<br>What blessing from God can you see in that situation? | **Blessings from the Bad**<br>What bad thing happened?<br>What blessing from God can you see in that situation? |
| **Blessings from the Bad**<br>What bad thing happened?<br>What blessing from God can you see in that situation? | **Blessings from the Bad**<br>What bad thing happened?<br>What blessing from God can you see in that situation? |

# UNIT 2—GOD BLESSES A NATION

## Theme

History reveals cycles of prosperity followed by times of hardship. But God remains constantly involved in human events, calling people to repent, forgiving them, and restoring them as His people. Old Testament history shows God's unfolding plan for the salvation of all people through the Child of Bethlehem, the Son of David, whose kingdom would know no boundaries nor have an end.

For those of us who live as God's New Testament people, our study of the events of these troubled Old Testament times reminds us that God is always faithful and gracious. Often, His goodness becomes especially apparent at those times "when every earthly prop gives way"—when His people are led to rely on Him most.

## Worship

As you cover this unit with your students, compare once again the worship life of Old Testament believers with the worship life of God's people today.

- As a class, explore actions performed during worship that honor Jesus as our King. Possibilities include bowing before entering the altar area or before the altar; calling Him Lord and King; recalling His great deeds performed on behalf of His people in the defeat of our enemies—sin, death, and Satan; and offering Him tribute in the form of our offerings and praise.
- Comment on the role of the Word in bringing the people back to God at the time of King Josiah. Talk about the various ways God's Word touches people in worship. God's Word is read, sung in hymns and choir selections, explained during the sermon, received during the administration of the Sacraments, and visually depicted in the symbols and artwork that are part of the environment in which worship takes place.
- Explain that the Sacraments of Baptism and the Lord's Supper unite God's people with fellow believers of all time and places, including the saints in heaven. These are the great cloud of witnesses referred to in Hebrews 12:1.

### UNIT 2

9. Rahab and the Spies; Israel Crosses the Jordan
10. Gideon Leads God's People
11. David Becomes King
12. Solomon Builds a Temple
13. Rehoboam and Jeroboam
14. God's People in Captivity
15. God's People Return from Captivity

# Extending Unit Concepts

## Community Building

*The Weight of Sin:* Have students hold their arms out straight in front of them, keeping their elbows straight and palms up. Place a heavy book in their outstretched hands and ask them to hold it as long as possible. Explain that this was a punishment often used in classrooms in the past. When they can hold the book no longer, ask how it felt trying to hold it up. How did it feel when their arms began to sag? How did it feel when they could finally put it down? How is this like unrepentant sin? How is it like forgiveness?

*Global Recall:* Give groups of students five minutes to list as many countries as they can. Talk about which nations have an openness to Christianity. Comment that Christians are persecuted in some nations. Pray for Christians undergoing persecution.

*Capture the City:* Divide students into two groups. Have each group construct a wall by taping sheets of tissue paper between two chairs. Allow each team to take siege against the enemy by standing behind a designated line and throwing wadded newspaper to bring down the enemy's wall. Declare the first team to bring down the opposition's wall the winner.

## Tools for Witness

- Design and create a church window, using construction and tissue paper for stained glass art to illustrate the strength God provides through the Word and Sacraments. Relate to the strength and sustenance God provided to His people throughout their captivity.
- Have students do some cuneiform writing on clay tablets they have made. Stress the ease of communicating today in written form, which we take for granted. Comment that God's people kept His Word with them, even in captivity, having committed it to memory when the written Word was not available to them.
- Have students develop comic strips to tell the story of God's grace in the life of Gideon or David.

## Service Projects

- Make small felt Baptism banners to be given to children baptized in the church.
- Collect money, food, clothing, and blankets to help others in God's kingdom. Talk about the kingdoms of power, grace, and glory—all ruled by Christ.
- Have students tutor someone in English or assist a student who is new to this country and needs a little help. Comment that God desires His people to be kind to those from other nations living among us. In a sense, all of God's people live as aliens with a true and lasting home in heaven.
- Have students choose a foreign mission to support.
- Contact a local prison ministry and perform a service to share God's love with those who are in prison or their families. Contrast those in prison with those who have not yet received the freedom only God provides.

## Reaching Every Individual

- Prepare a map of the twelve tribes of Israel. When discussing the division of the kingdom, cut the map in two sections to illustrate the division.
- Construct questions on all of the units. Divide students into teams and play Old Testament trivia.
- Prior to beginning the unit, on a tri-folded piece of paper, have students list (1) what they already know and remember about the story/topic, (2) what they would like to know, and, at the conclusion of the lesson, (3) what they learned that they didn't know before.
- Write the Law/Gospel focus on the board and draw attention to it at the beginning of each session.

# Integrating the Faith throughout the Curriculum

## Social Studies

- Investigate the culture, products, and dwellings of those living in Canaan at the time of the arrival of the people of Israel.
- Talk about the way God's people affect the culture in which they live; talk about the way the culture in which God's people live affects them.
- Trace on a map the homecoming journey of God's people. What are these countries called today?

## Science

- Research modern farming techniques compared to those at the time of Joshua.
- Investigate the processes of casting metal and burnishing bronze in the manufacture of the furnishings of Solomon's temple.
- From a sheet of paper create a raft that will float. See whose raft will support the most items before sinking. (Items may be a collection of washers, bolts, coins, etc.) Comment that rafts were used to bring cedar logs from Lebanon to Israel at the time of the construction of the temple.

## Mathematics

- Make a graph to compare the tribes of Israel according to size. See Numbers 2–4.
- Using graph paper, make a blueprint of the temple to scale, using the dimensions in the Bible (see 1 Kings 6:2–6).
- Construct an Old Testament timeline that begins with creation.
- Estimate how long it would have taken the exiles to reach Jerusalem if they walked twenty miles per day.

## Technology

- Write and present a radio play to illustrate one of the proverbs from the Book of Proverbs.
- Do an Internet search on recent archaeological findings regarding the life and times of David and Solomon.
- Report on ways technology is used to study and share God's Word. Comment that just as finding the Book of the Law brought about reform in the days of Josiah, so Luther's finding of God's truth revealed in the Bible brought about the Protestant Reformation.
- Embrace the gift of technology—cell phones and computers. Have your students select ten Bible verses that they really appreciate. They could be verses from memory work lessons or favorite verses they have read. If school policy allows, give students the opportunity to text one verse to their parents at some point during the school day for the next ten days. Students may choose to text the verse to their friends as well as their parents. Teach students to use technology to share the Gospel! Explore the daily Bible verse resource from the American Bible Society. You can check out their Web site www.americanbible.org to sign up to receive God's Word in the best way for you.

## Fine Arts

- Make a model of Solomon's temple.
- Study the paintings of Norman Rockwell. Which one best depicts faith and love of our homeland?
- Study Psalms 85 and 86, which are psalms of thanksgiving for return from captivity and for requesting grace and mercy for the future.

## Language Arts

- Name or read literature that deals with the theme of building and establishing new homes. Compare with the events of this unit.
- Debate the topic "good times are better than bad times for the people of God."
- Tell of a time when you were returning home after an extended absence. How did you feel?
- Write an eyewitness newspaper account about the fall of Jerusalem.

# Rahab and the Spies; Israel Crosses the Jordan

JOSHUA 2–5

## Central Truth

Like the Israelites, we are sinners, yet God in mercy, for Jesus' sake, leads us to His eternal promised land.

## Objectives

- Recognize that God uses all kinds of people to accomplish His will.
- Perceive the changes that took place upon entering the Promised Land.
- Acknowledge God in Christ as the Christian's source of strength and courage.

## Materials

- The Basics
- Reproducible 9

## Bible Prep

Post in advance so students can bookmark references before class time.

- Joshua 2:1–24; 3:14–17; 5:1–12

## Background

After Moses' death, God chose Joshua to lead His people. Joshua sent spies to see the land. When Moses sent spies earlier, Joshua was one of them. It did not turn out well. Moses sent spies to the entire land of Canaan. Joshua asked particularly for a report on Jericho. Moses' spies reported to many people; Joshua's spies reported only to him. The spies were hidden by Rahab, who is mentioned in New Testament verses such as Hebrews 11:31 and James 2:25, and then they returned.

Then God directed His people in their crossing of the Jordan River. He provided for them miraculously to cross on dry ground and commanded them to take twelve stones from the center of the river to construct a memorial of this great and dramatic event.

Once across the river, they made camp. The people of Jericho knew they were there, but they were too frightened to bother them. It was here that God commanded Joshua to have all the uncircumcised boys be circumcised. There are many reasons that circumcision may not have occurred in the wilderness. Some believe it was for medical reasons, while others believe it was a way that God showed that they were not in His favor. After the circumcision, they celebrated Passover. This had not been done since the one-year anniversary of the Passover. They used the fruits of the area, probably from abandoned farms. Since they were able to live off the land once again, there was no reason for God to provide the manna. Wandering days were over for God's people.

## Devotion

In today's story, you will meet a woman named Rahab. She was different from the Israelite spies who needed her help. She had different values, a different way of living. She represented a different culture. The one true God, however, worked through her to protect the spies.

We know the usual sources of God's protection and guidance. We can count on our pastors and teachers to provide godly help. Most of all, we always can trust the all-powerful God the Father to do what is best; He can do anything! We always can trust Jesus, the Son of God, to be the source of forgiveness when we fail; He lived, died, and rose to take away those sins too. Finally, we always can trust the Holy Spirit, who delivered faith into our souls and works through God's Word to guide, encourage, and comfort us.

God can do anything He wants. He *is* God, after all. We need not be surprised that He doesn't always use regular, ordinary means to help and provide for us. He can and does use whomever He chooses. Of course, we must be careful that we don't follow the devil. The devil is very good at deceiving and lying. That's why it is important to learn as much as we can about God. That's why it is important for God's Spirit to strengthen our faith and increase our understanding of God and what He has done and continues to do for us.

**PRAY: Dear Jesus, please be with us as we encounter new needs for courage and faithfulness. Thank You for giving us the Bible and godly people to guide us. Amen.**

Sing: "I Am Trusting Thee, Lord Jesus" (*LSB* 729).

# INTO the lesson

Comment that God often requires believers to be courageous. We can trust in God to help us sometimes in remarkable ways through unlikely people and circumstances. Read the following situations. Why would you need courage from God to do His will in each situation? Who might help you?

**1.** You're in a new school and you meet several students. These students are not Christians, and they talk to you about how foolish they think Christianity is. How do you respond?

**2.** You help out in the church nursery during a meeting. You see a little boy who is being teased by older children. How do you handle the situation?

Discuss the following for each situation:

- Why is there a need for courage?
- What might be the consequences for not helping?
- Whose help could be enlisted?

Lead students to understand the risks involved and the help required. First, help from God is the only sure help. This comes from prayer—even a very short one. Second, how might some creative students suggest how to turn one or more of the antagonists to their side?

# INTO the Word

## Changes for God's People

Introduce this section by discussing changes that students and you have experienced, focusing on the "before and after." Read through the examples of change reported in the Book of Joshua. Discuss which changes might require the most difficult adjustment.

Allow time for silent reading of Joshua 2:1–24. Ask students to use the boxes for brief notes to answer the three questions after they have read the entire selection. Conclude the section by discussing the reasons for their answers.

## Review

Write the definition of the words.

9 Joshua 2–5

### Rahab and the Spies; Israel Crosses the Jordan

**Changes for God's People**

The Book of Joshua tells the story of many changes.

Moses was dead. Joshua was in charge.

Israel stopped wandering. The people were ready to occupy the Promised Land.

A spy mission went from a previous failure to an exciting success.

After forty years, God stopped the flow of manna. Israel could eat from local crops.

Circumcision was once again practiced, something that had not been practiced regularly during the wandering.

Israel celebrated the Passover.

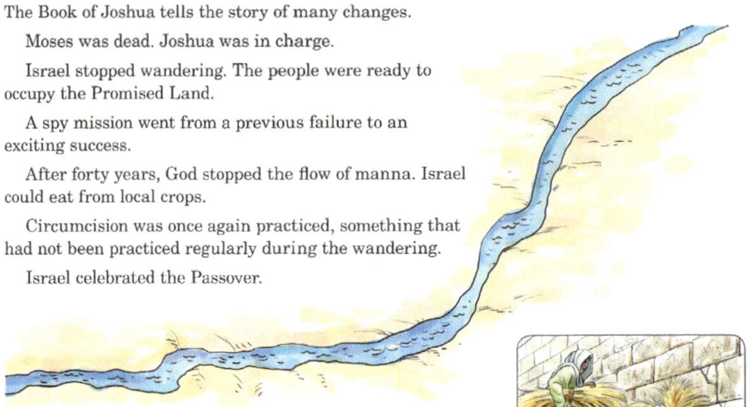

God caused this good change for His people. The change did not happen without an exciting story. Read that story in Joshua 2. Be ready to explain your answers to these questions:

| 1. What part of the story did you like best? | 2. What part of the story surprised you most? | 3. What did you learn about God? |
|---|---|---|

**Review**

Passover— annual festival held in remembrance of God's deliverance in Egypt

manna— bread miraculously provided by God for His people in the wilderness

circumcision—act performed on males to indicate their identity as followers of the true God

20

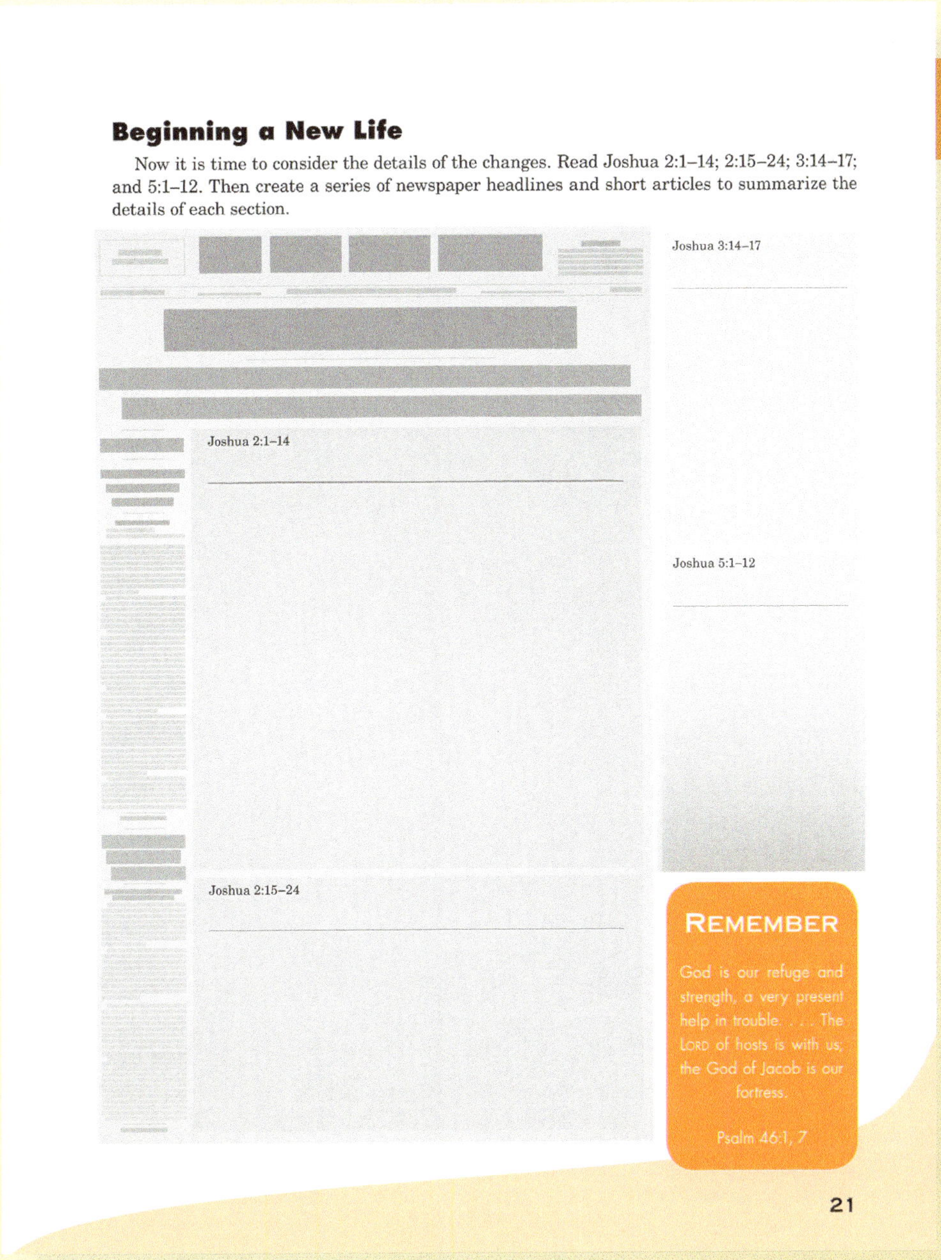

**Beginning a New Life**

Now it is time to consider the details of the changes. Read Joshua 2:1–14; 2:15–24; 3:14–17; and 5:1–12. Then create a series of newspaper headlines and short articles to summarize the details of each section.

Joshua 2:1–14

Joshua 2:15–24

Joshua 3:14–17

Joshua 5:1–12

REMEMBER

God is our refuge and strength, a very present help in trouble. . . . The LORD of hosts is with us; the God of Jacob is our fortress.

Psalm 46:1, 7

21

# INTO our lives

## Beginning a New Life

Separate the class into four groups, each group having the responsibility to write headlines and articles that summarize their respective verses. Students with the least Bible-reading experience might be assigned to the verses for chapter 3. Ask each group to report their headlines. If you choose to do so, distribute copies of **Reproducible 9** for students to complete as a review of the events of today's story.

Comment that the Jordan River Valley, especially during certain times of the year, is lush and green. Certainly, the people felt God's care and blessing on them as they crossed into the Promised Land on dry ground. Discuss the following: **What is courage? Who is the most courageous person you know? What makes him or her courageous?** Explain that there are times when we want to be courageous, but we're not. We may feel ashamed, scared, or have a variety of other feelings. We have God on our side. **He sent His Son to earn forgiveness and salvation for us.** And He gives us the power of His Spirit, who strengthens and encourages us through God's Word.

We can pray to God, and He will help us to do His will. He may not always answer our prayers in the way we expect. But He will answer our prayers according to what He knows is best for us.

Assure students that God gives the courage to face uncertain things and times in our lives, and He gives us something more special than that. He provides forgiveness of sins—forgiveness for the times we worry or we forget that He is with us. Someday, we will be in heaven with Him and will have no more fear.

## Remember

Discuss what this verse means. Pay special attention to troublesome words such as *refuge* and the phrase *is our fortress.* Ask students to tell what it means specifically to their lives. Comment that this verse was a favorite of Martin Luther, one in which he found strength and encouragement during the dark days of the Reformation.

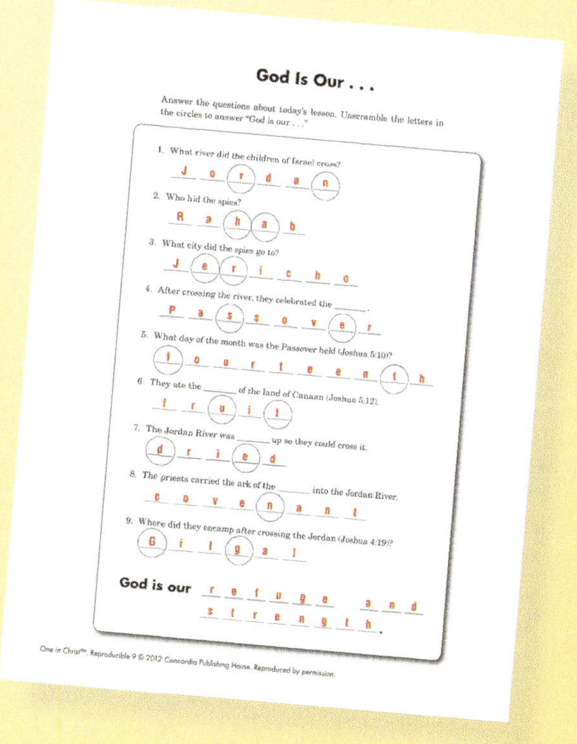

**God Is Our . . .**

Answer the questions about today's lesson. Unscramble the letters in the circles to answer "God is our . . ."

1. What river did the children of Israel cross? J o r d a n
2. Who hid the spies? R a h a b
3. What city did the spies go to? J e r i c h o
4. After crossing the river, they celebrated the ______. P a s s o v e r
5. What day of the month was the Passover held (Joshua 5:10)? f o u r t e e n t h
6. They ate the ______ of the land of Canaan (Joshua 5:12). f r u i t
7. The Jordan River was ______ up so they could cross it. d r i e d
8. The priests carried the ark of the ______ into the Jordan River. c o v e n a n t
9. Where did they encamp after crossing the Jordan (Joshua 4:19)? G i l g a l

**God is our** r e f u g e a n d s t r e n g t h.

# God Is Our . . .

Answer the questions about today's lesson. Unscramble the letters in the circles to answer "God is our . . ."

1. What river did the children of Israel cross?

   ___ ___ (___) ___ ___ (___)

2. Who hid the spies?

   ___ ___ (___)(___) ___

3. What city did the spies go to?

   ___ (___)(___) ___ ___ ___ ___

4. After crossing the river, they celebrated the _______.

   ___ ___ (___) ___ ___ ___ (___) ___

5. What day of the month was the Passover held (Joshua 5:10)?

   (___) ___ ___ ___ ___ ___ ___ ___ (___) ___

6. They ate the _______ of the land of Canaan (Joshua 5:12).

   ___ ___ (___) ___ (___)

7. The Jordan River was _______ up so they could cross it.

   (___) ___ ___ (___) ___

8. The priests carried the ark of the _______ into the Jordan River.

   ___ ___ ___ ___ (___) ___ ___ ___

9. Where did they encamp after crossing the Jordan (Joshua 4:19)?

   (___) ___ ___ (___) ___ ___

**God is our** ___ ___ ___ ___ ___ ___ ___ ___ ___

___ ___ ___ ___ ___ ___ ___ ___.

# Gideon Leads God's People

JUDGES 6–8

## Background

This episode in Israel's history takes place forty years after the time of Deborah. As part of the cycle of apostasy, servitude, supplication, salvation, God allows an enemy, the Midianites, to enslave His people.

When the angel of the Lord appears to Gideon, this "mighty man of valor" is threshing wheat—in a winepress! Why? A winepress provided a hiding place from the Midianites. This image illustrates the anxiety and desperation Gideon and his family feel.

First, the Lord tells Gideon to eradicate Israel's idolatry, an idolatry that has even infected his father's home. Starting in his own home, Gideon begins to cleanse Israel—but under the cover of darkness. The next morning, he refuses to claim responsibility for his actions.

These two episodes are emblematic of the doubt and timidity of Gideon revealed throughout the account. Gideon is an unworthy hero. He's afraid, he doubts, he whines a little, and his life comes to a less-than-admirable end. In it all, though, we come to recognize the triune God as the only true hero in all of Scripture—and in our lives too. Gideon's weakness reveals God's power.

As you prepare to teach today, read 1 Corinthians 1:18–31 and talk with Jesus about it. Ask Him to use you in your weakness to share His strong love and forgiveness with your students.

## Central Truth

God, in Christ, forgives the sinful doubts of His people, strengthens their faith, and enables them to do His will.

## Objectives

- Tell how God changed Gideon by strengthening his faith.
- Recognize God's power at work in Gideon's weakness, leading the Israelites to defeat the people of Midian.
- Show appreciation for God's forgiveness, restoration, and the new and eternal life He provides through faith in Christ Jesus.

## Materials

- The Basics
- Reproducible 10
- Students may want to use colored pencils for the storyboards they create.

## Bible Prep

Post in advance so students can bookmark references before class time.

- Proverbs 3:5–6
- Judges 6:11–24, 36–40
- Judges 7:1–23
- 2 Corinthians 12:9
- Isaiah 6:8

## Devotion

Mr. Daniels called Keisha to his desk one day, as the class was busy working on a set of math problems. "Keisha," he said quietly, "I'd like you to help Josiah with his math today." Keisha was surprised. "Mr. Daniels," she said, "I really don't think that's such a good idea. I barely understand the equations we're working on. Why don't you ask someone smarter?"

Mr. Daniels just shook his head. "Keisha, I have a very good reason for asking you, and I would like you to trust me. Will you please help Josiah?"

Grumbling under her breath about the unfairness, Keisha sat down near Josiah's desk and tapped him on the shoulder. "Can I help you with your math?" she asked, trying to keep the doubt from her voice.

"Sure!" Josiah said eagerly. "I don't get problem four; do you?" Keisha looked down at his paper. She was surprised to discover she actually did understand how to do that problem. When they finished discussing it, they moved on to the next and then the next. As they worked together, Keisha realized that helping Josiah was actually helping her understand the problems better herself.

Later in the day, Keisha stopped at Mr. Daniels's desk. "I guess you were right, Mr. Daniels," she said. "I just had to trust you."

We don't always understand the way Jesus works in our lives. We can't always figure out the reason behind the things He seems to be asking us to do. But Jesus went to the cross for us; He is our Savior. He wants us to trust Him. And He will never let us down!

**PRAY: Dear Lord, thank You for Your promise to reveal Yourself to us as we study Your Word. As we think today about what it means to be leaders, help us to remember that only You can provide us with the grace we need to become the kind of people You will use to bring honor to Yourself and help to other people. In Jesus' holy name we pray. Amen.**

Read Proverbs 3:5–6. Then sing either "I Am Trusting Thee, Lord Jesus" (*LSB* 729) or "Lord, Keep Us Steadfast in Your Word" (*LSB* 655).

# INTO the lesson

## What Makes a Good Leader?

In this section, students will consider leadership qualities and come to the realization that God uses people for His will in spite of their weaknesses.

Ask, **What does it take to be a great leader?** Let students brainstorm characteristics and record these on a thought web.

## Effective Leaders Are . . .

After students have created their webs, have them share their ideas with a partner. Encourage them to look for ideas they have in common and write those qualities as indicated. When students have had a chance to share, invite volunteers to share with the whole group.

Most likely, students will mention qualities such as bravery, determination, and self-confidence as key characteristics for a leader. These are the kind of characteristics the world values in its leaders. But God looks beyond the qualities our world demands when He is choosing leaders. He sees beneath the surface into the potential He has placed in each of us.

## Gideon's Leadership Qualities

Next, have students turn to Judges 6:11–24. It describes the beginning of Gideon's career as a judge in Israel. As they read, they should begin to see that the leadership qualities they listed are, in large part, missing from Gideon's character and personality.

Judges 6:11–24 makes it clear that Gideon does not think highly of himself. He questions God, he belittles himself, he demands a sign. God provides the sign, but in Judges 6:36–40, Gideon demands another, then another! In this classic narrative, we see God's patience with Gideon. Gideon knows he should have faith (e.g., see v. 39), but he still doubts!

When students finish reading, ask, **Which of the leadership qualities we identified earlier do you see in Gideon?** Most will realize that Gideon does not seem like a great leader at this point at all!

Ask students to think about why God chose Gideon. Point them to the idea that God uses us as we are, faults and all. Then, He gets the glory for anything we manage to accomplish. It's not us; it's Christ in us! **Jesus went to the cross to redeem and save us. Now His power is at work through the Word in the lives of those who, by faith, belong to Him.**

## Review

Allow time for students to define the words included in this section. Comment that the Israelites faced two kinds of oppression—that of placing themselves under the sin of idolatry and of oppression at the hands of the Midianites.

---

10 Judges 6–8

### Gideon Leads God's People

#### What Makes a Good Leader?

What does it take to be a good leader? In the box provided below, think of a great leader in the world today or someone you've learned about in history class. Write his or her name in the bubble provided, and then draw an idea web showing the different qualities that make (or made) that leader great.

**Gideon's Leadership Qualities**

Now, read Judges 6:11–24, 36–40. As you read, look for the qualities you listed in the activity at the right. Which of them do you see in Gideon? Discuss this with your partner, jot a few notes below, and be prepared to share your ideas with the class.

_______________

_______________

_______________

_______________

_______________

_______________

_______________

#### Effective Leaders Are . . .

When you complete the web, share your ideas with the person sitting next to you. Are there any common qualities you both included on your webs? Write those qualities below.

_______________

**Review**

Use your glossary to fill in definitions for the words below.

oppression— an unfair use of power

idolatry— worshiping a false god

Midianites— a group of people who lived south and east of Canaan

22

---

# INTO the Word

## God Gets the Glory

**Reproducible 10** includes a skit that narrates Judges 7:1–8. This text tells how God reduces Gideon's army from twenty-two thousand men to three hundred. If you choose not to use the skit, students may simply read the text from the Bible.

Say, **Even though Gideon wasn't very excited about being a leader, God did great things through him. (He wants to do great things through us too!) But for the good of His people, God wanted to make it very clear that HE was the one who brought victory to the army of Israel.**

When students finish reading, either the text or the skit, ask them to reflect on how God works through our weaknesses. Point out that God reduced the size of the army to an almost laughable number because He wanted Israel to see His power and contrast it with the weakness of the idols they had been worshiping.

Explain that Judges 7:9–14 tells of how God reassured Gideon by sending him sneaking into the camp of the Midianites, where he overheard one soldier telling another of a dream he'd had about a cake of barley that rolled into camp and flattened their tents. The soldier's friend interpreted this as a sign that the army of Israel, led by Gideon, was going to conquer their army.

### God Gets the Glory

Now read Judges 7:1–8. God makes it very clear through this that the victory will be His victory alone, not Gideon's and not his army's. And if Gideon had any lingering doubts about that, the way God planned the battle must have laid those doubts to rest.

Read Judges 7:15–23, and you'll see just what an awesome battle commander God is.

In the boxes provided, draw a storyboard that shows the sequence of events from the battle. When you're done, share your drawing with the student sitting next to you. Here are some questions you can ask each other:

- What surprises you about the battle plan?
  Students may be surprised by the attack at night, the clay pots with torches inside, the fact that the Midianite army destroyed itself. Israel carried no weapons.
- How do you think Gideon and the other soldiers felt?
  Perhaps a mixture of fear and determination
- What can we learn about God from this account?
  God is creative and surprising, and He works in ways that we cannot predict. He uses the resources at hand.

### God Gives Us His Strength

God took Gideon, a man who had some serious issues, and gave him the faith and the leadership qualities to conquer a huge army. Over and over again, Gideon doubted his own abilities, and he questioned God and tested Him. He didn't really show any qualities of great leadership at all!

God wants to work through you too. Your life can make an important difference. Take a minute and think about what God might have in store for you. Are there some things you are really good at? some things you really love to do? Maybe God's design for your life features you doing that.

**REMEMBER**

And I heard the voice of the __Lord__ saying, "Whom shall I __send__, and who will go for us?" Then I said, "__Here__ am I! Send __me__."

Isaiah 6:8

23

Next, read about the battle itself (Judges 7:15–23). Point out the fact that Midian's army was vast beyond belief. Gideon's army was tiny in comparison. With God's help, Gideon's little group of three hundred soldiers frightened the vast army of the Midianites so badly, the Midianites turn on each other in the dark. The slaughter was enormous.

When students have finished reading, have them show they understand the major events of the story by creating a storyboard in their books to illustrate the major events of this section. Suggested scenes for the storyboard include the following:

1. Gideon divides his army into three sections.
2. Each man has a trumpet in one hand and an empty jar covering a torch in the other.
3. At the edge of camp, they all blow their trumpets and break the jars.
4. They hold the burning torches up to create confusion and fear.
5. The army of Midian destroys itself.

When finished, have students share their storyboards with a partner and discuss the story using the guided questions. Ask volunteers to share their ideas.

# INTO our lives

## God Gives Us His Strength

In this section, students will reflect on their strengths and weaknesses and come to the understanding that God wants to use their lives to bring Him glory, just as He used Gideon. Tell students, **Think of some of the things you excel at, things you hope to do in the future.** Allow some time for students to think. Continue with, **God worked through Gideon's weaknesses to carry out His plan for Israel. Let's read 2 Corinthians 12:9.** Invite a volunteer to read that verse. Say, **What does that verse mean to you?** Accept student responses. Say, **Think about some of your weaknesses. Could God use them for His glory? How?** Invite students who are comfortable in doing so to share their ideas.

Conclude with, **It's easy to do what we're good at and to take credit for it. It takes God-given faith to trust God to use us in our weakness for His purposes. Jesus hung in weakness on Calvary's cross—and accomplished God's great work of our salvation. Sure of His forgiveness for our foolish pride in our accomplishments, we can walk confidently into any situation, trusting God to work in and through us.**

In closing, remind students that God created faith and trust in Gideon—a great and fearful doubter. What's even more important, God used Jesus' weakness and death to accomplish the great work of our salvation! Because of Jesus, God forgives our idolatry, pride, and doubt. He forgives our reluctance to step out in faith to serve Him by serving the people around us. He will use our lives to honor Jesus. We can trust Him to do that!

## Remember

After the students have found the verse from Isaiah and filled in the blanks in their books, explain that this verse was Isaiah's prayer after he heard God's call to service. Because God has brought us to Himself in Jesus, it can be our prayer too.

### Gideon's Tiny Army

Based on Judges 7:1–8.

Speaking parts: The Lord, Gideon, Frightened Soldier, Brave Soldier, Thirsty Soldier

Divide the rest of the class into three groups. Two of these groups will follow the Frightened Soldier when he leaves; of the remaining number, most will follow the Thirsty Soldier when he leaves. Only two or three will remain at the end.

**Gideon:** So, let me get this straight, Lord.

**The Lord:** *(Throughout the skit, THE LORD stands just behind GIDEON's shoulder, speaking to him alone)* Yes?

**Gideon:** You want me to gather an army and fight the Midianites, right?

**The Lord:** Exactly.

**Gideon:** But You think I have too many men?

**The Lord:** This is MY battle, Gideon, and I want you to remember that it is going to be MY victory. So, yes, you have too many men.

**Gideon:** How will I decide whom to dismiss?

**The Lord:** Ask them if any of them are frightened.

**Gideon:** *(Speaking to assembled SOLDIERS)* Okay, are any of you afraid to fight the Midianites? If you are, you can go back home.

**Frightened Soldier:** *Jumping up and down with hand in the air)* Oh! Oh! Pick me! Pick me!

**Gideon:** Yeeessss?

**Frightened Soldier:** May I go home, please? I hate fighting! So do . . . *(Looks around at other SOLDIERS)* umm . . . about 22 thousand other guys, give or take a few.

**Gideon:** *(In disbelief)* WHAT—22 thousand!? Is this a nation of sissies?

**Brave Soldier:** I'm not a sissy, Gideon. I'll stay. *(Looks around at other SOLDIERS and nods)* The rest of us will stay.

**Gideon:** *(In an aside to THE LORD)* Lord, is this what You meant? Two-thirds of my army is leaving!

**The Lord:** It's *not* your army, Gideon. It's Mine. Let them go.

**Gideon:** Okay, you guys can leave. *(FRIGHTENED SOLDIERS leave, and GIDEON speaks to remaining soldiers.)* Right, so now we need to figure out a battle plan.

**The Lord:** *(Taps GIDEON's shoulder)* Gideon, you still have too many men. We need to get rid of some more.

**Gideon:** Are You joking, Lord?

**The Lord:** No. Send your men down to the river and watch them drink. Then, do as I say.

**Gideon:** *(Sighing)* Men, I know you must be thirsty, so before I tell you our battle plan, let's go down to the river and drink.

**Thirsty Soldier:** Thank you, Gideon. I was getting parched out here. *(Kneels down to scoop up water and drink. Remaining SOLDIERS go to water and drink. Most kneel down to drink, but two or three lap up the water like dogs.)*

**The Lord:** See how some kneel and some lap the water? Separate them into two groups. The ones who lapped the water, they're your army.

**Gideon:** But that's only a handful of men, Lord! How can I ever win this battle?

**Lord:** Do you have faith in Me, Gideon? Trust Me.

**Gideon:** Yes, Lord. *(Turns to THIRSTY SOLDIER)* You and those who scooped the water up in your hands may go home.

**Thirsty Soldier:** *(Looking at other water-scoopers)* Yes, sir. *(Leaves with other SOLDIERS)*

**The Lord:** Now, Gideon, come here. I want to tell you My battle plan.

# Gideon's Tiny Army

Based on Judges 7:1–8.

Speaking parts: The Lord, Gideon, Frightened Soldier, Brave Soldier, Thirsty Soldier

Divide the rest of the class into three groups. Two of these groups will follow the Frightened Soldier when he leaves; of the remaining number, most will follow the Thirsty Soldier when he leaves. Only two or three will remain at the end.

**Gideon:** So, let me get this straight, Lord.

**The Lord:** (*Throughout the skit, THE LORD stands just behind GIDEON's shoulder, speaking to him alone)* Yes?

**Gideon:** You want me to gather an army and fight the Midianites, right?

**The Lord:** Exactly.

**Gideon:** But You think I have too many men?

**The Lord:** This is MY battle, Gideon, and I want you to remember that it is going to be MY victory. So, yes, you have too many men.

**Gideon:** How will I decide whom to dismiss?

**The Lord:** Ask them if any of them are frightened.

**Gideon:** (*Speaking to assembled SOLDIERS*) Okay, are any of you afraid to fight the Midianites? If you are, you can go back home.

**Frightened Soldier:** *Jumping up and down with hand in the air*) Oh! Oh! Pick me! Pick me!

**Gideon:** Yeeessss?

**Frightened Soldier:** May I go home, please? I hate fighting! So do . . . (*Looks around at other SOLDIERS*) umm . . . about 22 thousand other guys, give or take a few.

**Gideon:** (*In disbelief*) WHAT—22 thousand!? Is this a nation of sissies?

**Brave Soldier:** I'm not a sissy, Gideon. I'll stay. (*Looks around at other SOLDIERS and nods*) The rest of us will stay.

**Gideon:** (*In an aside to THE LORD*) Lord, is this what You meant? Two-thirds of my army is leaving!

**The Lord:** It's not your army, Gideon. It's Mine. Let them go.

**Gideon:** Okay, you guys can leave. (*FRIGHTENED SOLDIERS leave, and GIDEON speaks to remaining soldiers.*) Right, so now we need to figure out a battle plan.

**The Lord:** (*Taps GIDEON's shoulder)* Gideon, you still have too many men. We need to get rid of some more.

**Gideon:** Are You joking, Lord?

**The Lord:** No. Send your men down to the river and watch them drink. Then, do as I say.

**Gideon:** (*Sighing*) Men, I know you must be thirsty, so before I tell you our battle plan, let's go down to the river and drink.

**Thirsty Soldier:** Thank you, Gideon. I was getting parched out here. (*Kneels down to scoop up water and drink. Remaining SOLDIERS go to water and drink. Most kneel down to drink, but two or three lap up the water like dogs.*)

**The Lord:** See how some kneel and some lap the water? Separate them into two groups. The ones who lapped the water, they're your army.

**Gideon:** But that's only a handful of men, Lord! How can I ever win this battle?

**Lord:** Do you have faith in Me, Gideon? Trust Me.

**Gideon:** Yes, Lord. (*Turns to THIRSTY SOLDIER*) You and those who scooped the water up in your hands may go home.

**Thirsty Soldier:** (*Looking at other water-scoopers*) Yes, sir. (*Leaves with other SOLDIERS*)

**The Lord:** Now, Gideon, come here. I want to tell you My battle plan.

# David Becomes King

## 2 SAMUEL 1:1–6:23; 1 CHRONICLES 15:1–3, 12–15

## Background

Casual readers often fail to notice the time that elapsed between the day when Samuel anointed David and the day when David became ruler over a united kingdom. Months dragged into years, fourteen years to be precise. It took almost a decade and a half before David received the full blessing Samuel had promised.

Why so long? For one thing, the Lord still had unfinished business with Saul. God gave His anointed many opportunities for repentance and faith. He extended His grace and mercy to Saul again and again.

Second, the Lord used these fourteen long years—most of them, years of great danger and hardship—to shape and equip David for his future service. When David finally became king of all Israel, his relationship with God was one of true devotion.

As a result, David finally completed the command God had given His people centuries earlier when Israel first crossed the Jordan River under Joshua's leadership. King David subdued all of Canaan, conquering Jerusalem and making it his capital. The judges, presiding over a loose confederation of tribes, never created a consensus for that undertaking. Saul's confidence in the Lord to bring victory wavered, then died. But David obeyed, realizing at a deep level the Lord's commitment to His people and to His promise to send the world's Messiah through the people of Abraham, Isaac, Jacob, and Judah.

The story of David and his reign points forward to the King of kings, Jesus Christ, a direct descendant of King David. Christ's reign on earth was yet to come, but one day, this King would leave His heavenly throne to live as a human being on earth, keeping God's Law in our place and dying to pay the penalty for our sins.

## Central Truth

Through Jesus our King, God our Father and ruler of the universe offers forgiveness, strength as well as purpose for daily living, and eternal salvation to the citizens of His kingdom.

## Objectives

- Acknowledge that although earthly kingdoms rise and fall, our God reigns forever.
- Identify the rights and privileges God gives citizens of His kingdom of grace.
- Seek God's help in understanding and pursuing His goals for our life as we daily walk with Him and wait on Him.

## Materials

- The Basics
- Reproducible 11

## Bible Prep

Post in advance so students can bookmark references before class time.

- 2 Samuel 1
- 2 Samuel 2:1–7
- 2 Samuel 4
- 2 Samuel 5
- 2 Samuel 6

## Devotion

Would you like to be president of the United States someday? Maybe you'd rather be king or queen! Generally, people elect presidents, but kings and queens are usually related to the current ruler and assume power only when the current ruler dies. Sometimes, that takes years!

God chose Saul to serve as the first king of Israel. As Saul became more and more disobedient, God sent Samuel to anoint Jesse's youngest son, David, to reign after Saul's death. David had to wait; he waited for fourteen years! During that time, David first kept watch over his family's sheep. Then he served in Saul's entourage. For a while, he ruled a small part of the kingdom. God used all of this to prepare David for his service as king over all Israel. The Bible gives us God's verdict on David's life: "'I have found in David the son of Jesse a man after My heart, who will do all My will" (Acts 13:22).

Of course, David was a sinner. But in many ways, David set a good example for us, and his reign points us to another King, one who had no faults—Jesus Christ. Jesus' perfect life and sacrificial death brought salvation to David, and it brings salvation to us. That's a gift no earthly ruler can give.

Jesus is our King. He rules over us now in the kingdom of grace, and one day, we will live with Him forever in the kingdom of glory, the kingdom that will never end.

**PRAY: Dear Lord, thank You for our earthly leaders. Please guide them to do Your will. Thank You for King David and especially for King Jesus, who died for our sins. Lead us to the kind of special relationship with You that David had. Teach us to obey You now and to look forward to the joys of heaven that will last forever. Amen.**

Sing stanzas 1 and 5 of "Crown Him with Many Crowns" (*LSB* 525).

# INTO the lesson

Before you move into today's Scripture study, review the following political information, preferably while students are looking at a map of the Promised Land at the time David began his reign. The various tribal territory assignments should be clearly marked:

- The twelve tribes of Israel each descended from one of Jacob's sons and was named after that son (e.g., the tribe of Reuben, the tribe of Simeon, the tribe of Dan).
- Each tribe inherited specific territory in the Promised Land. Levi was the exception. The priests and temple workers belonged to this tribe, and they inherited their work. They lived scattered throughout the land as "teaching priests," and many settled near the central place of worship.
- Joseph's sons, Ephraim and Manasseh, each inherited a territory; thus, there were twelve tribal territories even though Levi inherited no land.
- God promised that the Messiah would come from the tribe of Judah.
- The Bible often refers to extended families in Scripture as "houses" (e.g., the house of Israel, the house of Judah).
- When Saul died, his kingdom was split in two parts—roughly north and south. Saul's son Ish-bosheth ruled eleven tribes—the "house of Israel."
- David ruled one tribe—the "house of Judah"—from the town of Hebron.

Refer to a map to illustrate conditions in the land of Israel at the time of the events of today's lesson. Eventually, all the tribes reunited under King David and, later, David's son King Solomon. Comment that after Solomon died, the kingdom split again, forming a "Northern" Kingdom and a "Southern" Kingdom. The two never reunited as an independent nation under a God-appointed king. Emphasize that God blessed His people and kept them united so that from this nation He might provide the world with **the Savior who would come to save all people from their sins.**

11

2 Samuel 1:1–6:23; 1 Chronicles 15:1–3, 12–15

## David Becomes King

### Why David Waited—God's Purposes Revealed

Scripture indicates that David waited fourteen years from the time Samuel anointed him king of all Israel until the day David finally took the throne. David waited, day by day, month by month. Not only did he wait, but he waited through some very unpleasant circumstances.

To David, those fourteen years of waiting may, at times, have seemed pointless. Actually, they were quite purposeful. God used them to transform David from a shepherd boy to a godly, wise adult—a leader God's people could confidently follow.

Read each chapter below, looking for the kind of person David had become. What does each incident reveal about the character the Lord had worked in David? How would each characteristic be important to a powerful monarch of God's chosen nation? The first row is done for you.

| Scripture | What This Chapter Reveals about David's Character | Why This Characteristic Was Important for Israel's King |
|---|---|---|
| 2 Samuel 1 | David was loyal to Israel's rightful king (Saul) and to his friend, Jonathan. David respected the leader of his nation, obeying the Fourth Commandment. | David modeled respect for authority; this was critical as he himself later worked to unify the kingdom. Assassinations would lead to instability. |
| 2 Samuel 2:1–7 | David sought guidance from the Lord, rather than charging ahead to claim the throne as his own—even though God had promised it to him. He also thanked the people who had buried Saul. | David had learned to follow God's guidance for himself; now he would follow it for the nation. Relying on the Lord, he would win victory over Israel's enemies. |
| 2 Samuel 4 | David could have celebrated the death of Saul's general (Abner) and rewarded Joab for killing him. Instead, David mourned Abner. The future king showed humility and self-discipline. | Israel could have plunged into a bloody civil war at any moment. David's restraint kept violence to a minimum and kept Israel's enemies from attacking at a time when the nation was weak and divided. |
| 2 Samuel 5 | Crowned king of all Israel, David leads his warriors in successful battle, crediting the Lord for making him king and (v. 12) recognizing the reason for it—the good of God's people, not David's honor. | By himself, David would lose every battle. To unify the tribes and defeat Israel's many enemies, he needed God's intervention. Also, people will more willingly follow a leader who has their good, not his own, at heart. |
| 2 Samuel 6 | David honors the Lord in worship. He repents of moving the ark of the covenant in the wrong way (Numbers 4:15). In this, he shows respect for God and an earnest desire to obey Him. | Israel had fallen into sinful idolatry off and on for over four hundred years. To break this vice, and to restore worship of the true God, David's wholehearted example would be invaluable. |

### Review

Define these words, using the glossary as necessary.

type of Christ— a biblical person or object having similarities to Christ and foreshadowing, foretelling, or pointing to the coming of Christ and His purpose

Zion— the hill in Jerusalem that was captured by David; it became another name for Jerusalem as well as a synonym for God's reign and His people

ephod— an outer apronlike garment made of linen worn by Jewish priests in ancient times

24

# INTO the Word

## Why David Waited—God's Purposes Revealed

Stress that David had to wait fourteen long years before he became king. He spent much of this time running and hiding from King Saul. As Saul grew more paranoid, he became more dangerous. He tried to murder David at least twice. Hiding from King Saul and his spear, David lived in damp, cold caves. He moved his family out of Israel (1 Samuel 22:1–3) to Moab, knowing his parents would be safer among the idolaters in a foreign land than in Judah, where Saul could find them! David himself fled to the Philistines, pretending at one point to be out of his mind (1 Samuel 21:10–15)!

Today's activity involves about five chapters. This is a lengthy section, but it is vital for students, especially at this age, to be in the Word rather than simply being told the facts. Students should fill in the chart as they glean the information from the text itself.

You may want to divide the class into four groups, each group reading one of the Bible accounts, filling in an appropriate section of the chart, and sharing what they found with the whole class when they have documented it. This is not the best method, because students will get a much better picture if they read the entire text.

## Faith for Life—Waiting on God

Put yourself in David's sandals or in his sleeping bag on the cold, hard ground. Imagine yourself thinking about Samuel's words and the oil the prophet poured over your head. What questions would be running through your mind? What would you be praying about? List your ideas here:

Talk about these questions with your class:

- Think about your life. For what things are you waiting?
- What makes waiting hard? What's the hardest thing you're waiting for?
- How might Jesus be using this time of waiting to grow or equip you? Where do you already see that happening?
- How might the truths you've encountered today change the ways you're praying (or not praying) for yourself?

**Remember**

They who wait for the Lord shall renew their strength; they shall mount up with wings like eagles; they shall run and not be weary; they shall walk and not faint.

Isaiah 40:31

25

However, it may be necessary if time is short.

After everyone has completed the chart, talk about it as a whole group. Answers will vary somewhat, but as you work through the third column, emphasize the benefits Israel received because of David's trust in God, his God-given humility, and his refusal to condone revenge and violence. Had a weaker, prouder, or less mature person vied for power, the outcome would have been very different. Many, many more people would have been hurt.

If you haven't already done so, explain that David wearing an ephod while he danced and sang in worship showed his humility; he took off his royal robes and praised God publicly like a "commoner" would. His wife Michal criticized David for his "unkingly" actions.

## Review

If you used **Reproducible 11** in connection with the lesson on Joshua, students should be familiar with the concept of a type of Christ. Discuss it before asking the class to find the definition in the glossary. Move quickly through the words *Zion* and *ephod*. Having these definitions in mind will help learners better comprehend the chapters from 2 Samuel they will read today.

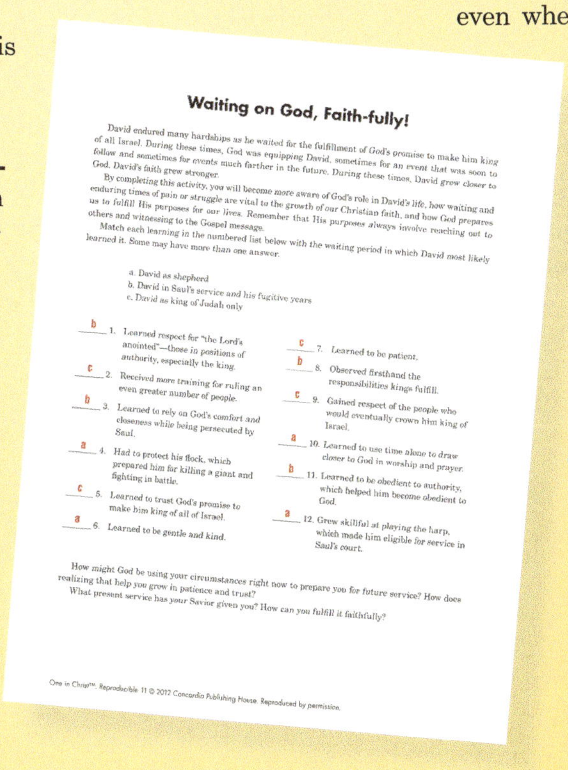

**Waiting on God, Faith-fully!**

David endured many hardships as he waited for the fulfillment of God's promise to make him king of all Israel. During these times, God was equipping David, sometimes for an event that was soon to follow and sometimes for events much farther in the future. During these times, David grew closer to God. David's faith grew stronger.

By completing this activity, you will become more aware of God's role in David's life, how waiting and enduring times of pain or struggle are vital to the growth of our Christian faith, and how God prepares us to fulfill His purposes for our lives. Remember that His purposes always involve reaching out to others and witnessing to the Gospel message.

Match each learning in the numbered list below with the waiting period in which David most likely learned it. Some may have more than one answer.

a. David as shepherd
b. David in Saul's service and his fugitive years
c. David as king of Judah only

b 1. Learned respect for "the Lord's anointed"—those in positions of authority, especially the king.
c 2. Received more training for ruling an even greater number of people.
b 3. Learned to rely on God's comfort and closeness while being persecuted by Saul.
a 4. Had to protect his flock, which prepared him for killing a giant and fighting in battle.
c 5. Learned to trust God's promise to make him king of all of Israel.
a 6. Learned to be gentle and kind.
c 7. Learned to be patient.
b 8. Observed firsthand the responsibilities kings fulfill.
c 9. Gained respect of the people who would eventually crown him king of Israel.
a 10. Learned to use time alone to draw closer to God in worship and prayer.
b 11. Learned to be obedient to authority, which helped him become obedient to God.
a 12. Grew skillful at playing the harp, which made him eligible for service in Saul's court.

How might God be using your circumstances right now to prepare you for future service? How does realizing that help you grow in patience and trust?

What present service has your Savior given you? How can you fulfill it faithfully?



# INTO our lives

## Faith for Life—Waiting on God

Clearly, God was at work in David throughout his years of waiting and hardship. But what does all this have to do with us today?

For one thing, in our "I-need-it-now" world, waiting has become especially hard. Junior high students wait on many things. Many want to attend high school—but can't yet. Many want to learn to drive—but can't yet. Some want to date—but can't yet. Most want more personal freedom—but it's not theirs yet.

In addition, some students may face special challenges. They may wait for an illness or health condition to heal. They may wait to outgrow an unwanted physical characteristic. They may wait for a sibling or parent to get well or get a job or return from a war zone or from a job overseas.

When we must wait, human beings—Christians included—often struggle to understand why God allows it. This section of the lesson will give you, the teacher, an opportunity to help your students begin to grasp at least part of the answer.

Talk through the questions honestly and thoughtfully. Admit that no one knows the specific answers we'd like to have about the whys of waiting and the ways Jesus wants to use these times in our lives. But looking at David's life helps us begin to see what God might be doing in our own lives.

Stress the truth that we can always bring our questions, frustrations, and even our anger to God in prayer. He already knows what we're feeling anyway. He forgives our fretting and rebellion. And even when He doesn't give us all the answers, in Jesus, He wants to give us peace and the ability to trust Him more deeply.

## Remember

Have students memorize these words as a reminder of God's sustaining love and grace for them in Christ Jesus, our Lord.

# Waiting on God, Faith-fully!

David endured many hardships as he waited for the fulfillment of God's promise to make him king of all Israel. During these times, God was equipping David, sometimes for an event that was soon to follow and sometimes for events much farther in the future. During these times, David grew closer to God. David's faith grew stronger.

By completing this activity, you will become more aware of God's role in David's life, how waiting and enduring times of pain or struggle are vital to the growth of our Christian faith, and how God prepares us to fulfill His purposes for our lives. Remember that His purposes always involve reaching out to others and witnessing to the Gospel message.

Match each learning in the numbered list below with the waiting period in which David most likely learned it. Some may have more than one answer.

a. David as shepherd
b. David in Saul's service and his fugitive years
c. David as king of Judah only

_______ 1. Learned respect for "the Lord's anointed"—those in positions of authority, especially the king.

_______ 2. Received more training for ruling an even greater number of people.

_______ 3. Learned to rely on God's comfort and closeness while being persecuted by Saul.

_______ 4. Had to protect his flock, which prepared him for killing a giant and fighting in battle.

_______ 5. Learned to trust God's promise to make him king of all of Israel.

_______ 6. Learned to be gentle and kind.

_______ 7. Learned to be patient.

_______ 8. Observed firsthand the responsibilities kings fulfill.

_______ 9. Gained respect of the people who would eventually crown him king of Israel.

_______ 10. Learned to use time alone to draw closer to God in worship and prayer.

_______ 11. Learned to be obedient to authority, which helped him become obedient to God.

_______ 12. Grew skillful at playing the harp, which made him eligible for service in Saul's court.

How might God be using your circumstances right now to prepare you for future service? How does realizing that help you grow in patience and trust?

What present service has your Savior given you? How can you fulfill it faithfully?

# Solomon Builds a Temple

## 1 KINGS 5–8

## Background

King David was a great and mighty king of Israel. He was a man "after God's own heart" (1 Samuel 13:14) who trusted God and had many military successes. Israel prospered through God's blessings under David's leadership. One thing is still missing—a permanent place of worship for the Israelites. Much detail and care went into building the tabernacle, the Israelite tent church, during their journey to the Promised Land. However, worship loyalties were divided during David's time, with the ark of the covenant residing in Zion (Jerusalem, 2 Samuel 6:2–3) and the Holy Place being in Shiloh (1 Kings 2:26–27). David desired to build a temple—one place where all the Israelites could assemble to worship and sacrifice.

God did not allow David to build the temple. God did, however, tell David that he could make preparations for the building of the temple. David's son, Solomon, a king during peaceful times, would be allowed to build the temple. Solomon recognizes in 1 Kings 5:4–5 that God has given Israel rest from their enemies and troubles. The time for the construction of Israel's magnificent temple has come! And Solomon will be the one to oversee the construction of the building where the one true God would make His dwelling among His people.

## Central Truth

Even as God commands that we worship Him, by grace through Jesus our Savior, He provides us with the resources and motivation to live lives of worship.

## Objectives

- Recognize that in worship God gives the Means of Grace to us, and through that means He directs and empowers our response.
- Acknowledge Christ Jesus our Savior as the central focus of true worship.
- Demonstrate an eagerness to participate in acts of worship.

## Materials

- The Basics
- Reproducible 12

## Bible Prep

Post in advance so students can bookmark references before class time.

- 2 Samuel 7:1–17
- Ephesians 2:20
- 1 Peter 1:23
- Galatians 3:27
- Luke 22:19–20

## Devotion

Are you familiar with the song about the wise and foolish builders? The foolish man built his house upon the sand, and the wise man built his house upon the rock. The focus of that song was the foundation upon which they built.

And then there's the story of the three little pigs. The first two pigs met their demise because they chose poor building materials. The third pig's home was a safe refuge because he chose solid building materials.

Consider this. Suppose you were building a new home. Would you rather wait patiently for the home to be built using the best construction materials and sound workmanship, or would you rather have a builder who uses cheap materials and shoddy construction methods so that you could move into your new home sooner?

I think you know the answer. Even though it is hard to wait for something to be accomplished well, it is worth the wait in the end. A home built with care, precision, and solid materials will last longer and have fewer problems.

Our lesson today is about Solomon building the temple. (Share some of the background material about why Solomon was chosen to build the temple.) While we may never be construction workers who build a home, office building, or even a church, our lives are being built each day. In this lesson, through the power of the Holy Spirit, may you be led to see the most solid foundation for your life. That solid foundation is Jesus Christ, your Savior and Lord, who lived and died and now lives again for you forever!

**PRAY: Dear heavenly Father, thank You for Jesus Christ, the Author and Perfecter of our faith. Thank You that Jesus Christ is the cornerstone and foundation of our lives. Please take away the temptations to build our lives upon other things besides the grace and mercy of Jesus Christ, who died and rose again that we may be assured of eternal life in heaven. Open our minds now as we study Your Word that we may continue to build our lives on You. In Jesus' name. Amen.**

Sing: "Built on the Rock" (*LSB* 645).

# INTO the lesson

Ask, **If you were going to design an ideal house of worship, what features would it contain?** Affirm student responses. Comment that Solomon's temple by its design gave glory to God, while providing its function as a place where people could assemble for corporate worship.

# INTO the Word

## The Significance of the Temple

David's desire to build a temple for the Lord is recorded in 2 Samuel 7:1–17. Students do not need to read this text, but share the important information. We find a stark contrast here between the building of the tabernacle as recorded in Exodus and the building of the temple recorded here. In Exodus, God commanded that the tabernacle be built using donations from the people and very specific instructions for each part of the tabernacle. Here in 2 Samuel, we see that the materials are going to be traded for by Solomon, not from donations by the people. We also see that David wants to build the temple because of his own desire, not because of the command of God. Explain to students that 2 Samuel 7 begins with David's desire to do something for God and ends with what God will do for David—establish his throne forever.

Because of the detailed amount of Scripture involved in this story, you may choose to summarize the text for the students. Direct students' attention to the drawing of the temple in the Student Book as the discussion moves along.

Depending on the amount of available time, you may choose to use **Reproducible 12** here to explain Solomon's Prayer of Dedication. If time does not permit sharing the information here, it can be used as a supplementary activity as outlined in the "Searching Further" section.

Comment that with the temple God comes to dwell among His people to bless and save them. This indwelling points us to Christ, who came to dwell among us to bless and save us and who comes to us still in the bread and wine of the Sacrament. Stress that the Holy Place reminds us of the kingdom of grace, God's Church on earth, and the Most Holy Place reminds us of heaven, the kingdom of glory. **Through Jesus' life and sacrificial death, we, forgiven sinners, are able to go from the kingdom to grace to the kingdom of glory.** The tearing of the temple curtain at the death of Jesus symbolizes this dynamic, most important effect.

## Review

Allow time for students to write definitions for these words. Review the definitions with the whole class.

---

12 | 1 Kings 5–8

### SOLOMON BUILDS A TEMPLE

#### The Significance of the Temple

When David was king of Israel, he had the desire to build a place of worship for God's people—one place where they could go to offer sacrifices. God told David, however, that he would not be the one to build the temple. His son, who would be king after him, would build the temple for the Lord. And now the time has come. First Kings 5–8 tells of the preparation and construction of this beautiful house of worship and all that it contained.

Study the drawing of the temple. Note that it consists mostly of two large rooms, one to be used for worship and the other to represent the very presence of God.

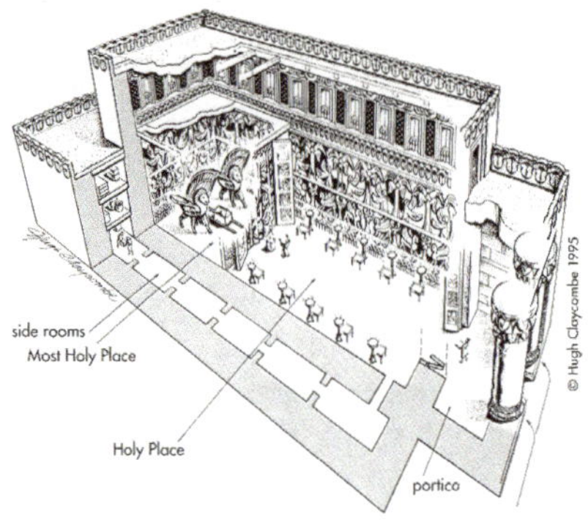


1. Which room is the dwelling place of God? Why do you think so?

**The Most Holy Place: it contains the ark of the covenant—the throne of God.**

2. Which room is used for worship? Why do you think so?

**The Holy Place is dedicated for the worship of God. It contains the altar, lampstands, and other furnishings similar to those found in Christian churches today.**

3. Note that a temple curtain separates the two rooms of the temple. A similar curtain tore from top to bottom upon Jesus' death on the cross for the sins of the world (Matthew 27:51). According to the following Bible verse, what does this tearing of the curtain signify?

"We have this as a sure and steadfast anchor of the soul, a hope that enters into the inner place behind the curtain, where Jesus has gone as a forerunner on our behalf, having become a high priest forever after the order of Melchizedek" (Hebrews 6:19–20).

**Because Jesus has gone through the curtain into the dwelling place of God, we sinful humans are able to do so also.**

#### REVIEW

Write the meanings of these words:

Means of Grace— **the Word (Gospel) and the Sacraments (Baptism and Lord's Supper)**

cherubim— **angels, especially in Old Testament, as they appear with wings spread over the ark of the covenant**

26

---

### Solomon's Prayer of Dedication

After the temple was built, Solomon gathered the people together to remind them of God's promises concerning the temple. He offered a lengthy prayer in 1 Kings 8:22–61. The prayer is summarized below: The prayer began with . . .

| When . . . | Then . . . |
|---|---|
| People make an oath to each other | Be a good judge, condemning the guilty and helping the righteous |
| We are defeated by an enemy because of our sins, but then are led to repentance | Forgive us and restore our nation |
| There is no rain because of our sins, but we are led to repentance | Forgive us and send rain to the land |
| We are affected by famine, pestilence, blight, mildew, locust, caterpillars, enemies, plagues, sickness, or other affliction | Forgive us our sins and act accordingly to help us |
| A foreigner prays to You | Listen to his prayer and answer him |
| We go out to battle | Maintain our cause and help us against our enemies |
| We are taken captive because of our sins, but are led to repentance | Forgive us and grant our captors compassionate hearts toward us |

"O LORD, God of Israel, there is no God like You, in heaven above or on earth beneath, keeping covenant and showing steadfast love to Your servants who walk before You with all their heart" (v. 23).

"And listen to the plea of Your servant and of Your people Israel, when they pray toward this place. And listen in heaven Your dwelling place, and when You hear, forgive" (v. 30).

Then, Solomon lists seven specific examples of when God's people will pray and need God's help. Solomon knows his people and their sins. In his prayer, Solomon reminds God of His promises to listen, forgive, and restore His people.

Solomon concludes with a benediction:

"The LORD our God be with us, as He was with our fathers. May He not leave us or forsake us, that He may incline our hearts to Him, to walk in all His ways and to keep His commandments, His statutes, and His rules, which He commanded our fathers" (vv. 57–58).

"Let your heart therefore be wholly true to the LORD our God, walking in His statues and keeping His commandments as at this day" (v. 61).

### My Prayer of Dedication

Use Solomon's prayer as an example for your own prayer of dedication to God. Your prayer can begin and end the same as Solomon's did. Fill in the boxes with special concerns that you have and how you would like God to help you with those concerns, remembering God's promise to hear and answer.

"O LORD, God of Israel, there is no God like You, in heaven above or on earth beneath, keeping covenant and showing steadfast love to Your servants who walk before You with all their heart" (v. 23).

"And listen to the plea of Your servant and of Your people Israel, when they pray toward this place. And listen in heaven Your dwelling place, and when You hear, forgive" (v. 30).

| When I am in this situation . . . | Dear God, please . . . |
|---|---|
| | |

### Under Construction

While we may never be personally involved in the building of such a house of worship, our lives are daily being built into a "spiritual house" as we daily die (confess our sin), receive forgiveness, and rise again to new life by the power of the Holy Spirit. Describe your Christian foundation—what makes you strong in Jesus Christ.

Read the words of 1 Peter 2:5 from the "Remember" section below.

Just like with the construction of any sound building, there is a need to have a solid foundation and building materials.

Check out the Bible verses below and label the cornerstone, the foundation, and the pillars to identify the things described in these verses that support lives being built in Christ.

**REMEMBER**

You yourselves like living stones are being built up as a spiritual house, to be a holy priesthood, to offer spiritual sacrifices acceptable to God through Jesus Christ.

1 Peter 2:5

27

# INTO our lives

## Under Construction

Just as the temple that Solomon built was constructed from the best building materials, God desires your life and the lives of your students to be built on the solid foundation of God's Word, with Jesus Christ as the cornerstone. Provide time for students to describe their own Christian foundation and its source of strength.

Give students time to look up the Bible verses and write words identified from the text relating to the foundation, cornerstone, and pillars. Discuss the term *Means of Grace* with the students. The Means of Grace are shown on the three pillars, and they are the ways through which the Holy Spirit offers us the blessings of Christ and His forgiveness. God uses the Means of Grace to strengthen our faith in Him.

**Where do we receive these Means of Grace?** We have our Bibles, which we can read anytime. Today's technology, online Bibles, and devotions make it very easy to read God's Word. However, the devil often tries to distract us from such daily reading. Our prayer is that God will help us with that daily reading and prayer life.

Holy Baptism and the Lord's Supper are important elements of the worship service. The words of the Invocation, "In the name of the Father and of the Son and of the Holy Spirit," remind us of our Baptism. While students in your class may not yet be able to partake of the Lord's Supper, they are very close to being able to do so. Until then, they can listen to the words of the pastor and be reminded of Jesus' sacrificial death for each of them.

Because these Means of Grace come to us in worship, it is important for students and their families to attend worship services. It is an opportunity for their faith to be fed and to grow stronger. Students may say that they can read their Bibles at home, but they are missing out on other important pillars when they stay away from worship.

Worship isn't about what we do for God. It is about what He has done for us. Remind students that when David tried to tell God what he wanted to do for Him, God turned it around and told David what He was going to do for him. The King from David's family who would rule forever is Jesus, our Savior and Messiah and the focus of our worship.

Now that students have an understanding of the foundation, cornerstone, and pillars of our lives, have them write their names within the pillars. Then, have them write five special things about themselves in the space provided. They might be hobbies, favorites, words that describe themselves, and so on.

Our lives are spiritual acts of worship to God each day. God has given each person special talents and abilities with which we serve Him. However, by God's grace, each person's life can be built and focused on the love of Jesus Christ as our Savior from sin. Without His mercy and grace, our lives are meaningless.

## Remember

Comment that the Bible verse underscores God's Word in building us up into the people He would have us be, people who live lives devoted to God as empowered by the Means of Grace with which He continues to bless and fortify us.

# Solomon's Prayer of Dedication

After the temple was built, Solomon gathered the people together to remind them of God's promises concerning the temple. He offered a lengthy prayer in 1 Kings 8:22–61. The prayer is summarized below: The prayer began with . . .

"O Lord, God of Israel, there is no God like You, in heaven above or on earth beneath, keeping covenant and showing steadfast love to Your servants who walk before You with all their heart" (v. 23).

"And listen to the plea of Your servant and of Your people Israel, when they pray toward this place. And listen in heaven Your dwelling place, and when You hear, forgive" (v. 30).

Then, Solomon lists seven specific examples of when God's people will pray and need God's help. Solomon knows his people and their sins. In his prayer, Solomon reminds God of His promises to listen, forgive, and restore His people.

| When . . . | Then . . . |
|---|---|
| People make an oath to each other | Be a good judge, condemning the guilty and helping the righteous |
| We are defeated by an enemy because of our sins, but then are led to repentance | Forgive us and restore our nation |
| There is no rain because of our sins, but we are led to repentance | Forgive us and send rain to the land |
| We are affected by famine, pestilence, blight, mildew, locust, caterpillars, enemies, plagues, sickness, or other affliction | Forgive us our sins and act accordingly to help us |
| A foreigner prays to You | Listen to his prayer and answer him |
| We go out to battle | Maintain our cause and help us against our enemies |
| We are taken captive because of our sins, but are led to repentance | Forgive us and grant our captors compassionate hearts toward us |

Solomon concludes with a benediction:

"The Lord our God be with us, as He was with our fathers. May He not leave us or forsake us, that He may incline our hearts to Him, to walk in all His ways and to keep His commandments, His statutes, and His rules, which He commanded our fathers" (vv. 57–58).

"Let your heart therefore be wholly true to the Lord our God, walking in His statues and keeping His commandments as at this day" (v. 61).

## My Prayer of Dedication

Use Solomon's prayer as an example for your own prayer of dedication to God. Your prayer can begin and end the same as Solomon's did. Fill in the boxes with special concerns that you have and how you would like God to help you with those concerns, remembering God's promise to hear and answer.

"O Lord, God of Israel, there is no God like You, in heaven above or on earth beneath, keeping covenant and showing steadfast love to Your servants who walk before You with all their heart" (v. 23).

"And listen to the plea of Your servant and of Your people Israel, when they pray toward this place. And listen in heaven Your dwelling place, and when You hear, forgive" (v. 30).

| When I am in this situation . . . | Dear God, please . . . |
|---|---|
| | |

# Rehoboam and Jeroboam

## 1 KINGS 11:1–12:24

## Background

King Saul. King David. King Solomon. These three served successively as kings of a united Israel. They ruled all twelve tribes. With the death of King Solomon, we now begin to explore Israel's history as a divided nation. What caused that division?

We might subject Solomon to the adage "It all went to his head." Solomon had it all—wisdom, wealth, power, the honor of building the temple, a beautiful palace. But that wasn't all that Solomon was gaining. In this lesson, students will explore how Solomon also gained many wives, not out of love, but out of political alliances. Along with those wives came their false gods. We will discover in this lesson that Solomon turned away from worshiping the one true God for whom he had built the temple in order to appease his wives who worshiped false gods.

God warned Solomon in 1 Kings 9:6–7, "But if you turn aside from following Me, you or your children, and do not keep My commandments and My statutes that I have set before you, but go and serve other gods and worship them, then I will cut off Israel from the land that I have given them, and the house that I have consecrated for My name I will cast out of My sight."

Solomon did exactly what the Lord had warned him not to do, and now Israel will face the consequences.

## Central Truth

God in Christ always preserves a remnant of His faithful people.

## Objectives

- Recognize that unfaithfulness can lead to final rejection of God's grace and salvation.
- Describe Solomon's apostasy as a primary cause of the division of Israel.
- Demonstrate the intent to rely on God for power to abide in His grace and to honor Him in our lives as citizens of an earthly nation.

## Materials

- The Basics
- Reproducible 13
- Dominoes
- Ruler labeled "Sin"

## Bible Prep

Post in advance so students can bookmark the reference before class time.

- 1 Kings 11:1–12:24

## Devotion

(Before the devotion begins, set up some dominoes on end. Make a pattern of dominoes that goes across the table. Have them close enough so that when you knock down one domino, it will knock down all the rest.)

Have ever heard of the domino effect? One thing happens, and that causes another to happen, and so on.

No person lives in a bubble. Our actions influence the lives of others, and their actions influence our lives.

(Use the ruler labeled "Sin" to knock down the first domino. Watch the rest of the dominoes fall.)

When sin affects our lives and the lives of those around us, it may seem like we are all knocked down. These dominoes are all knocked down. They cannot stand themselves up again. They need someone to stand them up. We are like those dominoes. Our sins knock us down and away from God. We need His love and forgiveness to pick us up and help us to stand tall.

When King Solomon began to worship other gods and turn away from the one true God, the domino effect began. His actions influenced the lives of those he was ruling. They, too, began to worship false gods. Today's Bible story will show the consequences of those sins. But we also have a Savior. Christ Jesus came to forgive our sins and to get us back on our feet. Thank God for His loving and forgiving grace!

**PRAY: Dear Father in heaven, thank You for creating us to live in a world where we get to experience so many blessings. Sometimes, Lord, we get distracted by these blessings and devote too much of our time and attention to these things rather than to You. For this and all other sins, forgive us, Father, for Jesus' sake. Please lift us up when we feel knocked down by our sins, and help us fully to devote ourselves to You. In Jesus' name we pray. Amen.**

Sing: "Son of God, Eternal Savior" (*LSB* 842).

# INTO the lesson

## Other Gods

The passage from 1 Kings 11:1–12:24 may be unfamiliar to your students. They may not have heard of Rehoboam and Jeroboam. For this reason, it will be helpful to read through the entire text with the students and then complete the activities in the Student Book.

The downfall of Israel as a unified nation begins when King Solomon begins to share the glory that belongs to God with numerous false gods. He made many political alliances through marriage, and along with those alliances came the gods of those nations. Each of Solomon's wives played the "You don't love me if you don't worship my god" game, and soon the nation of Israel has more gods and more troubles.

# INTO the Word

## God Takes Action

God had warned Solomon repeatedly to obey the Lord's commands and statutes. God was keeping His side of the covenant that He would be their God, but the Israelites, led by their king, were not being the people of God.

When Solomon built the temple, God warned him that if the people turned away from the Lord, the true God, the building would end up in a heap of ruins. Solomon's welcoming of other gods is the beginning of the downfall of the Israelite kingdom.

Solomon had generally enjoyed a peaceful reign for the last twenty years. That is why he was able to accomplish all the building that he did.

Work through the questions in this section with your class. Comment that God raised up enemies and adversaries as a way of getting the attention of Solomon and the people of Israel. Share these brief descriptions of the adversaries:

Hadad the Edomite, as a young boy, had fled to Egypt to be safe during David's military campaign against the Edomites. After David dies, Hadad returns to cause trouble for David's son Solomon.

Rezon is another enemy of David; he becomes king in neighboring Syria and causes problems for Israel because of his hatred toward Israel.

Jeroboam was the servant to whom God promised to give most of Solomon's kingdom. As such, Jeroboam could also be considered Solomon's enemy. Jeroboam gained popularity among the people of Israel because he paid attention to their complaints of being overworked.

## God's Word Fulfilled

Distribute copies of **Reproducible 13** and have the class act out the story of Rehoboam and Jeroboam. The section in the Student Book reviews the highlights of the kingdom split. Solomon kept a large labor force busy with the building of the temple and the building of his palace. This workforce became tired and dissatisfied. Jeroboam came to Rehoboam and asked him to lighten the load, and Rehoboam said he would give an answer in three days. During those three days, he consulted with advisers to his father and his own advisers. His father's advisers told him to be kind to the people and be a servant to them. Rehoboam's advisers told him to crack down on them for their dissatisfaction. Rehoboam arrogantly refused to help them and spoke harshly to them. The people then expressed their displeasure by making Jeroboam their king.

Comment that we now see a division in the kingdom of Israel. The Northern Kingdom consists of ten tribes. Two tribes, Judah and Benjamin, make up the Southern Kingdom, the remnant of God's people who are ruled by the descendant of Solomon. Have students skim through the headings of 1 and 2 Kings to see the names of the kings

---

13 1 Kings 11:1–12:24

### Rehoboam and Jeroboam

#### Other Gods

God elevated Solomon to the position of king of Israel in place of David, his father. God blessed Solomon with wisdom, wealth, power, and influence. And Solomon posed himself as a key player in the political realm. Note what God's Word says about Solomon's actions and their consequences.

"Now King Solomon loved many foreign women, along with the daughter of Pharaoh: Moabite, Ammonite, Edomite Sidonian and Hittite women, from the nations concerning which the LORD had said to the people of Israel, 'You shall not enter into marriage with them, neither shall they with you, for surely they will turn away your heart after their gods.' Solomon clung to these in love. He had 700 wives, princesses, and 300 concubines. And his wives turned away his heart. For when Solomon was old his wives turned away his heart after other gods, and his heart was not wholly true to the LORD his God, as was the heart of David his father. . . . And the LORD was angry with Solomon, because his heart had turned away from the LORD, the God of Israel, who had appeared to him twice and had commanded him concerning this thing, that he should not go after other gods. But he did not keep what the LORD commanded" (1 Kings 11:1–4, 9–10).

1. Circle the five foreign peoples listed in the above verses with which Solomon aligned himself through marital contracts.

2. In the paragraph above, underline the numbers that indicate Solomon's wives and concubines.

3. Draw a line around the words in the paragraph above that indicate the sad result in Solomon's life. **Answers will vary somewhat.**

#### God Takes Action

1. Read 1 Kings 11:11–13. After the Lord warned Solomon twice about the problems that would come from his idolatry and Solomon refused to listen, God announced His judgment against Solomon. What did God promise to do as a consequence of Solomon's sin?

**God would tear the kingdom from Solomon and give it to his servant. For the sake of David, however, God would retain one tribe for Solomon's son.**

#### Review

concubine— **a woman legally bound in an arrangement similar to marriage**

alliance— **a bond or union between individuals, groups, or states**

remnant— **what is left when something is removed from a larger item**

28

2. Now skim 1 Kings 11:14–25. Give the names of the two adversaries God raised up against Solomon.

**Hadad the Edomite and Rezon**

3. Skim 1 Kings 11:26–43. Name the servant to whom God promised to give most of Solomon's kingdom.

**Jeroboam**

### God's Word Fulfilled

After King Solomon died, his son Rehoboam became king. No sooner did Rehoboam become king than he faced an important decision. Should he honor their request to lighten the workload imposed on the people by his father, King Solomon or should he continue to make them work hard?

He chose to make them work even harder!

This decision caused the people of Israel to revolt against Rehoboam. They then made Jeroboam their king. So now the kingdom of Israel is divided—ten tribes in the Northern Kingdom and two tribes (Judah and Benjamin, commonly regarded as one tribe) in the Southern Kingdom. And so, God's judgment against Solomon because of his sin of idolatry came to pass just as He had said.

### Perspectives for Today

Baal and Asherah were among the false gods of Elijah's day. They were crafted from wood and stone, but the wood and stone from which the idols were derived are natural resources—blessings from God also used for many good purposes including the construction of the temple.

Today, there are also elements of creation that draw people's attention away from the one true God. But none of these things is bad in and of itself. These things do not become idols until we allow them to draw our focus away from Jesus, our Savior. Tell how each of the following might be used as either an idol or as a means to give God glory.

| Money | friends | computers |
|---|---|---|
| food | sports | cell phones |

Dear heavenly Father, thank You for the gifts that You have given me. You take good care of me and make sure that I have all I need to support this body and life. I have so many other blessings too. Please forgive me for the times that I have put those things in front of You or focused on them instead of Your great love for me. Please show me ways to use those things to bring glory to You and to share Your great love with others. In Jesus' name. Amen.

**Remember**

Choose this day whom you will serve. . . . But as for me and my house, we will serve the Lord.

Joshua 24:15

29

# INTO our lives

## Perspectives for Today

Work through this activity as a whole class, or allow time for students to work with a partner to discuss each item and generate their thoughts and ideas. Help students see the difference between allowing God's blessings to distract us from God and allowing the Holy Spirit to use the Means of Grace to build our lives in Christ.

Emphasize that all these are blessings from God and God desires us to enjoy them. The problem comes when they become more important than God. The stone and wood used to create Baal and the Asherah poles were not bad in and of themselves. The stone and wood were bad because they were used to draw people away from God. For example, people may think the Bible says that money is the root of all evil. Actually, the Bible says that "the *love* of money is a root of all kinds of evils" (1 Timothy 6:10). Have students name ways that these blessings can be used to draw people closer to God. Stress **the full and complete forgiveness for all sins, which Jesus earned for us on Calvary.**

Close the lesson with a prayer of confession and repentance written in the Student Book.

## Remember

This verse comes from the text of Joshua when the Israelites were entering the Promised Land. The age-old problem of other gods continues through the life of Solomon and to our lives today.

in both Israel and Judah. Most of these kings did not follow God's will. However, God kept His promise and continued David's line of succession in the kingdom of Judah. Eventually, here in Judah, Jesus, the Savior of the world, would be born among David's descendants.

## Review

Allow time for students to define these terms. Relate them to the Bible account on which today's lesson is based. Comment that having a concubine was actually a legal arrangement. Therefore, Solomon is sometimes said to have had one thousand wives.

### Rehoboam and Jeroboam Skit

Characters Needed: REHOBOAM, JEROBOAM, SOLOMON'S ADVISORS (2), REHOBOAM'S ADVISORS (2), NARRATOR 1 (who will need a sheet of paper), and NARRATOR 2

The rest of the class can be divided into two groups, with one group being larger than the other.

**NARRATOR 1:** King Solomon was a well-known king of Israel. He was blessed with great wisdom and wealth. It was during his reign that the temple of the Lord was built.

**NARRATOR 2:** However, King Solomon had a problem. Each of his many wives wanted Solomon to worship her god instead of the one true God. Solomon gave in.

**NARRATOR 1:** Because of this, God told him that the kingdom of Israel would be divided during the reign of his son.

**NARRATOR 2:** When Rehoboam became king, he faced a difficult decision early on.

**JEROBOAM:** *(to REHOBOAM)* You know that your father made us work very hard. Please let up on us and don't make us work so hard.

**REHOBOAM:** Come back in three days, and I will give you my answer.

*(JEROBOAM EXITS.)*

**REHOBOAM:** I don't know what to do. I will talk to my dad's advisors.

**REHOBOAM:** *(to SOLOMON'S ADVISORS)*: What should I do? The people want me to lessen their workload.

**SOLOMON'S ADVISORS:** Treat the people with respect and serve them well. They will then serve you well.

**REHOBOAM:** Okay. Now I will talk to my friends and advisors.

**REHOBOAM:** *(to his advisors)*: What should I do? The people want me to lessen their workload.

**REHOBOAM'S ADVISORS:** No way! Show them who is boss. Don't lessen their workload. Make them work harder.

**NARRATOR 1:** Three days later . . .

**JEROBOAM:** *(to REHOBOAM)* I have returned because you told me to come back in three days.

**REHOBOAM:** I will not lessen the workload of the people. In fact, I will make them work harder than my father did.

**PEOPLE IN THE LARGER GROUP:** No! Rehoboam is not a good king. We do not want him to be our king. We want Jeroboam to be our king. Jeroboam is our king! Jeroboam is our king!

**NARRATOR 1:** *(Tears a piece of paper into twelve pieces)* And that is how the kingdom of Israel split into the Northern Kingdom and the Southern Kingdom.

**NARRATOR 2:** Jeroboam became the king of the Northern Kingdom, which consisted of ten tribes. *(NARRATOR 1 gives JEROBOAM 10 pieces of paper.)*

**NARRATOR 2:** Rehoboam remained the king of the Southern Kingdom, which consisted of two tribes—Judah and Benjamin. *(NARRATOR 1 gives REHOBOAM 2 pieces of paper.)*

**NARRATOR 1:** And that is the beginning of the fall of the kingdom of Israel, all because they did not trust in the true God and follow His commands.

# Rehoboam and Jeroboam

Characters: REHOBOAM, JEROBOAM, SOLOMON'S ADVISERS (2), REHOBOAM'S ADVISERS (2), NARRATOR 1 (who will need a sheet of paper), and NARRATOR 2

The rest of the class can be divided into two groups, with one group being larger than the other.

**NARRATOR 1:** King Solomon was a well-known king of Israel. He was blessed with great wisdom and wealth. It was during his reign that the temple of the Lord was built.

**NARRATOR 2:** However, King Solomon had a problem. Each of his many wives wanted Solomon to worship her god instead of the one true God. Solomon gave in.

**NARRATOR 1:** Because of this, God told Solomon that the kingdom of Israel would be divided during the reign of his son.

**NARRATOR 2:** When Rehoboam became king, he faced a difficult decision early on.

**JEROBOAM:** (*To REHOBOAM*) You know that your father made us work very hard. Please let up on us and don't make us work so hard.

**REHOBOAM:** Come back in three days, and I will give you my answer.

(*JEROBOAM EXITS.*)

**REHOBOAM:** I don't know what to do. I will talk to my dad's advisers.

**REHOBOAM:** (*To SOLOMON'S ADVISERS*): What should I do? The people want me to lessen their workload.

**SOLOMON'S ADVISERS:** Treat the people with respect and serve them well. They will then serve you well.

**REHOBOAM:** Okay. Now I will talk to my friends and advisers.

**REHOBOAM:** (*to his advisers*): What should I do? The people want me to lessen their workload.

**REHOBOAM'S ADVISERS:** No way! Show them who is boss. Don't lessen their workload. Make them work harder.

**NARRATOR 1:** Three days later . . .

**JEROBOAM:** (*To REHOBOAM*) I have returned because you told me to come back in three days.

**REHOBOAM:** I will not lessen the workload of the people. In fact, I will make them work harder than my father required.

**PEOPLE IN THE LARGER GROUP:** No! Rehoboam is not a good king. We do not want him to be our king. We want Jeroboam to be our king. Jeroboam is our king! Jeroboam is our king!

**NARRATOR 1:** (*Tears a piece of paper into twelve pieces*) And that is how the kingdom of Israel split into the Northern Kingdom and the Southern Kingdom.

**NARRATOR 2:** Jeroboam became the king of the Northern Kingdom, which consisted of ten tribes. (*NARRATOR 1 gives JEROBOAM 10 pieces of paper.*)

**NARRATOR 2:** Rehoboam remained the king of the Southern Kingdom, which consisted of two tribes—Judah and Benjamin. (*NARRATOR 1 gives REHOBOAM 2 pieces of paper.*)

**NARRATOR 1:** And that is the beginning of the fall of the kingdom of Israel, all because the people did not trust in the true God and follow His commands.

# God's People in Captivity

## 2 Kings 23–25; 2 Chronicles 36; Jeremiah 34–39

## Background

When we read 2 Kings, 2 Chronicles, and Jeremiah, we may react with shock and dismay at how wickedly God's people acted and how obstinate they were. Yet, despite the impenitence and unbelief that marked this era, we also read about the righteous example of King Josiah. He became King of Judah at age 8 and faithfully led God's people for thirty-one years. The Scriptures tell us that Josiah "did what was right in the eyes of the LORD" (2 Kings 22:2). He opposed the idolatry so rampant in his day and restored temple worship to its rightful place. Further, King Josiah properly responded to the true God in faith, witness, and good works. In King Josiah, we find an exception to the overwhelming number of wicked kings of God's people.

Although God is merciful, His patience can and eventually will run out. His wrath falls on unbelief and wickedness. We see this illustrated in the violent ends met by Judah's evil kings and also in the harsh captivity into which Babylon's armies carried God's people.

The message for us is clear. While God loves us, He also hates sin, and He hates what sin does to us. In fact, God loves us so much that He will not permit us to continue long in a sinfully destructive life.

As Moses wrote long ago, "Be sure your sin will find you out" (Numbers 32:23). Like the arrogant disobedience of the people in our text, our own unchecked rebellion can lead to spiritual death. And so, in love, our Lord continues to call us to repentance. We ignore His Word to our peril, but, "In returning and rest [we] shall be saved; in quietness and in trust shall be [our] strength" (Isaiah 30:15). In the shadow of Christ's cross, we find eternal salvation and the strength to live our lives for Jesus.

## Central Truth

Even as God allows the consequences of sin to take their course, He remains faithful to His people; through Jesus, He rescues and protects captive sinners from the devil and restores them to His eternal kingdom.

## Objectives

- Verbalize that our freedom from the captivity of sin is only by the grace of God through Jesus.
- Spread the Good News of freedom from captivity, won for all through the life, death, and resurrection of Christ.
- Describe the consequences of sin as illustrated by the fate of Judah's wicked kings and people prior to the exile.

## Materials

- The Basics
- Reproducible 14

## Bible Prep

Post in advance so students can bookmark references before class time.

- 2 Kings 23–25
- Jeremiah 1
- Romans 4:5

## Devotion

Read Romans 6:1–4. Then continue with the following.

Most teenagers could tell many stories about times when other people have tempted them to do wrong things. Whether it's cheating on a test, gossiping, lying, stealing, drinking alcohol, or doing drugs, we've all been tempted—sometimes by friends, sometimes by Satan, sometimes by our own sinful nature.

How do we respond to temptation? We might say, "No, I don't do that." Or we might say, "I'm a Christian, so that's not an option for me."

Or we might say, "Sure!" and then, under our breath, remind ourselves, "God will forgive me."

Whoa! Really? Certainly it's true that God forgives us. But it is wrong to turn God's grace into a license to sin. God's love for us keeps us from ever wanting to sin on purpose. True repentance includes both confession and the intention to change our behaviors so as to leave sin behind.

The Bible warns about "the deceitfulness of sin" (Hebrews 3:13). Sin is tricky, treacherous. One lie, for example, probably won't kill our faith. But one lie often leads to another and another. Lying desensitizes our hearts to other sins—stealing, perhaps. More and more, sin can crowd into our lives, crowding God out and choking off our faith.

And God doesn't want that for you. When we pray, "Lead us not into temptation," we ask God to keep us close to the cross, always mindful of His love for us in Jesus, our Savior.

**PRAY: Jesus, thank You for Your death, which brings me forgiveness. Help me to keep You first in my life, so sin won't gain a foothold in my heart and keep me from living as a child of God. Amen.**

Sing: "I Want to Walk as a Child of the Light" (*LSB* 411).

2 Kings 23–25;
2 Chronicles 36;
Jeremiah 34–39

## 14 God's People in Captivity

### Voices during Troubled Times

Connect the names of the kings and prophet below to the category that describes them better. Were they wicked rebels or faithful servants of God? (Look for their names in these passages: 2 Kings 23–25 and Jeremiah 1. The bold headings in your Bible may help you spot them. Be ready to defend your answers.)

Wicked Rebels — Jehoahaz, Jehoiakim, Jehoiachin, Zedekiah

Faithful Servants — Josiah, Jeremiah

| | |
|---|---|
| Wicked Rebels | Jehoahaz |
| Faithful Servants | Josiah |
| | Jehoiakim |
| | Jehoiachin |
| | Jeremiah |
| | Zedekiah |

### Today's Checkup

Have you ever . . .

_____ forgotten about God's commands?

_____ ignored God's commands?

_____ ignored good advice?

_____ relied on your own goodness to make God happy with you?

_____ thought you were too young to be God's representative?

_____ tried to live a happy life without paying attention to God?

### Review

captivity— **state of being confined or imprisoned**

rebellious— **opposed to rules or authority**

faithful— **steadfast, loyal, resolute to a person or cause**

30

# INTO the lesson

Say, **Some people believe the Bible is a collection of moral sayings and stories that show people how to live. What are the dangers of viewing the Bible as only a moral guide?** When we see the Bible as primarily a moral touchstone, we miss the salvation story; we fail to see our need for a Savior and God's provision for our salvation in Jesus. Such a view of Scripture also rejects its claim to be God's inspired Word, living, true, and intended by God for each of us personally.

Help students focus on the concept that the Bible reveals both our sin and our need for a Savior. It teaches us what our Savior has done to make forgiveness and eternal life possible. And, yes, it does tell how we are to live—not so that God will love us, but because He already does love us, in Jesus.

# INTO the Word

## Voices during Troubled Times

Introduce today's Bible study by saying, **People like Abraham, Isaac, Jacob, Judah, Tamar, Ruth, David, and many others understood and believed God's message of repentance and salvation in the coming Savior. They were still sinners, just like we are. But they lived lives of repentant faith, and for the sake of Jesus, God forgave their sins.**

**Many other people in Israel, though, lived in rebellion against God. They totally dismissed His Word and His prophets. They refused to acknowledge their sinfulness and repent.**

When everyone has completed the matching exercise, talk through the answers. Why did they designate Jeremiah and King Josiah as "faithful servants" and the other kings on the page as "wicked rebels"? Didn't Jeremiah and Josiah sin too?

## Today's Checkup

Tell students that they will not be asked to share their answers to the questions in this exercise, but the purpose in answering these questions is so that everyone understands just how much we all have in common with the people we've read about, even Judah's wicked kings. We may be tempted to think of them as somehow different from us.

## Review

Review all the words and definitions together. Then ask students to write a sentence that uses all of the review words to describe Judah before and during the Babylonian captivity.

## Captive to Sin

You may choose to draw a simple, two-column chart on the board with the headings "Babylonian Captivity" and "Captives of Sin Today." Then ask students to suggest items for either column. Possible points of comparison include the following:

- We, like Judah of old, commit sins of idolatry, ignoring God's Word and looking for satisfaction in all the wrong places.
- In justice, God must punish our sin, just as He had to punish the sins of ancient Judah.
- Jesus took the punishment of the people of Judah and our punishment too.
- God forgives His penitent people of every era.
- God uses the consequences of our sin as a tool to lead the impenitent to true repentance and faith.

Still, some in Judah refused to repent; by God's grace, we have been led to repentance. Say, **Throughout the Old Testament, we read prophecies that point forward to Jesus. Because of Jesus, we can find release from slavery to sin. Sin and Satan cannot rule our lives any longer.** If time will allow, consider using **Reproducible 14** at this point.

### Captive to Sin

Judah sinned and sinned and sinned again. Her sins of idolatry and unbelief were bad enough. But no matter what God's prophets said, Judah's kings ignored His Word. Like their leaders, the people also rejected God's Word and refused to repent. Both leaders and the common people rebelled and refused to obey. Their hearts were as hard as stone!

Finally, God let the Babylonian army defeat His people and rule over them. His goal? To bring His people to repentance and true faith.

What parallels do you see in the lives of God's people today? (Think primarily about your own life!)

### WWJD? Why Would Jesus Die?

1. A few years ago, people began using the acronym *WWJD*. It appeared on bracelets, Bible covers, bumper stickers, and in graffiti on walls and railroad cars. It stood for "What Would Jesus Do?"

It meant that if you were in a situation and didn't know what to say or how to act, you could make a good decision by asking yourself, "What would Jesus do?" WWJD implied that we should use Jesus as an example of how to behave.

- What is good about that idea?
- What is not so good about it?

2. Jesus' life does model for us what our lives can be like when we trust in Him. It's important to think and pray about being more like Jesus in our words and actions. But before we can do that, before we would *want* to do that, we need to know and believe the answer to the other WWJD question: "Why Would Jesus Die?" That question is the difference between eternal life and eternal death. So what's the answer? Why *would* Jesus die?

3. In our culture, leaders (celebrities, politicians, and even some religious people) sometimes suggest that there are many valid ways to find freedom and peace. They say that all religions lead to the same place. They claim that all those paths will get us where we want to go.

How would you answer that claim? What Scripture verses would support your answer?

**Remember**

Jesus answered them, "Truly, truly, I say to you, everyone who commits sin is a slave to sin. The slave does not remain in the house forever; the son remains forever. So if the Son sets you free, you will be free indeed."

John 8:34–36

31

# INTO our lives

## WWJD? Why Would Jesus Die?

**1.** If you have any WWJD posters, T-shirts, or bracelets, show them to the class. Some students may be aware of WWJD, while others may not. Ask what the letters mean. Then have a volunteer read question 1. Draw students toward the understanding that Jesus came not as our example or model, but as our Savior.

**2.** Of course, as God's Spirit works within us, we do want to change our sinful lives. We do want to live as "little Christs" in our families, school, church, and community. But Christianity is not a self-help project. If we could free ourselves from sin's captivity, then Jesus didn't need to come to earth. Faith in Him is the only way to be free. Trying hard won't work. It never has and never will. **Jesus died so we could live. Jesus died because He loves us and wanted to rescue us when we were rebellious and helpless.**

**3.** Ask, **Is faith in Jesus the only way to be saved?** Listen to the responses. According to recent polls, many Lutheran teens think it is intolerant to insist that there is only one way to heaven. Some students may be wrestling with the idea that a close friend or family member is without faith. Be careful to give those students extra support and encouragement in their personal witness. Encourage students to use a concordance or online reference material to locate pertinent Scriptures. These may include John 14:6; Acts 4:12; and Galatians 2:21.

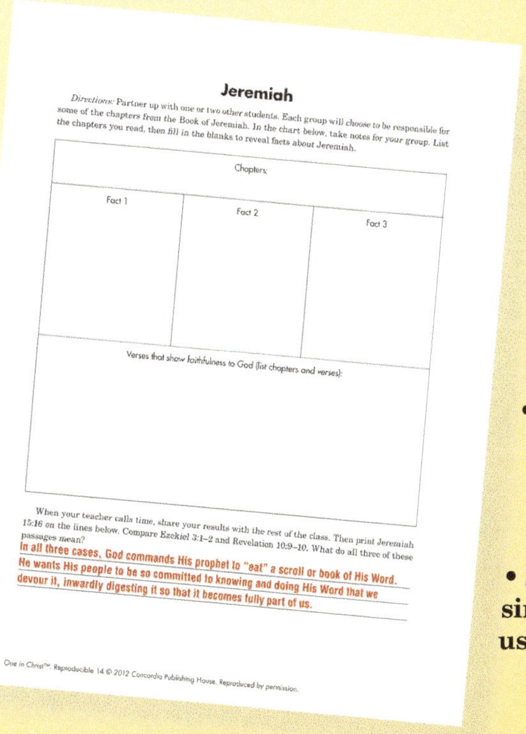

**Jeremiah**

*Directions:* Partner up with one or two other students. Each group will choose to be responsible for some of the chapters from the Book of Jeremiah. In the chart below, take notes for your group. List the chapters you read, then fill in the blanks to reveal facts about Jeremiah.

| Chapters: | | |
|---|---|---|
| Fact 1 | Fact 2 | Fact 3 |
| Verses that show faithfulness to God (list chapters and verses): | | |

When your teacher calls time, share your results with the rest of the class. Then print Jeremiah 15:16 on the lines below. Compare Ezekiel 3:1–2 and Revelation 10:9–10. What do all three of these passages mean?

In all three cases, God commands His prophet to "eat" a scroll or book of His Word. He wants His people to be so committed to knowing and doing His Word that we devour it, inwardly digesting it so that it becomes fully part of us.



## Remember

Ask students to highlight all the words in this verse that begin with *S*. Then make these points:

- ***Sins*—Sins don't just happen to us. We commit them. We are responsible for our actions.**
- ***Slave*—When we sin, we show a lack of self-control. Sin controls us; we don't control it. That makes us slaves!**
- ***Slave*—Look at the next time this word comes up. It says that slaves are not part of a family, and they're not! They don't belong. When Jesus died on the cross and rose again in victory, He made us part of God's family. We are God's adopted sons and daughters! We're no longer slaves to sin.**
- ***Son*—In ancient times, sons inherited the family's fortune. The Bible uses the term *son* here to refer to God's heirs. Boys and girls, men and women, all God's faithful people are His "sons." We inherit heaven's riches!**
- ***So*—This little word points to the theme of our lesson: Since Jesus set us free, let's start acting like we are free. Let's stop acting like slaves and live like the heirs we are!**
- ***Son*—The last "Son" is capitalized. The Son of God gave His life so that you can live with Him in heaven forever. We celebrate that joy by sharing Jesus' love with others.**
- ***Sets*—Jesus unlocked the shackles of sin that kept us in bondage. He has set us free.**

# Jeremiah

*Directions:* Partner up with one or two other students. Each group will choose to be responsible for some of the chapters from the Book of Jeremiah. In the chart below, take notes for your group. List the chapters you read; then fill in the blanks to reveal facts about Jeremiah.

| Chapters: | | |
|---|---|---|
| Fact 1 | Fact 2 | Fact 3 |
| Verses that show faithfulness to God (list chapters and verses): | | |

When your teacher calls time, share your results with the rest of the class. Then print Jeremiah 15:16 on the lines below. Compare Ezekiel 3:1–2 and Revelation 10:9–10. What do all three of these passages mean?

________________________________________

________________________________________

________________________________________

# God's People Return from Captivity

EZRA 1–10

## Background

The Book of Ezra tells an amazing story of God's sinful, exiled people returning to their Lord in repentance and faith. We can learn much as we read about their struggles.

For example, at first blush, it seems unreasonable that the people of Judah would reject the offer of help made by the "people of the land" to help rebuild the temple. Weren't they bypassing an opportunity to develop neighborly relations and an opportunity to witness to unbelievers?

No. Remember, they were rebuilding the temple! By refusing help from pagans, God's people were resisting temptations to what we today call "syncretism"—mixing worship of the one true God with the worship of false deities. Just as the Jews did not want to muddy the waters of their pure worship practices, so we also strive to keep our practices pure. It is especially important that we teach our children and all new believers to understand why we do what we do in worship, since worship involves receiving God's gifts to us and responding to His goodness.

Today's lesson also includes the account of Ezra's opposition to intermarriage with the "people of the land." Be sure to note that this had nothing to do with skin color or race. Instead, here again, Ezra wanted to protect God's people from the practice of syncretism. Solomon had introduced idolatry into Israel a thousand years before—by marrying pagan wives! Judah was in danger of repeating this very same sin. Ezra and those who followed him wanted nothing to do with the worship of idols, especially since at the time, that worship involved sexual immorality, incest, and even human sacrifice!

Thus this text serves as a wonderful means for teaching students that disobeying God's laws is like giving up an umbrella of protection. Conversely, living in obedience to them and trusting the promises God has made brings His joy and peace, even when life is hard.

## Central Truth

God assures His people that His promises are true by reminding them of His faithfulness in the past.

## Objectives

- Recognize the return of God's people to Judah as the fulfillment of His promise.
- Describe Ezra's role in stabilizing the resettlement of Judah.
- Explain that peace, joy, and happiness await all who trust in Jesus for salvation when God takes us to live with Him in heaven.

## Materials

- The Basics
- Reproducible 15

## Bible Prep

Post in advance so students can bookmark references before class time.

- Ezra 1–10
- Romans 8:18

## Devotion

"Let's cut through here so we're not late!" Ann heaved her backpack over her shoulder and used both hands to pull the weeds aside.

"I don't know if we should. The counselors said to stay on the paths," said Liz. "Besides, there could be snakes in there!"

"This is a registered campground. They've gotta make it safe!" Ann plunged into the woods.

"Don't make me come in after you!" joked Liz. "You always do this, you know!"

"Do what?" Ann was already several steps ahead.

"Make me break the rules," replied Liz. "Remember when you talked me into asking . . . "

Liz's words were interrupted by a shriek.

"Ann!" Liz ducked through the trees to see what was happening.

"Shh!" Ann's was standing in a clearing, waving frantically for Liz to back away. "I think it's a copperhead! What should I do?" Ann whispered.

"Um . . . " Liz was frantically looking for a stick. In her panic, she stumbled and landed on the log behind her. As she raised her head, she was staring straight into a pair of eyes about five feet away.

Often, like Ann and Liz in the story, we disregard the rules—the rules God has provided for us for our help and benefit. Like Ann and Liz, we often find ourselves in trouble as a result. Thank God! He sent Jesus to keep all of God's rules in our place. He desires to help us, regardless of the troubles we get ourselves into. He wants us to turn back to Him and to be the recipients of His forgiving, restoring love.

**PRAY: Dear Lord Jesus, thank You for the protection You give us under Your Law. Because of Your death and resurrection for us, forgive us for the times we have failed to obey Your Commandments. Empower us to start anew, trusting in Your grace and mercy. In Your precious name we pray. Amen.**

Sing: "O Word of God Incarnate" (*LSB* 523).

# INTO the lesson

## Where Are You?

Ask a volunteer to read the first paragraph. Then read the second paragraph yourself, and explain the directions further as necessary. Give the class time to work on their graphs. As they do so, talk about some of the scenarios. For example, if some of the students have actually experienced any of the traumatic events described, allow them to tell their stories—but only if they feel comfortable doing so.

Have volunteers show their line graphs to one another, focusing special attention on the ones that illustrate the most dramatic highs and lows. Point out that each of us experiences different things in life, and these experiences shape who we become. At all times, especially in the hard times, we can remember "whose" we are—God's dearly loved, baptized sons and daughters in Christ's cross.

Display the "average" score for the class, and again point out that we each experience life's challenges differently. The "average" in this case tells us nothing about how an individual might react to any of the opportunities or challenges described on the graph.

If time will allow, this would be an ideal point to introduce **Reproducible 15**. If time is short, simply distribute it and assign the reproducible as homework. Otherwise, have students work in groups of four to complete the activity. Have each student in each group find one of the verses and read it aloud to the group. Ask students to highlight the verses they personally find and read. Some students may want to highlight verses read by their classmates too. Each student should record answers on the handout. When all the groups have finished, discuss the answers.

Summarize by pointing out that the Means of Grace are all about God! He comes to us and bestows His gifts of forgiveness and life everlasting through His Word and through the "visible word"—Baptism and Holy Communion. We do nothing to receive His grace; God gives it to us through Word and Sacrament just because He loves us!

## Review

Allow time for students to match each vocabulary word with its correct definition. Review responses with the whole class, connecting each word with today's Bible story.

---

15 Ezra 1–10

### God's People Return from Captivity

**Where Are You?**

Imagine how the emotions of the Jews rose and plunged throughout the times of war with Babylon, the waves of deportation, the process of resettlement in a new land, the Persian takeover of Babylon, the threat of extermination during the reign of King Ahasuerus, and their deliverance from that danger. What a roller coaster! Life for the nation and the individuals in it included a few highs, many terrible lows, and many emotions in between. Only faith in the one true God could have carried His people safely through all this!

We, too, experience a wide array of emotions. The sketches below the graph show different events in the lives of people today. Above each, place a dot on the line that would represent the level of your feelings if you experienced that event. A "1" means you'd be extremely happy, ecstatic with happiness; "10" means you would experience extreme fear or sadness during this event. When you've rated each event, connect the dots from left to right.

**Review**

Match these words with their definitions. Use the glossary in the back of this book if you need help. The words come from Ezra 7–8.

vessel — a plea or earnest request
genealogy — a container, like a bottle, bowl, or cup, for holding something
implore — to call or pray for earnestly
entreaty — an account or list of one's ancestors

32

---

# INTO the Word

## Who Are They?

Have each student, in turn, read one sentence from the first paragraph aloud until the entire paragraph has been read.

Then read Ezra 1–6 as a class, paragraph by paragraph. Or read it to the group aloud yourself, asking that students follow along in their own Bibles. Alert them to the fact that when you finish, they will answer the ten true/false questions.

After the text has been read, ask each student to complete the true/false activity and to unscramble the letters to form the name for God Ezra often uses in his book: "the God of heaven." This name is especially important because the Jews at one time associated their God with a specific geographical place on earth (the land of Israel), but now they knew Him as God of the universe, the God of all that exists.

Then read Ezra 7–10, noting before you start that these events take place fifty years after those in chapter 6. When you finish, talk briefly about these four questions:

1. **How did God use a pagan king, Artaxerxes, to help Ezra's ministry?** (God prompted Artaxerxes to allow Ezra to journey to Jerusalem with other volunteers to find out about the conditions there. The king also

### Who Are They?

The Jews, exiled in Babylon, soon came to appreciate all they had lost. They could no longer worship with other believers in the temple in Jerusalem. The joy of the feasts God had commanded was no longer theirs. Then, one day, they learned that Jerusalem had been destroyed and the temple had been burned. It was a final, terrible blow. But God was not finished with His people. Through Cyrus, the great king of Persia, God would bring His people home and fulfill His promise to send the world's Savior through the descendants of Abraham.

Read Ezra 1–6 and circle *T* for "true" or *F* for "false" by each statement below. Then unscramble the blue letters within the **true** statements and place them on the blanks provided below the True/False activity to reveal a very special name for God.

(T) F 1. Those whom God "stirred up" to return to Jerusalem were supported before leaving Persia by their neighbors' gold, silver, and goods.

T (F) 2. Nebuchadnezzar kept the temple vessels in a safe place so they could be returned.

T (F) 3. The exiles all returned to live in the same town.

(T) F 4. Jeshua, his fellow priests, and Zerubbabel built the altar in the temple.

(T) F 5. The people built the altar because they feared for their safety.

T (F) 6. Everyone shouted cheers of joy when the foundation of the temple was laid.

T (F) 7. The leaders allowed the people of the land to assist in building the temple.

(T) F 8. Threats by the people of the land made the Jews very fearful; reconstruction was stalled for fifteen years.

(T) F 9. Prophecies by Haggai and Zechariah encouraged the people to begin building again.

(T) F 10. Darius, king of Persia, made a decree protecting and providing for those who were to rebuild the temple.

What name for God often appears in the Book of Ezra? What makes this name so appropriate?

T H E   G O D   O F
H E A V E N

Now skip ahead more than fifty years by reading Ezra 7–10. Then talk about the text with your class.

**REMEMBER**

For I consider that the sufferings of this present time are not worth comparing with the glory that is to be revealed to us.

Romans 8:18

33

# INTO our lives

Remind the group that God gives us many opportunities to share His Word with those around us and to build one another up through that Word.

Lead from here into today's memory verse. Tell students that just as the people of Israel trusted in the Lord to work for good in their lives, we can trust Him to do that for us too.

## Remember

As you discuss and review this memory verse with your class, stress God's faithfulness to His promises.

### Where Is He?

Does the line graph you made in class today look a bit choppy? a bit like a roller coaster? Life is often like that! We live in a sinful world and therefore must deal with times of fear, anxiety, and sorrow throughout life. Even so, times of peace, joy, and laughter often punctuate our lives too.

How could each of these passages encourage us during life's hard times, the down times in life?

Romans 8:38

Malachi 3:6

Revelation 22:13

James 1:17

### God's Grace Conveyed to Us

We need God's strength all the time. This need is especially strong when troubles come into our lives. It's often then that Satan tempts us to believe that God is angry with us because of our sins or that He isn't there or that He doesn't love us. Through the Means of Grace, we experience His presence and unending love. There, we receive forgiveness and the assurance of our Lord's gracious care for us.

Place a check next to each item below that is one of the Means of Grace.

- [ ] Parents
- [x] Holy Communion
- [ ] The offering
- [x] God's Word
- [ ] Hymns
- [x] Baptism
- [ ] Confirmation
- [ ] Doughnuts before the service

Although God is with us all the time wherever we are, we typically come into contact with the Means of Grace when we gather with other believers in church each week. What makes church attendance so important?

When we gather for the Divine Service, God comes to us in His Word and Sacraments and offers us forgiveness of sins and life everlasting. He strengthens us to defeat temptation, encourages us in our troubles, and empowers us to carry out our various vocations—especially that of witnessing to the Savior.



allowed them to deliver the temple vessels stolen by Nebuchadnezzar and to take donations for the rebuilding of the temple. He even opened up his own treasury to provide the extra money needed. Finally, Artaxerxes allowed Ezra and those returning with him to enforce God's Law in Judah.)

**2. When Ezra arrived, how did he help make the resettlement of Judah more stable and peaceful?** (He interceded for the people, leading them to repent for their intermarriage with pagans. Then he dissolved those ungodly marriages in a peaceful and organized manner so that the doctrine and lifestyle of God's people could remain distanced from pagan influences.)

**3. Still today, we enjoy the blessings of living under God's "umbrella of protection." That doesn't mean we won't face troubles and hardships. But if we think of the Law as an umbrella, what blessings do we receive from staying under it?** (Obeying God isn't easy—except when we compare it with life when we do not obey Him! Proverbs 13:15 says, "The way of transgressors is hard" [KJV]. When we obey, our hearts are generally more peaceful. Our relationships usually work better. Even though trouble and hardship may come, we find comfort in God's unchanging love for us. Of course, none of us can obey perfectly. Because of Jesus, we receive forgiveness and the renewed hearts that grow in knowing God's Law and wanting to live according to it.)

**4. Considering everything Ezra did, what was most important?** (Teaching the people God's Word as he opened up the Scriptures for them. The truth they most treasured was, undoubtedly, the promise of the Savior who was to come. That Savior would teach in the very same temple they were building! **One day on a cross nearby, the Savior would suffer and die for the sins of the world.** How encouraging it must have been for them to hear this.)

## Where Is He?

Does the line graph you made in class today look a bit choppy? a bit like a roller coaster? Life is often like that! We live in a sinful world and therefore must deal with times of fear, anxiety, and sorrow throughout life. Even so, times of peace, joy, and laughter often punctuate our lives too.

How could each of these passages encourage us during life's hard times, the down times in life?

Romans 8:38

Malachi 3:6

Revelation 22:13

James 1:17

## God's Grace Conveyed to Us

We need God's strength all the time. This need is especially strong when troubles come into our lives. It's often then that Satan tempts us to believe that God is angry with us because of our sins or that He isn't there or that He doesn't love us. Through the Means of Grace, we experience His presence and unending love. There, we receive forgiveness and the assurance of our Lord's gracious care for us.

Place a check next to each item below that is one of the Means of Grace.

- ☐ Parents
- ☐ Holy Communion
- ☐ The offering
- ☐ God's Word
- ☐ Hymns
- ☐ Baptism
- ☐ Confirmation
- ☐ Doughnuts before the service

Although God is with us all the time wherever we are, we typically come into contact with the Means of Grace when we gather with other believers in church each week. What makes church attendance so important?

# Unit 3—Jesus Comes to Serve

## Theme

As you teach this unit, help students to recognize the life, death, and resurrection of Jesus as the "heart and soul" of Christianity. Remind students that the New Testament brings us the message the ancients longed to hear—redemption has come! God sent Jesus "not to be served but to serve, and to give His life as a ransom for many" (Matthew 20:28). Jesus served by living a sinless life in our place and by calling us to, and teaching us about, the new and eternal life He offers freely in His name.

Stress Jesus Christ as the ultimate hero, the founder of the religion that bears His name and the One who brings forgiveness and new and eternal life to you and to each of your students. Celebrate God's goodness as, through your study of these early books of the New Testament, you help to acquaint your students with their Savior and best and truest friend, the Savior and Servant of all.

### Unit 3

16. Jesus Is Born
17. Jesus' First Disciples
18. Nicodemus Visits Jesus
19. Jesus Heals at Bethesda
20. Parables of the Kingdom
21. Jesus and the Miraculous Catch of Fish
22. The Good Samaritan
23. The Lost Son

## Worship

Throughout this unit, talk with your class about how God would have us honor Him with respect to Sunday—our day of worship and rest. Stress that, like Jesus, we honor God best by serving Him on Sundays as on all other days. Remind students that we celebrate Jesus' defeat over sin, death, and the devil's power whenever we assemble for Sunday worship. Point out that the choice of Sunday as the day of worship sets Christians apart from Old Testament believers, for whom Saturday was a special day dedicated to the Lord.

Review with students the portions of the Gospels that may be recognized from their repeated and customary usage in Sunday worship. Explore with students the context of each the following verses:

"In the name of the Father and of the Son and of the Holy Spirit" (Matthew 28:19; Invocation).

"Lord . . . have mercy on us!" (Matthew 20:30; Kyrie).

"Glory to God in the highest, and on earth peace!" (Luke 2:14; Gloria in Excelsis).

"Lord, to whom shall we go? You have the words of eternal life" (John 6:68; Verse).

"Blessed is He who comes in the name of the Lord! Hosanna in the highest!" (Matthew 21:9; Sanctus).

"Our Father in heaven, hallowed be Your name . . . deliver us from evil" (Matthew 6:9–13; Lord's Prayer).

"Peace be with you" (John 20:19; Peace).

"The Lamb of God, who takes away the sin of the world!" (John 1:29; Agnus Dei).

"Lord, now You are letting Your servant depart in peace, . . . for my eyes have seen Your salvation . . . for glory to Your people Israel" (Luke 2:29–32; Nunc Dimittis).

"My soul magnifies the Lord, and my spirit rejoices in God my Savior . . . as He spoke to our fathers, to Abraham and to His offspring forever" (Luke 1:46–55; Magnificat).

## Extending Unit Concepts

### Community Building

*Gospel Jeopardy.* Play the game according to Jeopardy! rules. Plan answers for the four Gospels (Matthew, Mark, Luke, and John) as categories.

*Amoebas.* A roll of inexpensive clear plastic wrap will be needed for this community-building activity. Organize the class into teams of four to seven and have them stand together in a close group. Encircle each group with plastic wrap twice to create an amoeba. The object is for the amoebas to race a distance without breaking the plastic wrap. After a few races, ask the class how they cooperated to move as a group. Was there a leader? How was the leader chosen?

*Rope Drawing.* You will need a 30-foot rope tied into a circle, a fairly large area, and the class organized into teams of no less than five per team. Each team member should grasp the rope and not let go until the game is over. The object of the game is for the team to move so as to create the outline of a shape such as a tree or house. You may need to provide a sketch of the end product. The first team to successfully organize into the shape wins.

### Tools for Witness

Ask each student to draw a picture of a symbol to illustrate one of the attributes of God. Compare students' work. Compare these true but different pictures of God with the different information provided by the Gospels about the person and work of Jesus.

### Service Projects

Talk about God's power for the restoring of broken relationships—broken relationships between God and people and relationships with one another. Involve students in the distribution of tracts in local public places.

Mark 9:41 records Jesus' words, "I tell you the truth, anyone who gives you a cup of water in My name because you belong to Christ will certainly not lose his reward." Encourage students to write thank-you notes to those (pastor, teachers, etc.) who have been kind to them because they are fellow believers.

## Reaching Every Individual

Provide a large map of the Holy Land. As much as possible, plot the location of each Bible story on the map.

Have a group of students act out each of the Bible narratives in this unit as a narrator reads the text. Ask questions to review the facts of the story.

Tell each Bible story to the students. After reviewing the facts of the story, ask, **What does this story show us about Jesus, our Savior?**

# Integrating the Faith throughout the Curriculum

## Social Studies

- Review with students the role and function of an eyewitness. Comment that while Luke was not an eyewitness to the events recorded in his Gospel, he checked out the events he wrote with the power and direction of the Holy Spirit.
- Have groups take a part in preparing a display on the Sea of Galilee, including pertinent information such as coastal towns and villages prominent in Jesus' ministry, types of fish the sea contains, the sea's size and depth, and types of storms there.
- Have students work in groups to construct maps of Jerusalem and the surrounding area, tracing Jesus' steps from the days immediately preceding His crucifixion to His ascension.

## Science

- Scientifically investigate the role of the vine in bringing life to the branches of a plant. Relate to John 15:1.
- Investigate the biological processes that shut down when death occurs. Talk about the miracle of the resurrection and what it means that Jesus is "the resurrection and the life."

## Mathematics

- Chart the details of the birth of Jesus according to which of the Gospels, Matthew or Luke, records them.
- Bible scholars have found that 91 percent of the Book of Mark is found in the Book of Matthew and 53 percent of the Book of Mark is found in the Book of Luke. Talk about what this information suggests about the origin of the Gospels.

## Technology

- Create a radio play of one of the events from the ministry of Jesus.
- E-mail selected favorite portions of one of the Gospels to those in special need of the strength and encouragement God's Spirit provides through His Word.
- Personalize and send a free Internet greeting card celebrating the joy of Easter.
- Social media can be useful in accomplishing many good purposes, too, including sharing the Gospel.

Have students formulate ways that they could use social media in their calling as fishers of men.

## Fine Arts

- Choose and report on Christmas hymns that praise God for the life and atoning work of Jesus.
- Find various depictions of one or more of the Bible stories studied during this unit. Compare the portrayal with regard to the aspects of the story to which each artist draws attention.

## Language Arts

- Pretend you are one of those who saw Jesus after His resurrection. Write a journal entry telling what you saw and how it influenced you.
- Equip your students with a tool for finding solid Lutheran answers to important doctrinal questions instead of simply allowing them to "Google" them and believe whatever the first hit says.
- In 1964, Martin Gansberg wrote an article titled "38 Who Saw Murder Didn't Call the Police" (some versions print 37) in response to the brutal stabbing death of a young woman in Queens, New York. Either have students find this article online or provide copies. Students should work in groups to read this article and reflect on the similarities and differences between the event portrayed in this article and the parable of the Good Samaritan.
- Alternatively or additionally, students can research "Good Samaritan" laws and write a paragraph or two summarizing what these laws do and how they were inspired by the parable. Note that in the United States (and other countries as well), citizens are not required to help others in need, and these Good Samaritan laws were primarily written to protect from liability those who do elect to help someone should that person suffer permanent damage or death as a result of the voluntary assistance.

# Jesus Is Born

LUKE 2:1–20

## Background

We say "Merry Christmas" on December 25, but when was the first Christmas? This question has had scholars scratching their heads since the very early days of the Christian Church.

In the sixth century, Pope John I asked Dionysius Exiguus to determine the dates for Easter for the next few decades. In the process, Dionysius also determined a date for Christmas—and created a welter of misconceptions about the actual year in which Christ was born.

Working backward from dates he thought were accurate, Dionysius set up the Anno Domini calendar system with the BC and AD designations for dating we still use today. Since then, scholars have determined that Dionysius was working with incomplete information. Based on other historical records of the time, they have determined that Jesus was probably born somewhere between 6 and 4 BC in the system Dionysius invented. This would fit with the information Luke gives us about Quirinius, Caesar Augustus, and the census.

As for December 25, most scholars agree that December is an unlikely month for shepherds to be out in the fields outside Bethlehem. The earliest mention of December 25 as the date of Christmas comes from records dated AD 336. It is likely that Church Fathers chose this date to coincide with the winter solstice and the pagan celebrations common to that event. In doing so, perhaps they wanted to make the transition to Christianity more palatable to potential pagan converts.

Whatever the reason, the Bible simply does not tell us when Christ was born. That makes our suppositions merely guesses—educated guesses, perhaps, but guesses nonetheless. Still, as His followers, we delight in the remembrance of His coming. It's an event worthy of celebrating every day, including today!

## Central Truth

In love and mercy, God sent His Son to be born into the world, to live a sinless life, to suffer and die, and to be raised again so that, through faith, all might have life in Him.

## Objectives

- Acknowledge that Jesus, the Savior, is both true God and true man.
- Profess faith in God's desire to save all people.
- Praise God for sending Jesus to be our Savior.

## Materials

- The Basics
- Reproducible 16

## Bible Prep

Post in advance so students can bookmark references before class time.

- Matthew 4:2
- Luke 2:1–20
- Luke 24:39
- John 1:14
- John 19:28
- John 20:28
- Philippians 2:10
- Colossians 2:9
- 1 Timothy 1:15
- 1 Timothy 2:3–6
- Hebrews 2:17
- 1 John 5:20

## Devotion

As soon as the minivan's headlights turned the corner, Tyler turned to his younger brother, James. "You know what to do, right?" Tyler asked.

James nodded solemnly, his thumb in his mouth. "I look in Mama's closet for the presents."

"That's right, James. You're so smart. I can't get caught this year, okay? If I do, Mama and Daddy will be really, *really* mad at me." Checking his watch, Tyler said, "And they'll be home in twenty minutes. They're just going to drop a check off at the bank and pick up burgers for supper. So get started."

With a push in the right direction, Tyler sent James toddling into their parents' bedroom, praying that James would have the sense to be subtle in his search.

Two minutes later, Tyler heard a crash and then a shattering sound. Tyler knew he would soon find himself in a heap of trouble for investigating his Christmas presents for the second year in a row. Why did Christmas have to be so difficult?

Clearly, Tyler has the wrong idea about Christmas. For him, it's all about the presents. He is consumed with solving the mystery of what will be under the tree on Christmas morning—so much so that he's willing to get both himself and his younger brother into trouble to find out.

Christmas isn't causing Tyler's troubles; his impatience is. God's Old Testament people may have been impatient too. They waited many, many years for the Savior to be born. But then He came—born under humble circumstances to Mary and Joseph. Born to live, die, and rise again for every sin, including sins relating to being impatient!

**PRAY: Dear Father in heaven, too often we want the things we want right away instead of waiting until Your time is right. Work in our hearts the patience we need to wait for Your best for us in every situation. Thank You for sending Jesus to be our Savior. We pray in Jesus' name. Amen.**

Sing: "What Child Is This" (*LSB* 370) or "Chief of Sinners Though I Be" (*LSB* 611).

# INTO the lesson

Since, in most settings, this lesson will be taught soon after Christmas, it is likely that most students will easily be able to answer the first of the following reflective questions, listing everything they got for Christmas this year.

Say, **Take out a sheet of paper and list every present you got for Christmas this year.**

After students have finished, ask, **Do you think you remembered everything? Now, how about listing everything you got for Christmas last year? and the year before?** These memories will likely be much more difficult to dredge up. **That makes it a little more difficult, doesn't it?**

Even though we all get excited about Christmas presents, after the haze of unwrapping and initial pleasure wears off, we usually can't remember exactly what we got so excited about. **There's really only one Christmas gift important enough to remember for a lifetime.**

Ask students to talk about why Jesus' arrival was such a significant, history-changing event. It is important for them to state (again and again) their understanding of the gift of salvation. **Jesus is the Savior, promised of old, who came to earn forgiveness of sins, new life, and eternal salvation for us and for all people.**

16 Luke 2:1–20

## Jesus Is Born

### The Greatest Gift

Last time, we saw that God had revealed His plan of salvation through the promised Messiah in many ways through His prophets. We saw how Jesus fulfilled those prophecies. Today, as you read Luke's account of the nativity (Luke 2:1–20), keep in mind God's plan to save us.

1. The prophet Micah foretold that the Messiah would be born in Bethlehem (Micah 5:2). What did God do to get Mary and Joseph from their hometown of Nazareth to Bethlehem, Joseph's ancestral home, in time for Jesus to be born there?
   **God worked through Caesar Augustus and the census the emperor introduced to get Mary and Joseph from Nazareth to Bethlehem.**
2. Matthew 23:12 says: "Whoever exalts himself will be humbled, and whoever humbles himself will be exalted." How did the birth of Jesus illustrate this concept perfectly?
   **Jesus was born in some sort of shed or outbuilding, not even a proper inn. Mary had to lay Him in a manger! This is not the typical arrangement for most newborn earthly kings, let alone the King of kings.**
3. The multitude of angels glorified God as they announced the arrival of the Prince of Peace, the One who would save His people from their sins. According to their words, who will receive God's gift of salvation?
   **God's gift of peace—salvation—will be given to those who believe in Him.**
4. How did the shepherds respond to the message of the angels and to arriving at the birthplace of the infant Jesus?
   **They hurried to find the baby Jesus. After they had seen Him, the shepherds praised God and told everyone that the promised Savior had come.**

### Review

Draw a line to match each term with its definition.

|  |  |
|---|---|
| humility | one of Isaiah's names for Jesus |
| Prince of Peace | deliverance from sin and its effects |
| salvation | looking at yourself through God's eyes |
| incarnation | the act of taking on flesh |

34

# INTO the Word

## The Greatest Gift

As students read through Luke's account of Jesus' birth, remind them that God sent Jesus into the world at just the right time to fulfill His perfect plan. If time will allow, have someone find and read Galatians 4:4—a key verse that asserts this truth about God and His timing. Numerous prophets foretold the details surrounding Christ's birth, and those prophecies were fulfilled.

Then have students pair up with a partner to read Luke 2:1–20 and answer the questions in the Student Book. When they finish, discuss the questions with the whole class.

**1.** God can influence people, especially those in positions of authority, to accomplish His will. (See Proverbs 21:1.) So it is not unreasonable to consider that He used the census of Caesar Augustus as a means to fulfill the prophecy that Jesus would be born in Bethlehem (Micah 5:2).

**2.** We assume Jesus' birthplace was an animal shelter because it had a manger in it, but that doesn't necessarily mean dozens of animals crowded around.

**3.** While God certainly *wants* all people to be saved (1 Timothy 2:4), many harden their hearts and refuse His gift of peace and eternal life. This saddens God, who has done everything necessary to win our salvation.

**4.** Truly, the shepherds responded appropriately to the Messiah's birth. As God's Spirit works within us, we, too, want to join them in telling everyone the great truths God has revealed to us in His Word.

## Review

As time allows, point out that *incarnation* and *carnivore* both come from the same Latin root word. Underline the letters *carn* in each word. Mention that *chili con carne* is made with meat as well as chili peppers, beans, and tomatoes. The word refers to "meat" or "flesh." Jesus took on human flesh and "became man," as the Nicene Creed indicates.

## True God, True Man

The two natures of Christ made our salvation possible. If Jesus had not

## True God, True Man

So, baby Jesus was born and laid in a manger in Bethlehem. What makes that the best Christmas gift ever? Jesus was true God and true man at the same time. This made it possible for Him to live a perfect life in our place and then give Himself up as the final sacrifice for the sins of all people. This gift of salvation lasts for all time and is freely offered to every person who ever lived here on earth. It will never break or get lost. It doesn't need batteries. Most important, it's something everyone everywhere truly needs!

Read the following verses and decide whether they tell us that Jesus is true God or true man or both at the same time. Then, write the Bible reference in the appropriate place in the diagram.

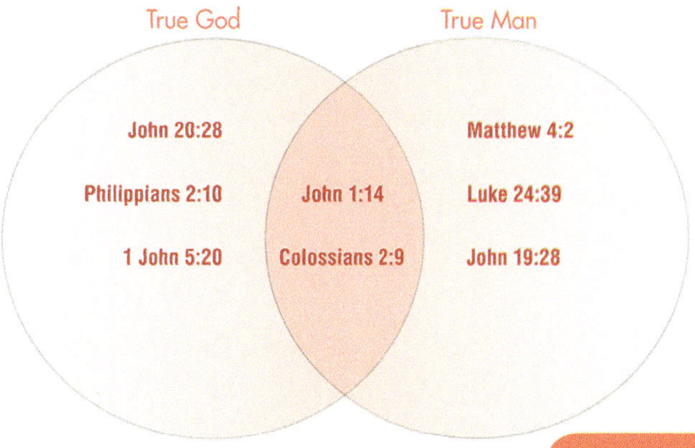


Matthew 4:2— **true man**

Luke 24:39— **true man**

John 1:14— **both true God and true man**

John 19:28— **true man**

John 20:28— **true God**

Philippians 2:10— **true God**

Colossians 2:9— **both true God and true man**

1 John 5:20— **true God**

Jesus became a true human being in order to save us from our sin. As we celebrate the gift of His birth at Christmas, we look ahead to what His incarnation meant. We look ahead to the cross—and to our own salvation. It's the reason He was born in Bethlehem.

**REMEMBER**

For unto **you** is born **this day** in the city of David a **Savior**, who is **Christ** the **Lord**.

Luke 2:11

35

been true God, He could not have lived a sinless life, nor would His sacrifice for our sins have been sufficient. If Jesus had not been true man, He could not have taken our place under the Law and died in our place. For more detail, see the section on the Second Article of the Apostles' Creed, especially "The Two Natures of Christ," questions 118–124, in *Luther's Small Catechism with Explanation*. This doctrine is difficult to understand and easy to misstate. If students have questions, you may want to invite your pastor to class to field them.

Have students follow the directions as they complete the diagram, adding the Scripture references in the correct places. It will help if students work with a partner and talk about the texts as they decide where to put the references.

For each reference, they must decide whether the verse talks about Jesus' human nature, His divine nature, or both.

When students have finished, initiate a discussion focused on any verses students misplaced.

## INTO our lives

Ask students to work in small groups to find and read one of the following passages and then summarize it. Assign one of the three passages to each group. (Alternatively, students may work independently or with a partner, or students may all look up each of the three passages.) When students have finished, ask volunteers to share their summaries.

- Hebrews 2:17 (Christ had to be a true human being so that He could die in payment for our sins.)
- 1 Timothy 1:15 (Jesus came into the world to save sinners, and I am a sinner.)
- 1 Timothy 2:3–6 (God wants all people to be saved; He sent Christ to earth to work this salvation.)

These verses—and many others just like them in the Bible—remind us that we are sinners and there is no way we could ever bring about our own salvation. Only by the gift of God's grace in Jesus do we enjoy a relationship with Him, now and forever.

All of the passages remind us that Christ Jesus came into the world to save us. He was committed to this task from before time began (see Ephesians 1:3ff.). Remind students that this is our focus during the Christmas season—not the gifts we get, but the gift the world got more than two thousand years ago.

Stress that Jesus was sent to earth to be the final and perfect sacrifice for sin. We are now washed clean. When God looks at us, He sees not our sin, but souls purified by Jesus. Throughout the seasons of Christmas and Epiphany, we keep Good Friday and Easter in mind too, for it is there that Christ's redemptive work was brought to its glorious completion.

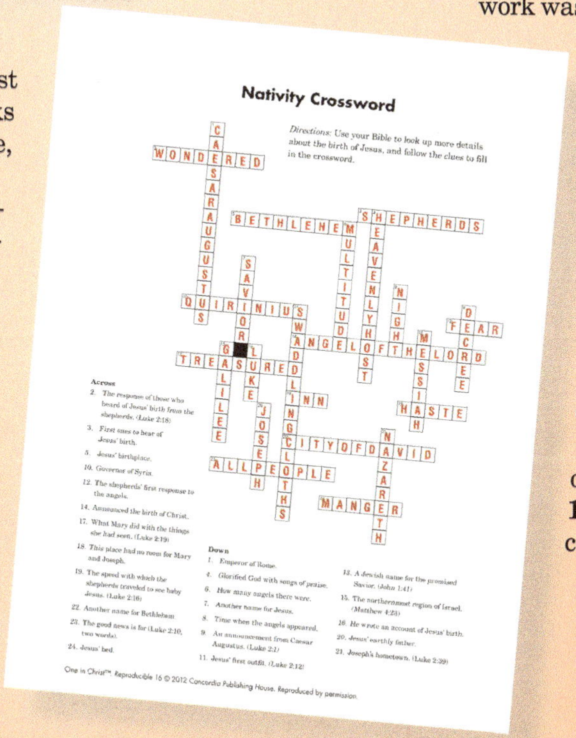


### Remember

Emphasize that these words from the angels to the shepherds apply to us as well: "For unto you is born this day in the city of David a Savior, who is Christ the Lord."

Distribute copies of **Reproducible 16** for students to complete.

# Nativity Crossword

*Directions:* Use your Bible to look up more details about the birth of Jesus, and follow the clues to fill in the crossword.

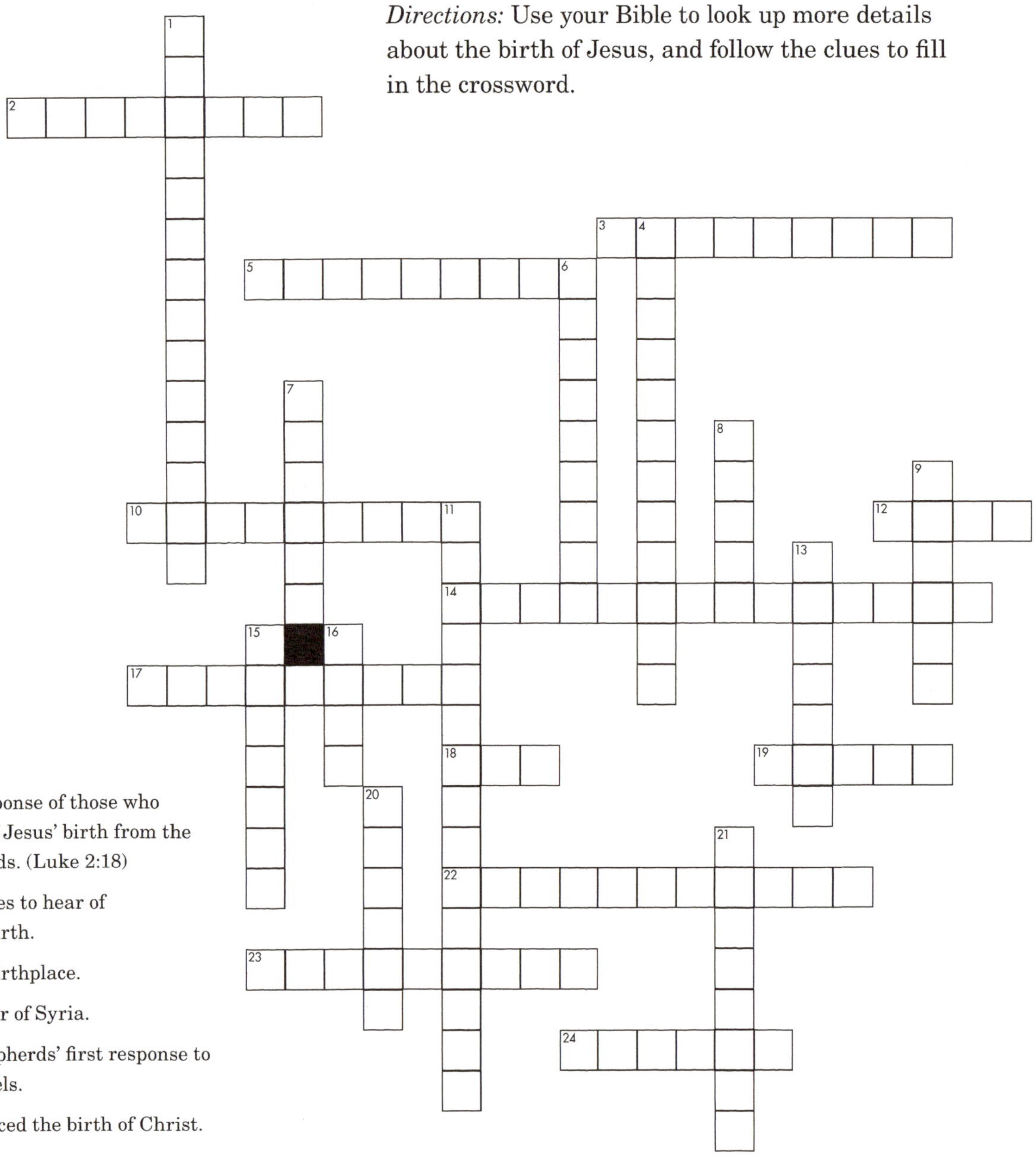

**Across**

2. The response of those who heard of Jesus' birth from the shepherds. (Luke 2:18)
3. First ones to hear of Jesus' birth.
5. Jesus' birthplace.
10. Governor of Syria.
12. The shepherds' first response to the angels.
14. Announced the birth of Christ.
17. What Mary did with the things she had seen. (Luke 2:19)
18. This place had no room for Mary and Joseph.
19. The speed with which the shepherds traveled to see baby Jesus. (Luke 2:16)
22. Another name for Bethlehem.
23. The good news is for (Luke 2:10, two words).
24. Jesus' bed.

**Down**

1. Emperor of Rome.
4. Glorified God with songs of praise.
6. How many angels there were.
7. Another name for Jesus.
8. Time when the angels appeared.
9. An announcement from Caesar Augustus. (Luke 2:1)
11. Jesus' first outfit. (Luke 2:12)
13. A Jewish name for the promised Savior. (John 1:41)
15. The northernmost region of Israel. (Matthew 4:23)
16. He wrote an account of Jesus' birth.
20. Jesus' earthly father.
21. Joseph's hometown. (Luke 2:39)

# Jesus' First Disciples

MARK 1:14–20

## Background

The word *disciple* essentially means "learner." The New Testament uses the term in several ways. Sometimes it refers to the twelve early followers of Jesus whom He later named "apostles" (Mark 3:14). Sometimes it refers to the people who accompanied Him during His earthly ministry. This group had grown to around 120 by the time of His ascension (Acts 1:12–15). Later, it came to refer to all who believed in Jesus, as the number of disciples expanded rapidly (Acts 6:1; 11:26). At this point, the terms *disciple* and *Christian* meant the same thing.

Jesus told His first four disciples, "I will make you become fishers of men" (Mark 1:17). Notice the future tense in that statement; the disciples would take their first steps on the path to becoming witnesses to the Savior. They knew exactly what it meant to be a fisherman in the literal sense, but they had little knowledge of what it would mean to bring persons into the kingdom of heaven. Jesus would teach them all about it—in both word and example.

It's interesting to note the number of early disciples: four at first, and later, twelve. For Jews, the number *4* often signified the creation or the created world. The four new followers, all fishermen, are told that now they will leave their physical fish and nets to instead bring people into the kingdom of God. Eventually, the influence of their message would extend to the four corners of the world.

More significantly, Jesus chooses a total of twelve disciples for His inner circle. In this number, we hear echoes of the twelve tribes of Israel. In a significant sense, Jesus Himself now *is* Israel—God's chosen servant (see Isaiah 44). He will obey God perfectly in our place, and then, in His death, absorb the punishment all human beings have deserved for our sins. In doing so, He will establish the new Israel, making disciples of "all nations" (Matthew 28:18–20).

## Central Truth

Through Jesus' death on the cross, God forgives us our failure to acknowledge His call to discipleship. The Holy Spirit empowers us to use the gifts God has given us to serve Him as obedient, faithful witnesses.

## Objectives

- Acknowledge that Christ calls His disciples to follow Him and serve Him.
- Identify factors that keep people from following Jesus.
- Express the intent to seek Christ's forgiveness and pray for the power to follow Him faithfully.

## Materials

- The Basics
- Reproducible 17

## Bible Prep

Post in advance so students can bookmark references before class time.

- Mark 1:14–20
- Matthew 16:13–17
- Matthew 16:21–23
- Luke 18:15–17
- Luke 18:34
- John 21:4–7
- Acts 2:37–38

## Devotion

During the American Civil War, doctors and nurses followed the troops into battle, positioning themselves dangerously close to the fighting. They carried all of their equipment on their backs and would begin to treat injured soldiers while shells were still flying overhead. These medics knew they had to act quickly in order to save the lives of those injured in battle. Mere minutes could mean the difference between life and death. The more immediately the medics responded, the more lives they saved.

When Jesus called His first disciples, they responded immediately. Simon, Andrew, James, and John were working as fishermen in the Sea of Galilee. As they mended and cleaned their nets one day, Jesus came past and said, "Follow Me, and I will make you become fishers of men."

The Lord meant that they would no longer spend their days catching fish. Rather, they would gather people for the kingdom of God. The disciples put down their nets, left their boats and business behind, and immediately followed Jesus. Like the fearless medics of the American Civil War, they did not let their fears or doubts keep them from doing what they had to do—and doing it right away.

Jesus has chosen us to be His disciples as well. He called us out of sin's darkness. In Baptism, He claimed us as His own. He intends that we follow Him immediately and fearlessly. Sadly, that doesn't always happen. We sometimes let doubts or fear slow us down. In those moments when we are fearful or slow to obey, we look to our Teacher because He is also our Savior. He died on the cross in our place for every sinful thought, word, and action. Certain of His forgiveness and of His love for us, we follow Him—living lives of love and witness.

**PRAY: Lord Jesus, assure us of Your forgiveness, and teach us to follow You in obedience and witness. Amen.**

Sing: "You Are the Way; through You Alone" (*LSB* 526).

# INTO the lesson

As a class, brainstorm words that are synonymous with the word *immediately* (e.g., *instantly*, *right now*, *suddenly*, *rapidly*, and *quickly*). Then ask the class what these words suggest. Steer the conversation toward the idea that all these terms suggest a sense of urgency, a sense that the matter at hand is so important that it cannot wait until tomorrow. Tie this discussion into the devotion you shared earlier by mentioning the existence of "urgent care centers," who provide medical treatments that can't wait. Have students think about what ailments require visiting an urgent care center as opposed to waiting for one's yearly routine checkup.

Now have students read Mark 1:14–20, noting the word "immediately" in the text. Ask, **How is it used?** (The disciples drop what they are doing to follow Jesus immediately.)

**So why did the disciples respond immediately?** (The Holy Spirit was at work in their hearts, impressing upon them that following Jesus was an important—an urgent—matter.)

Summarize by noting that as Jesus called these four to follow Him, He used an analogy—fishing—familiar to them. They knew how to fish on the Sea of Galilee; they would have to learn how to fish in the sea of people around them.

17 Mark 1:14–20

## Jesus' First Disciples

### Fishers of Men

As He began His earthly ministry, Jesus gathered a group of students—the disciples—around Himself. They learned from Jesus and then taught others. They saw Jesus perform miracles and then performed miracles themselves. They watched as Jesus was crucified, and many of them followed Him even into death.

Eventually, Jesus would have hundreds and thousands of disciples. We sometimes take note of the Twelve who were part of our Lord's "inner circle." At first, Jesus called just four individuals—fishermen—to follow Him in "catching" people: Simon, Andrew, James, and John.

At that time, many people made a living by fishing on the Sea of Galilee. These fishermen did not use a rod and reel, worms, or lures to catch one fish at a time. Instead, much like commercial fishermen today, they used big nets to catch hundreds of fish at a time.

Jesus told Simon and Andrew that He would make them "fishers of men." Rather than spending their days netting fish to feed others' bodies, they would instead now invest their lives in bringing people into the kingdom of God.

Even after the Twelve had spent several years hearing Jesus teach and watching Him minister, they still sometimes misunderstood His methods and priorities. Then Jesus had to correct them. Other times, they knew exactly what He wanted, and Jesus praised them for their work.

Find the following passages and write the letter beside each in the correct column.

| Understanding Their Calling | Misunderstanding Their Calling |
|---|---|
| a | b |
| e | c |
| f | d |

a. Matthew 16:13–17
b. Matthew 16:21–23
c. Luke 18:15–17
d. Luke 18:34
e. John 21:4–7
f. Acts 2:37–38

### Review

Circle the correct meaning of each word below.

A **disciple** is (a) a student who learns from a master/teacher; (b) one of Jesus' inner circle of twelve followers; (c) one of hundreds who followed Jesus during and after His earthly ministry; (d) anyone today who follows Jesus.

A **fisher of men** is (a) someone who works in the sporting goods department; (b) someone who has a job in the church, like a pastor or teacher in a Christian school; (c) someone like me who knows Jesus' love and wants others to know it too; (d) two of the above.

36

# INTO the Word

## Fishers of Men

Read Mark 1:14–20. Then review the paragraphs in this section. Have students work together to brainstorm ways in which the disciples "caught" people for the kingdom of God. People are caught for God's kingdom when they believe the Good News—**Jesus Christ is the Savior of the world.** Use **Reproducible 17** in connection with this activity if you choose. Distribute it now and work on it together, or ask students to partner up to do so.

When everyone has finished, ask students to share the "fishing methods" they have identified. Write the ideas students suggest on the board, being sure to spread them around in a random order. Once the class has suggested a dozen or so examples, draw lines connecting each idea to the others, creating a net, or web, of evangelism approaches. Explain that these are the "nets" the disciples cast into the world as they fished for people.

Then tell the students that Mark records that just before Jesus called His first disciples, He was in Galilee, proclaiming an important message. Jesus later passed this message on to the Twelve, and they proclaimed it. Then other disciples picked the message up, and it has now come to us. We, too, are disciples who witness to it.

Point out that the first disciples had the message, but—as is sometimes the case with us—they didn't always understand (or believe!) it.

## Review

Allow time for students to complete this activity as they explore the meanings of these words. Review concepts with the whole class.

### Now Is the Time!

When Jesus called His first disciples, He expected them to follow Him immediately. He expects the same from us. But we don't always drop what we are doing to obey Him. Suppose the Lord walked into your classroom right now or into your gym during practice after school. Would you leave your books or your basketball behind to go with Him? What if He told you to stay where you are, doing your best, and living out His love in your relationships with others? Would worries or fears keep you from doing what He asked?

Sadly, words like *immediately*, *now*, and *instantly* do not always describe our life as Christ's disciples. Jesus forgives our slowness of heart to believe and the reluctance of our feet and hands to act. Though we sometimes misunderstand His calling in our lives, He continues to patiently explain and wait for us. Though we often struggle with temptation and often disobey, in His cross we find forgiveness for our every failure to live as His disciples.

Talk about each of these questions with one or two other people. Be prepared to report to the class.

1. In Scripture, Jesus commands His disciples to follow Him. What does that mean specifically for you personally and for your classmates right this minute?
2. What fears or concerns keep Christians today from following Jesus? What keeps you from following Him immediately and completely?
3. How does the message Christ proclaimed help you in times like that?

### Fishers of Men? Me?

Jesus did not leave His disciples on their own to figure out what He meant when He told them to be "fishers of men." He taught them all about it—lovingly and patiently. He gave them everything they needed—knowledge, skills, practice, His own example to follow. On top of all that, He gave them the Holy Spirit to empower them after He went back to heaven.

The Holy Spirit is at work in our lives too. As He works in us, we sometimes do a great job of following Jesus, leaving our fears and doubts behind. At other times, we do not do as well. We delay, deny, and disobey. At those times especially, we look back to Christ's sacrifice on the cross—His sacrifice for us!

On the line below, put an X on the continuum to show where you think you are as you consider your words and actions as Jesus' disciple and witness. Then, beneath the box on the left, jot down the biggest hindrance to your discipleship. Beneath the box on the right, jot down two or three things that help you most as you grow in your life of discipleship and witness.

Totally Hopeless Fisher of Men ———————— Productive, Successful Fisher of Men

**Answers will vary; accept thoughtful responses.**

**REMEMBER**

Jesus said to them again, "Peace be with you. As the Father has sent Me, even so I am sending you." And when He had said this, He breathed on them and said to them, "Receive the Holy Spirit."

John 20:21–22

37

# INTO our lives

## Now Is the Time!

Have a volunteer read the first two paragraphs under this heading. Then ask questions like these:

- If the school secretary called your house and told you someone had dropped off a big package for you at the school, and it looked like a gift, how long would it take you to come pick it up?
- If the principal announced that the first ten students to come to the office would get to go with him for a day at the amusement park, what would you do?
- If your teacher said that a brand-new gaming system would go to the first student to put his or her name on a piece of paper, would you sharpen your pencil first?
- What if Jesus told you to drop everything and follow Him? What would you do?

Then talk about the questions at the end of this section.

**1.** It means obeying Jesus all the time and right away, not just when it's convenient or pleasant for us. We are sometimes slow to respond when our Lord wants us to act. Would it be different if He asked us face-to-face? Most will say they would drop everything if Jesus came and asked them in person to follow Him. Explain that Jesus has told us to follow Him. We should not hesitate or quibble because of the method He has chosen to communicate that message.

**2.** Let students name fears or concerns that keep Christians today from following Jesus. Sometimes it's not fears or worries, however; sometimes it's selfishness and a reluctance to give up our own priorities or comforts.

**3.** Jesus calls us to repent—to recognize and confess our sin. Then He calls us to "believe in the Gospel"—the Good News that He died for us and now forgives us. Our sin is gone, and His Holy Spirit lives inside us, motivating and empowering us to witness in words and actions. This is tremendously helpful as we seek to live lives of holy service to those around us.

## Fishers of Men? Me?

The Holy Spirit is at work in us, just as He was at work in Jesus' first disciples. Because He is, we are becoming more and more fully the fishers of men Jesus calls us to be. Scripture guides us, and other Christians walk with us as we learn to follow Jesus.

Although we often stumble in our efforts to follow Jesus, He never faltered in fulfilling His purpose as our Savior. When we realize our failures as followers of Jesus, we rejoice knowing that Jesus did not stumble (Mark 14:36; John 19:30). God counts His perfect obedience as our own.

As necessary, help students complete the exercise in this section. Keep on reinforcing the fact that the Holy Spirit is at work in us to produce everything we need as Jesus' disciples and witnesses. Point to today's memory verse as one promise of that.

## Remember

As you review this memory verse with your class, stress God's power at work through the Holy Spirit teaching us the meaning of discipleship as He works in us through God's Word.

# Nets for Fishing

The disciples "fished" for people in a number of ways, using many different kinds of "nets," "worms," and "lures."

Find and read each of the passages referenced below. As you read, ask yourself what approaches were used. (Note that some texts mention several, while others have only one.)

Then summarize the approaches in one, two, or three words. Scatter your answers around the page to make a random collection. When you finish, connect all the answers, drawing lines to make one large net.

Here are the Bible texts to use: Matthew 10:8; Luke 9:10–17; Acts 2:14; Acts 11:29.

# Nicodemus Visits Jesus

JOHN 3:1–21

## Background

From the very beginning, Jesus' message seems to have caused quite a stir. As evidence, consider the Lord's visit with Nicodemus. As a member of the Sanhedrin, Nicodemus was among a handful of highly respected leaders in Israel. (The seventy-two members of the Sanhedrin were all powerful and, presumably, wealthy.) The Sanhedrin resembled the U.S. Supreme Court in their duties, influence, and authority. At the end of His ministry, Jesus would stand trial before this very body.

But now, one of its members had come to Him under the cover of darkness to discuss the state of his own soul! John records their conversation using the metaphors of light and dark from chapter 1 of his Gospel and in the context of Jesus' first cleansing of the temple in chapter 2. *That* dramatic event—imagine Jesus with a whip, turning over tables, scattering money everywhere and chasing away escaping animals!—certainly would have drawn everyone's attention. Most were likely still shaking their heads. But Nicodemus wanted to go further. He wanted to know more. Perhaps he had heard the Baptist's message. Now, a poor unknown rabbi had picked it up: "The kingdom of God is at hand; repent and believe in the gospel" (Mark 1:15).

But what did it mean? Was this some new law, a new requirement Nicodemus was to add to the mountain of requirements God had already obligated him to fulfill? Nicodemus, "the teacher of Israel" (John 3:10), didn't know.

Our Lord tenderly explains salvation as purely God's work of grace. He does it in terms so simple that even a child could understand (see John 3:16), although the preconceptions Nicodemus had brought into the conversation block his understanding. Nevertheless, the Holy Spirit continued His work, and by the time Jesus died for Nicodemus—and for us—Nicodemus seems to have become a disciple, a bolder and bolder one! (Compare John 7:40–52 and 19:38–42.)

## Central Truth

God sent His only Son, Jesus, into the world to save sinners. The Holy Spirit gives us faith to believe in Jesus as our Savior.

## Objectives

- Explain the meaning of "born of water and the Spirit."
- Acknowledge with joy the saving faith that the Holy Spirit works in human hearts.
- Thank God for calling us to faith and preserving us in that faith.

## Materials

- The Basics
- Reproducible 18

## Bible Prep

Post in advance so students can bookmark references before class time.

- John 3:1–21
- John 7:40–52
- John 19:38–42

## Devotion

Nick loved to hike—the lonelier the wilderness, the better. One day, Nick filled his canteen to the brim with water and headed out for a hike in the desert. As the day went on, the sun beat down hotter and hotter. Nick drank more and more water, but no matter how much he drank, he grew more and more thirsty.

That wasn't the only problem. After awhile, he didn't know where he was. Soon he was sunburned, parched, out of water, and lost. What could he do?

Then, in the distance, he saw a small lake! With all the strength he had left, Nick sprinted toward it. But when he arrived, all he saw was sand. The lake had been a mirage. Then, in the distance, Nick saw a deserted shack—and a pump nearby. Was *this* a mirage—or the real thing? Nick didn't know, but, exhausted, he crawled toward it.

When Nick got to the pump, he saw a sign with a water bottle tied to it. The sign said, "Don't drink the water in this bottle. Pour it into the pump. Believe, and you will receive!" Puzzled and unsure, Nick opened the bottle and poured the water into the pump's mechanism. Then he grabbed the pump handle and began to pump. Suddenly, water began gushing out!

This is a picture of our Christian life. It seems foolish that something so simple as Baptism could have such remarkable saving power. It seems foolish that a holy God would send His Son to live with sinners and then die for us! But it's true, all true.

Every morning when your feet hit the ground, you can remember: "God loves me. He's made me His own child. I belong to Him."

**PRAY: Jesus, You are our living water. Thank You for all You've done to give us everlasting life! Continue to teach, rule, and make each of us more and more like You. Amen.**

Sing: "We Know That Christ Is Raised" (*LSB* 603).

# INTO the lesson

## Good and Evil—the Ultimate Conflict

Read the opening paragraphs in the Student Book to the class or have a volunteer do so. Ask if anyone has heard the term *dualism* before. We might deduce the philosophy of dualism by looking at the circumstances around us and by watching or reading the news. Earthquakes strike (evil) and relief agencies rush in to help (good). Babies are born, bringing happiness into families (good), but they later grow up and become estranged from their parents and siblings (evil).

The evidence we see may lead us to believe dualism is true. But the Bible teaches us not to believe it. Jesus is already victorious, despite all evidence to the contrary. The sin, tragedy, and death around us will one day give way to the glories of heaven for all who cling to Christ by faith.

From the brief opening discussion, lead into the chart activity. It introduces the opposites apparent in John 3:1–21. Lead students in working through today's Bible narrative and discovering the contrasting themes there.

As you do that, draw attention to this fact: **Many in our world insist that moral questions seldom fit neatly into categories like good or evil, black or white. What would Jesus say to this?** (Just because we don't always understand what's right and wrong in a given situation, that doesn't mean that right and wrong don't exist.)

## Review

Have students find the word *conversion* in their glossary and guide them as they complete the two sentences in this section of the lesson. Conversion is God's act from beginning to end. He gives us faith as His gift, then nurtures that faith through His Word and Sacraments, transforming us into "little Christs" ("Christians"). Conversion is not anything that we do or could do. We can't decide to follow Jesus. He chooses us and works in us, deepening our realization of His love and our response of discipleship.

John 3:1–21 reinforces this truth. Just as no baby decides to be born, so we do not decide to believe in Jesus. He gives us true faith.

Remind the class that older children, teens, and adults who are not yet baptized come to faith through the proclamation of God's Word. People who are baptized as infants receive the gift of faith through the Sacrament of Holy Baptism. Either way, God is the author of our faith. He makes it possible for us to be "born again," as Jesus puts it in today's text.

18 John 3:1–21

## Nicodemus Visits Jesus

### Good and Evil—the Ultimate Conflict

God is holy. Man is sinful. From the day Adam and Eve fell into sin, life on earth has been marked by the struggle between good and evil. One human philosophy—dualism—proposes that neither will ever win; life in our universe will remain locked in an ongoing battle forever.

Scripture, though, teaches that Jesus has already won the battle between good and evil on His cross and in His empty tomb. Meanwhile, while we live here on earth, we fight a mop-up operation. When Jesus returns, we will sing, "The kingdom of the world has become the kingdom of our Lord and of His Christ, and He shall reign forever and ever" (Revelation 11:15). Until then, we endure situations that are often scary and dark.

The battle between good and evil, particularly between God and demons, marked Jesus' earthly ministry. Our Savior often confronted Satan head-on—not just during His temptation in the desert, but also when He healed people tormented by devils.

Jesus' conversation with Nicodemus helps us understand these confrontations and what's at stake. Read John 3:1–21. As you do, you will note several opposites. Unscramble the words in column 1 and their opposites in column 3. Then write the contrast in column 4. Use the hints from John 3 (column 5) if you need help. The first one is done for you.

| | | | | |
|---|---|---|---|---|
| GTHIL | and | KDRA | LIGHT and DARK | John 3:19 |
| TEAH | and | VEOL | HATE and LOVE | – |
| NEEVAH | and | LELH | HEAVEN and HELL | John 3:16 |
| FIEL | and | TEHAD | LIFE and DEATH | John 3:14–15 |
| DAVES | and | MEDDENONC | SAVED and CONDEMNED | John 3:17 |
| AYD | and | THIGN | DAY and NIGHT | John 3:2 |
| REALTHY things | and | LYEVANEH things | EARTHLY things and HEAVENLY things | John 3:12 |
| DEANCS | and | SNECDDE | ASCEND and DESCEND | John 3:13 |

The Bible tells us every person on earth is on one side or the other. There is no middle ground. Why do people sometimes like to "hang out" on the wrong side? When have you chosen that side? Why?

### Review

Conversion is . . .

Conversion is not . . .

38

# INTO the Word

## Who Was Nicodemus?

Use this brief activity to illustrate the concept of conversion/rebirth Jesus describes in John 3:1–21. (Refer also to the "Background" section of this guide.) After students list observations about Nicodemus based on the text, add to their knowledge by explaining that as a member of the Sanhedrin, Nicodemus was among a handful of highly respected leaders in Israel. Have half the class find and read John 7:40–52 and the other half find and read John 19:38–42. Ask, **What appears to be happening to Nicodemus?** (He came to faith in Jesus and began to speak and act boldly on that faith, despite the risk of losing his power and position.)

The Holy Spirit was at work in the life of Nicodemus.

## Born Again!

As students talk through these questions, help them understand that the term "born again" describes the radical change that God works in the lives of sinners—human beings who are born sinful, as rebels and enemies of God. We were once on the "wrong side" of the contrasts the class identified as today's session began.

1. The Holy Spirit was at work in Nicodemus even before he came to see Jesus. We know this because Nicodemus is evidently concerned about his personal relationship with God.

### Who Was Nicodemus?

Look back over John 3:1–21. Find all the facts about Nicodemus you can glean from this text. Who was he? What did he believe about God and about light and dark, good and evil? What sparked his interest in Jesus?

**Possible answers include:**

- **Nicodemus was a Pharisee, trying to please God by obeying the Law in every detail.**
- **He was a member of the Sanhedrin (the ruling council, the Jewish supreme court).**
- **As a member of the Sanhedrin, he would have been powerful and wealthy.**
- **He was probably questioning his relationship with God—by asking a poor rabbi (Jesus) questions.**
- **He may have been afraid of what others would think of him, so he came to Jesus under the cover of darkness.**

### Born Again!

Talk about the questions below with your class. As you do so, think about Nicodemus being "born again." What does that phrase mean?

1. Why did Nicodemus come to Jesus? What did he hope Jesus could tell him?

   **He wanted to know about his own soul and his salvation.**

2. How did Jesus answer this?

   **"You must be born again of the water and Spirit."**

3. What made Jesus' answer hard for Nicodemus to understand?

   **He had been taught to obey the Law precisely. He was trying to obey rules rather than trusting the Savior whom God had promised to send.**

4. What can you deduce from Jesus' words in this text about why evil persists in our world?

   **Human beings are sinful and flee from the light, from the goodness, from the holiness of God.**

5. What has God done to address this problem?

   **He sent His only Son so that whoever believes in Him, trusting the sacrifice He made for us, will be rescued from sin and all the evil it brings into life.**

6. If God did this, why isn't everyone on the side of the light? Why isn't everyone saved?

   **They refuse to come into the light. They reject the Savior God sent.**

### REMEMBER

For God so loved the world, that He gave His only Son, that whoever believes in Him should not perish but have eternal life. For God did not send His Son into the world to condemn the world, but in order that the world might be saved through Him.

John 3:16–17

### God So Loved ____________________

Put your name on the blank line above. Sometimes, it's easier for us to think of God loving "the world" than it is to believe that He loves each one of us—deeply and personally.

When is it hard for you to trust God's love for you personally? How can your Baptism help you then?

39

# INTO our lives

## God So Loved ____________

Follow the directions, talking through the questions as students apply Jesus' words to Nicodemus to their own lives. If they have trouble explaining how Baptism helps us trust God's love for us personally, point out the individual nature of this Sacrament. Here, God calls us by name (through the pastor) and claims each of us as His very own.

## Remember

Most students will already know at least the first portion of this passage by heart.

As you close today, you may want to lead the class in singing "All Who Believe and Are Baptized" (*LSB* 601).

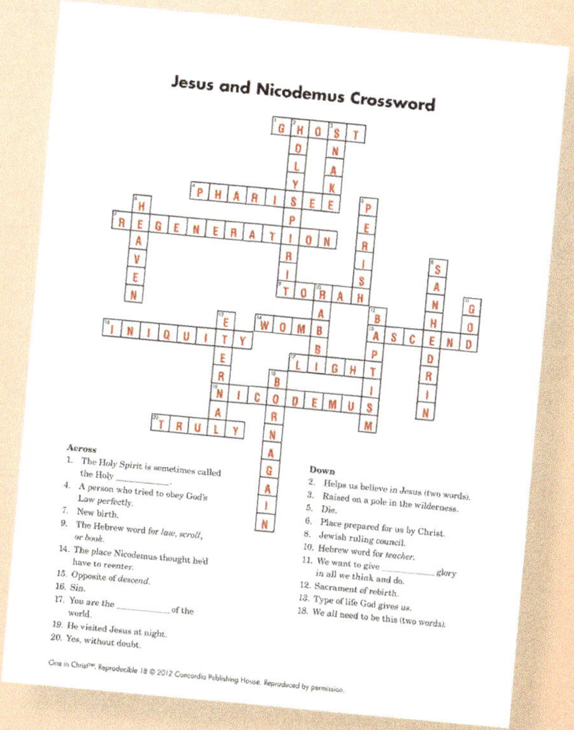

Jesus and Nicodemus Crossword

**Across**

1. The Holy Spirit is sometimes called the Holy ________.
4. A person who tried to obey God's Law perfectly.
7. New birth.
9. The Hebrew word for *law, scroll,* or *book.*
14. The place Nicodemus thought he'd have to reenter.
15. Opposite of *descend.*
16. Sin.
17. You are the ________ of the world.
19. He visited Jesus at night.
20. Yes, without doubt.

**Down**

2. Helps us believe in Jesus (two words).
3. Raised on a pole in the wilderness.
5. Die.
6. Place prepared for us by Christ.
8. Jewish ruling council.
10. Hebrew word for *teacher.*
11. We want to give ________ glory in all we think and do.
12. Sacrament of rebirth.
13. Type of life God gives us.
18. We all need to be this (two words).



**2.** Jesus' answer must have seemed cryptic to Nicodemus. The Pharisees tried to please God by perfectly obeying the Law, going above and beyond what they understood it to require. Now Jesus was saying that God wanted the impossible! No one could find a way to be "born again" by his or her own efforts. Only God could give a rebirth—and that is Jesus' point. Human effort is futile.

Point out that the phrase "born of water and the Spirit" refers to the Sacrament of Holy Baptism.

**3.** Nicodemus considered Jesus' answer gibberish, but the Holy Spirit prompted him to keep thinking, asking, talking.

**4.** Like the other Pharisees of his day, Nicodemus had been taught to obey the Law precisely. He was trying to obey rules rather than trusting the Savior whom God had promised to send.

**5.** One day, all the darkness, hatred, condemnation, hell, and other manifestations of evil that plague God's born-again children will be gone from our experience forever. For now, we live in a fallen world, and we experience that fallenness in ourselves to some degree, as the saint/sinner war rages in our own hearts.

**6.** Refer students to John 3:16. Here, Jesus clearly states His mission and identifies Himself as the Messiah, long promised by God.

As you talk through this question, be sensitive to students who may have parents, grandparents, and friends who are as yet unbelieving. Encourage them to keep praying for these people. Often, as in the case of Nicodemus, the Holy Spirit continues to work in the hearts of skeptics, leading them little by little to true faith.

Point out that by nature, human beings can choose to reject the gift of faith the Holy Spirit wants to give. We cannot, however, decide to believe. Faith is a gift God works in human hearts. By nature, human beings are blind, dead, and enemies of God. We can no more bring ourselves to trust Him than a dead person can crawl out of a coffin and order breakfast at the neighborhood diner.

Distribute copies of **Reproducible 18** for students to complete.

# Jesus and Nicodemus Crossword

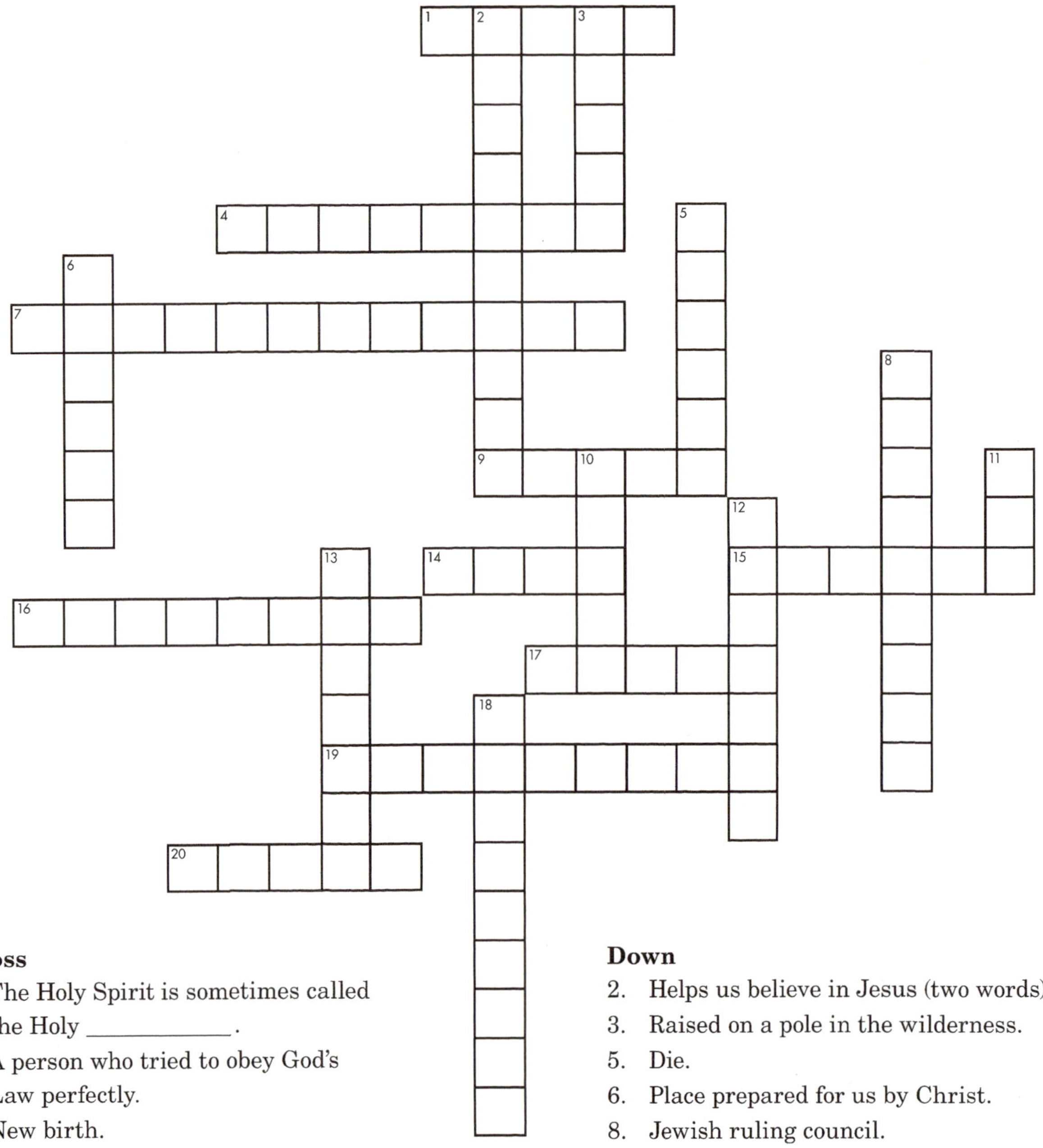

**Across**

1. The Holy Spirit is sometimes called the Holy ____________.
4. A person who tried to obey God's Law perfectly.
7. New birth.
9. The Hebrew word for *law*, *scroll*, or *book*.
14. The place Nicodemus thought he'd have to reenter.
15. Opposite of *descend*.
16. Sin.
17. You are the ____________ of the world.
19. He visited Jesus at night.
20. Yes, without doubt.

**Down**

2. Helps us believe in Jesus (two words).
3. Raised on a pole in the wilderness.
5. Die.
6. Place prepared for us by Christ.
8. Jewish ruling council.
10. Hebrew word for *teacher*.
11. We want to give ____________ glory in all we think and do.
12. Sacrament of rebirth.
13. Type of life God gives us.
18. We all need to be this (two words).

# Jesus Heals at Bethesda

John 5:1–18

## Background

After Jesus spoke to the Samaritan woman at the well and spent some time teaching in Samaria, He continued on His way to Galilee. There, His ministry of teaching and helping others through His miracles continued. The people of Galilee welcomed Him. Then, Jesus went back to Jerusalem for the celebration of one of the special feasts. His ministry of teaching and serving continued there as well. However, the Pharisees in Jerusalem did not welcome His miracles. They questioned His authority to do such things. In this lesson and the next, the Pharisees especially question His regard for Sabbath law.

Help students recognize Jesus' increasing popularity as a reason the Pharisees wanted to get rid of Him. John 5:18 states that "the Jews were seeking all the more to kill Him." But God used the Pharisees' jealousy of Jesus and their failure to recognize Him as the promised Messiah as part of His plan to bring salvation to the whole world.

When our students were younger, they were taught about the miracles of Jesus, but generally not within the context of His total ministry. They simply learned about the power of Christ. Helping students connect His miracles and corresponding rise in popularity with His death on the cross gives the students a deeper understanding of Christ's ministry proclaimed in the Bible.

## Central Truth

Jesus came to bring all people healing.

## Objectives

- Acknowledge that Jesus loves and cares for all people.
- Explain that physical and spiritual healing come only from Jesus.
- Recognize that all believers will have perfect wholeness of body and soul in heaven.

## Materials

- The Basics
- Reproducible 19

## Bible Prep

Post in advance so students can bookmark references before class time.

- John 5:1–18
- Acts 4:12

## Devotion

Today's lesson is about the healing of a paralyzed man at the pool of Bethesda. What a great and amazing day for him! But what about all the other disabled people at the pool? Why didn't Jesus heal them? Why was this man chosen to be healed? Didn't Jesus care about the other people too?

Sometimes, God chooses to heal a person from their sickness or disability, and sometimes He chooses to give them strength to endure their struggle. Our human minds want to say, "That's not fair." But may our prayer be: "Dear God, please show Your plan for this struggle." Because of Jesus' sacrifice of His own body on the cross, we can be sure that God loves and cares for all people. He desires to bring good into the lives of all people. His perfect and holy will for our lives may be different from *our* plans for our lives.

One person who struggled with God's plan for her is Joni Eareckson Tada. She was involved in a diving accident in 1967 and, as a result, became a quadriplegic. She cannot move any part of her body below her neck. But God has allowed her to use her struggle to share the Gospel of Jesus Christ. She has learned to draw and paint while holding the art tools in her mouth. She is also a talented vocalist and speaker. God uses Ms. Tada's talents, in spite of her disability, to reach others for Jesus. God has a plan for the lives of His people that we may not even imagine.

**Pray: Lord, today we pray for all those who are sick or dealing with some kind of physical problem. Send Your Holy Spirit to strengthen them and give them patience. Heal them according to Your will. Bless those who help them. In Jesus' name. Amen.**

Sing: "When I Survey the Wondrous Cross" (*LSB* 425, 426). This beautiful hymn is closely related to the theme of today's lesson—that Christ is the source of our healing and that we can use our bodies to give glory to God.

19

John 5:1–18

## Jesus Heals at Bethesda

### The Pool of Bethesda

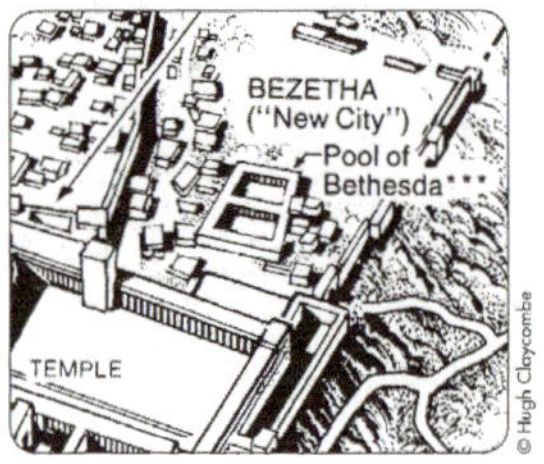


Jesus traveled from Galilee to Jerusalem to observe one of the feasts of the Jews. While He was there, Jesus went to the pool called Bethesda (John 5:2), which is near the Sheep Gate, one of the entrances to the temple. Study John 5:3–4; look at your Bible's notes for help. For what was this pool known?

**Suggested student response: Stories were told that an angel of the Lord would come and stir the waters of the pool. The first person to step into the pool after the stirring of the waters would be healed of their sickness or disease.**

As the text continues, we find that true healing does not come when the sick try to go to the pool. True healing comes when Jesus comes to the sick.

### Two Types of Disabilities

In John 5, two groups of people are introduced: the Physically Disabled and the Spiritually Disabled. In the left-hand circle below, write some of the characteristics of the physically disabled group described in verses 1–9. In the right-hand circle, write some characteristics of the spiritually disabled group described in verses 10–18.

Physically Disabled

**They were blind, lame, and paralyzed.**

**They were aware of their disability every day of their lives.**

**They thought that their hope for a cure came in the waters of the pool of Bethesda.**

**The true source of their healing was Jesus Christ.**

Spiritually Disabled

**They were blind to the coming of the Messiah.**

**They were lame and paralyzed in their faith because they were held back by observing the man-made laws.**

**They did not think they needed a cure because they had their own self-righteous acts.**

**They proudly did not think they had any problems or disability.**

Which group's sickness is ultimately more detrimental to them?

**Suggested student response: The spiritually disabled people are in more danger because they do not see that they need any help or cure. They will continue in their sins, and they will push away their source of healing—Jesus Christ.**

### Review

righteousness— **being without fault**

self-righteousness— **an individual self-perception of being without fault**

40

# Into the Lesson

## The Pool of Bethesda

After witnessing to the woman at the well in Samaria and healing the child of an official in Capernaum, both of whom professed their faith in Him, Jesus returned to Jerusalem. That same faith is not evident in the people of Jerusalem. Jesus stopped by the Pool of Bethesda near the temple's Sheep Gate (John 5:2). Here, He found people who trusted in the water to heal them rather than trusting the almighty God to heal them.

Stories were told that an angel of the Lord would come and stir the waters of the pool. People thought that the first person to step into the pool after the stirring of the waters would be healed. Many blind, disabled, and paralyzed people waited by the pool, but few could actually make it into the pool at all, let alone be the first one to enter. If students look closely in their Bibles to find John 5:4, they may need to look in the footnotes of the chapter because some manuscripts leave verse 4 out of the text. Do not spend a lot of time dwelling on the reasons for this. Verse 4 is helpful in understanding verse 7. The man wanted to get to the pool to be healed, but he was frustrated because others would get there first.

Help students see a connection between this story and the story of the Samaritan woman at the well. In both situations, Jesus began His ministry to them by asking them something about what they were doing. He did not expect them to come to Him. Jesus was at the temple for a feast of the Jews. He could have very easily bypassed the Pool of Bethesda and its patient patients (pun intended). Help students to see that pattern in Jesus' ministry. He goes to those who need Him.

He comes to us, who need Him as well. Review Luther's explanation of the Third Article, where it states that we cannot by our own reason or strength believe in Jesus Christ, our Lord, or come to Him; but He calls us by the Gospel. Right now, He calls us through His Word and through the faithful ministry of His disciples today.

# Into the Word

## Two Types of Disabilities

In the first eighteen verses of John 5, we meet two groups of people. In verses 1–9, we meet the *physically disabled* people.

The paralyzed man had been that way for thirty-eight years. He knew very little of any other life. Every day, he would be at the Pool of Bethesda, waiting and hoping that he could be the first one in the pool so that he could be healed. He and his ailing friends at the pool knew that they needed help.

When Jesus approached the man and asked him if he wanted to be healed, he gave Jesus the reason why he hadn't yet been healed: no one could help him down to the pool fast enough. He believed the pool was the source of healing. He did not know that Jesus is the true source of healing until Jesus told him to take up his bed and walk. Jesus' healing of the man was total and complete.

In verses 10–18, we meet the *spiritually disabled* people. These people were spiritually blind, lame, and paralyzed because they depended on themselves for all things. Falsely, they also believed that they were obeying the Law more than the healed man, who was violating Sabbath regulations by carrying his bed, and better than Jesus, who violated Sabbath regulations by healing on the Sabbath. Their self-righteousness was the cause of their disability. Had they recognized Jesus as their source of spiritual healing, they would have been forgiven. But they did not.

To the casual observer, it might appear that one of the groups is dangerously disabled because of their outward appearance. However, the spiritually disabled people are in much greater danger—*eternal* danger—than the physically disabled people. They do not acknowledge their sinful condition. Many times, Jesus tried to

### Earthly Cure vs. Eternal Cure

God has blessed us with many advancements in technology and medical know-how to improve the quality of life for persons with disabilities or sicknesses. Still, God does not provide earthly healing for everyone. Take the apostle Paul, for example. In 2 Corinthians 12:7–9, Paul writes about an unnamed physical condition: "So to keep me from becoming conceited because of the surpassing greatness of the revelations, a thorn was given me in the flesh, a messenger of Satan to harass me, to keep me from becoming conceited. Three times I pleaded with the Lord about this, that it should leave me. But He said to me, 'My grace is sufficient for you, for My power is made perfect in weakness.' Therefore I will boast all the more gladly of my weaknesses, so that the power of Christ may rest upon me."

Explain Paul's words.

**Sometimes the things that limit us physically remind us to rely more closely on our Savior and His power in our life. Therefore these things remain with us, and God uses them to deepen our reliance on Him.**

What is the only cure for spiritual sickness and disability? Read Acts 4:12 and Ephesians 2:8–9.

**Salvation is only found in Jesus Christ. Salvation is God's gift to believers. The cure for our sin-sickness is not our good works; it is Jesus' sacrifice for us on the cross, taking the punishment for our sins.**

**Remember**

For by grace you have been saved through faith. And this is not your own doing; it is the gift of God, not a result of works, so that no one may boast.

Ephesians 2:8–9

41

point out the spiritual disability of the Pharisees. They were not receptive to His healing. It only made them more irritated.

Discuss how Jesus' message was received by the woman at the well in Samaria and how it was received by these Jewish people at the Pool of Bethesda, and the difference between the two. Same Jesus—two different reactions. In John's Gospel, Jesus calls us to acknowledge our sin and receive His forgiveness and healing in faith.

## Review

The acknowledged source of righteousness and healing was the primary difference between the two groups of people in John 5:1–18. In your review of the definitions of the words in this section of the Student Book, help students understand that Jesus gives us His righteousness through faith, and *that* is the source of our healing.

# INTO our lives

## Earthly Cure vs. Eternal Cure

Today, we live in a world of great technological advancement in medicine. Cures for terrible diseases are being discovered. We have doctors, nurses, physical therapists, x-ray technicians, pathologists, surgeons, medicines, x-rays, MRIs, CAT scans, cardiac stents, pacemakers, and so forth. The array of medical technology available to us goes on and on.

People still have sicknesses and disabilities because we live in a sinful world. Sickness, pain, sadness, and death are consequences of sin that we endure as long as we live in this sinful world.

However, no medical advancement is able to cure us of sin. Only through God's amazing plan (John 3:16) are we saved. That same plan was available to the spiritually disabled Jews in John 5. However, they did not see a need for Jesus. Emphasize that our spiritual health and well-being are of far greater importance than our physical health or abilities. Ironically, sometimes when we struggle with illness or physical challenges, we are led to rely more deeply and completely on our Savior.

Nevertheless, Jesus desires both physical and spiritual wholeness for us and for all people. **One day, because of Jesus' suffering, death, and resurrection, we, too, will rise from the dead.** If we die before Jesus returns, our physical death will be swallowed up in the wonders of heaven. At the Last Day, our earthly bodies will be made glorious. How will that all happen? We do not know. We wait in faith and eager expectation for that to occur.

What our bodies will be like in the resurrection is one of those great questions students and adults like to ask. We have brief glimpses of our glorified body in 1 Corinthians. Use the activity on **Reproducible 19** to explore what the Bible does say about our glorified bodies.

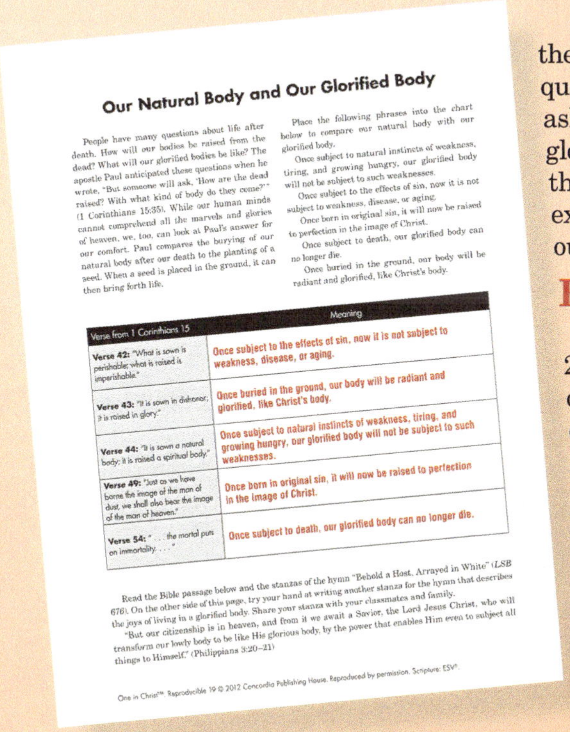

**Our Natural Body and Our Glorified Body**

People have many questions about life after death. How will our bodies be raised from the dead? What will our glorified bodies be like? The apostle Paul anticipated these questions when he wrote, "But someone will ask, 'How are the dead raised? With what kind of body do they come?'" (1 Corinthians 15:35). While our human minds cannot comprehend all the marvels and glories of heaven, we, too, can look at Paul's answer for our comfort. Paul compares the burying of our natural body after our death to the planting of a seed. When a seed is placed in the ground, it can then bring forth life.

Place the following phrases into the chart below to compare our natural body with our glorified body.

Once subject to natural instincts of weakness, tiring, and growing hungry, our glorified body will not be subject to such weaknesses.

Once subject to the effects of sin, now it is not subject to weakness, disease, or aging.

Once born in original sin, it will now be raised to perfection in the image of Christ.

Once subject to death, our glorified body can no longer die.

Once buried in the ground, our body will be radiant and glorified, like Christ's body.

| Verse from 1 Corinthians 15 | Meaning |
|---|---|
| **Verse 42:** "What is sown is perishable; what is raised is imperishable." | Once subject to the effects of sin, now it is not subject to weakness, disease, or aging. |
| **Verse 43:** "It is sown in dishonor; it is raised in glory." | Once buried in the ground, our body will be radiant and glorified, like Christ's body. |
| **Verse 44:** "It is sown a natural body; it is raised a spiritual body." | Once subject to natural instincts of weakness, tiring, and growing hungry, our glorified body will not be subject to such weaknesses. |
| **Verse 49:** "Just as we have borne the image of the man of dust, we shall also bear the image of the man of heaven." | Once born in original sin, it will now be raised to perfection in the image of Christ. |
| **Verse 54:** ". . . the mortal puts on immortality. . . ." | Once subject to death, our glorified body can no longer die. |

Read the Bible passage below and the stanzas of the hymn "Behold a Host, Arrayed in White" (*LSB* 676). On the other side of this page, try your hand at writing another stanza for the hymn that describes the joys of living in a glorified body. Share your stanza with your classmates and family.

"But our citizenship is in heaven, and from it we await a Savior, the Lord Jesus Christ, who will transform our lowly body to be like His glorious body, by the power that enables Him even to subject all things to Himself." (Philippians 3:20–21)



## Remember

The memory verse (Ephesians 2:8–9) emphasizes that salvation is offered to us in the Gospel and is received by faith. Help your students memorize this important Scripture passage by writing it on a whiteboard, having the class repeat it. Then, erase a word or two, and have the class repeat it. Repeat this process until the passage is completely erased.

# Our Natural Body and Our Glorified Body

People have many questions about life after death. How will our bodies be raised from the dead? What will our glorified bodies be like? The apostle Paul anticipated these questions when he wrote, "But someone will ask, 'How are the dead raised? With what kind of body do they come?'" (1 Corinthians 15:35). While our human minds cannot comprehend all the marvels and glories of heaven, we, too, can look at Paul's answer for our comfort. Paul compares the burying of our natural body after our death to the planting of a seed. When a seed is placed in the ground, it can then bring forth life.

Place the following phrases into the chart below to compare our natural body with our glorified body.

Once subject to natural instincts of weakness, tiring, and growing hungry, our glorified body will not be subject to such weaknesses.

Once subject to the effects of sin, now it is not subject to weakness, disease, or aging.

Once born in original sin, it will now be raised to perfection in the image of Christ.

Once subject to death, our glorified body can no longer die.

Once buried in the ground, our body will be radiant and glorified, like Christ's body.

| Verse from 1 Corinthians 15 | Meaning |
|---|---|
| **Verse 42:** "What is sown is perishable; what is raised is imperishable." | |
| **Verse 43:** "It is sown in dishonor; it is raised in glory." | |
| **Verse 44:** "It is sown a natural body; it is raised a spiritual body." | |
| **Verse 49:** "Just as we have borne the image of the man of dust, we shall also bear the image of the man of heaven." | |
| **Verse 54:** " . . . the mortal puts on immortality. . . . " | |

Read the Bible passage below and the stanzas of the hymn "Behold a Host, Arrayed in White" (*LSB* 676). On the other side of this page, try your hand at writing another stanza for the hymn that describes the joys of living in a glorified body. Share your stanza with your classmates and family.

"But our citizenship is in heaven, and from it we await a Savior, the Lord Jesus Christ, who will transform our lowly body to be like His glorious body, by the power that enables Him even to subject all things to Himself." (Philippians 3:20–21)

# Parables of the Kingdom

MATTHEW 13:24–52

## Background

Jesus often spoke to the crowds and His disciples in parables. These fictional stories always illustrate the deeper principles of God's work. For example, in Luke 15, Jesus wasn't speaking of specific instances when a shepherd lost a sheep, a woman a coin, or a father his sons. And yet, those stories contained deeper truths about our Lord's compassion for those who are lost.

Also important to remember is the audience with whom Jesus shared the parables. Knowing who originally listened to the parable can help us understand the story's deeper meaning. For example, in the parable of the dishonest manager (Luke 16:1–9), a reader might think that Jesus is suggesting that a person can buy his way into heaven (v. 9). However, since this parable was originally told to the disciples, who already had a relationship with Christ through faith, we can understand that Jesus is speaking of sanctification, not justification.

Jesus' parables also can teach us one more important lesson. When He taught, He drew illustrations from everyday life (e.g., weeds in a field, leaven in bread dough, fish in a net) to help illustrate what He was discussing, thus making the lessons more memorable and accessible to a wider audience.

## Central Truth

God gives His kingdom to all who believe in Jesus and enables us to share His kingdom with others.

## Objectives

- Explain God's kingdom as Jesus explains it in the parables.
- Apply Jesus' teachings to our life of faith.
- Demonstrate a desire to share God's Word with others.

## Materials

- The Basics
- Reproducible 20

## Bible Prep

Post in advance so students can bookmark the reference before class time.

- Matthew 13:24–52

## Devotion

Mom could hear Dan's reaction all the way upstairs. She had sent him to the cellar to get some apples so that she could make an apple pie for dinner that evening.

"Oh, yuck!" was all she could hear upstairs before she saw his head emerging through the door.

"Mom, the apples are all rotten, and I'm not touching them!"

Every so often, Dan's mom sorted the apples in the barrel to throw out the rotten ones. It seems that she had forgotten to do that task recently, and now it was too late.

"Oh, no!" she responded. "One rotten apple ruins the whole bunch."

Dan rolled his eyes. "That's what my teacher said today when our class lost its recess. It seems we were talking too much and not listening. Does that mean that we were rotten?"

"No, it just means that sin entered your classroom. Like one apple caused our whole barrel of apples to rot, sin caused one person to talk and be disrespectful, and the disobedience spread throughout your classroom."

"That sounds like what the pastor was saying at chapel last week. Sin entered the world through Adam and Eve, and with their disobedience, it spread throughout the human race," responded Dan.

Mom nodded. "And that is why God had to send His perfect Son to die on the cross for the whole human race. Though He was sinless, He took on the world's sins so that we can be forgiven—even for those sins we don't know we have committed. Today, even as sin spreads throughout the world, God's gift of salvation in Jesus is spreading too, as God's people tell others about Him."

"Maybe I can be part of spreading *that* kind of talk instead of the kind that got us into trouble in school today," Dan said with a smile.

**PRAY: Lord Jesus, we are grateful for the love that You show us every day. Thank You for the continual blessing and forgiveness we receive. Help us to spread Your love as we tell the Good News to everyone we meet. Amen.**

Sing: "Almighty God, Your Word Is Cast" (*LSB* 577).

20 Matthew 13:24–52

## Parables of the Kingdom

### Jesus, the Teacher

As Jesus traveled, He encountered many types of people: some who doubted or refused to believe in Him and others who possessed a strong faith and were committed to following Him to the end. Jesus addressed all types of hearers. Because Jesus is a teacher, He used words and actions to weave pictures of what was happening in the present and what will happen in the near and distant future.

### What the Kingdom of Heaven Is Like

In Matthew 13:24–52, Jesus uses parables to teach simple yet profound truths about human existence. He teaches about the Church—the sum of those who by faith know and believe in Him as the Son of God and Savior of the world—and also about those outside the Church—those without faith in Him. Read these verses. Then consider the three Venn diagrams that follow. Each diagram compares two of Jesus' parables about the kingdom of heaven. Fill in blanks to name the parable identified by each set of verses. Then draw lines to place each phrase in the correct area of each Venn diagram.

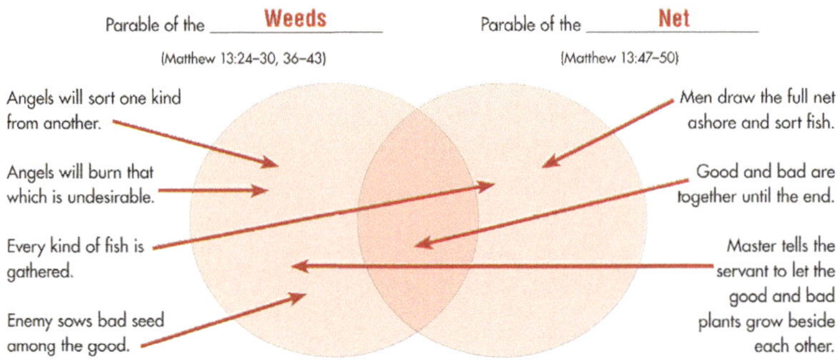


**Review**

leaven— yeast, a rising agent used in baking items made with flour

harvest— time when the crop is mature and ready to be gathered for use or storage

42

# INTO the lesson

## Jesus, the Teacher

Imagine you were alive when Jesus was living on earth. Ask, **How did people react or respond to Him?** People followed Him, ignored Him, or thought He was a heretic, as many of the Pharisees and Sadducees did. Those without faith may have found Jesus' stories interesting or entertaining. But those with faith would have found spiritual insights and encouragement in the things Jesus said as they came to understand these stories by the power of the Holy Spirit.

# INTO the Word

## What the Kingdom of Heaven Is Like

Read through the parables with your class, pausing periodically for comment. Then allow time for students to work through the Venn diagram activities to review the parables. Comment that farming and fishing were common means of making a living during Bible times. The illustrations Jesus used would have been readily identified as ordinary occurrences.

In the parable of the weeds, we encounter a great horror. The weeds have been planted amidst the good plants. The master, knowing what could happen if the weeds were pulled (some good plants could be uprooted as well), encourages the servants to wait until a later harvest.

The people of the crowd might have interpreted this combination of weeds and plants as follows:

1. God is restoring His rule; do not mess with His followers.
2. Jesus' ministry will continue in the way it is happening right now. In the future, it will change (at harvesttime), but for now, be satisfied with how He is ministering.
3. For now, the kingdom of God may be small. Leave it alone until the harvesters come and do their job.

But when the same parable is explained to the disciples—those who recognize Jesus as the Messiah—it takes on a whole different tone. Their message is one of assurance:

1. Keep your hopes up, for soon the day will come when things will be set right again. The conflict will be finished.
2. Sin is present in the world, but it is not your place to judge others.

The parable of the weeds compares closely with the parable of the net. In both cases, the same end comes to both good and bad, but the ultimate conclusion is quite different.

When you discuss the parable of the mustard seed, point out that mustard seeds were among the smallest seeds in Jesus' day. If possible, bring in a mustard seed to show the students. As you read the parable, remind students that this tiny seed will grow into a large shrub, typically about six feet in height—not exactly a tree, but that could be an exaggeration to show how great the Kingdom will become. The Kingdom will grow large enough for "the birds of the air" (an Old Testament symbol for the nations of the world) to roost in it (figuratively speaking, to be part of God's kingdom).

Thus this parable could be interpreted to mean that Jesus' ministry may seem small now, but it will grow to encompass many people.

Likewise, the parable of the leaven illustrates that what is small can grow into something large. Leaven is the yeast or another similar ingredient that makes bread rise. Compared with the amount of flour used in a recipe, the amount of leaven is relatively small—and yet, it works through the entire mass of dough. Such was the influence of the relatively small num-

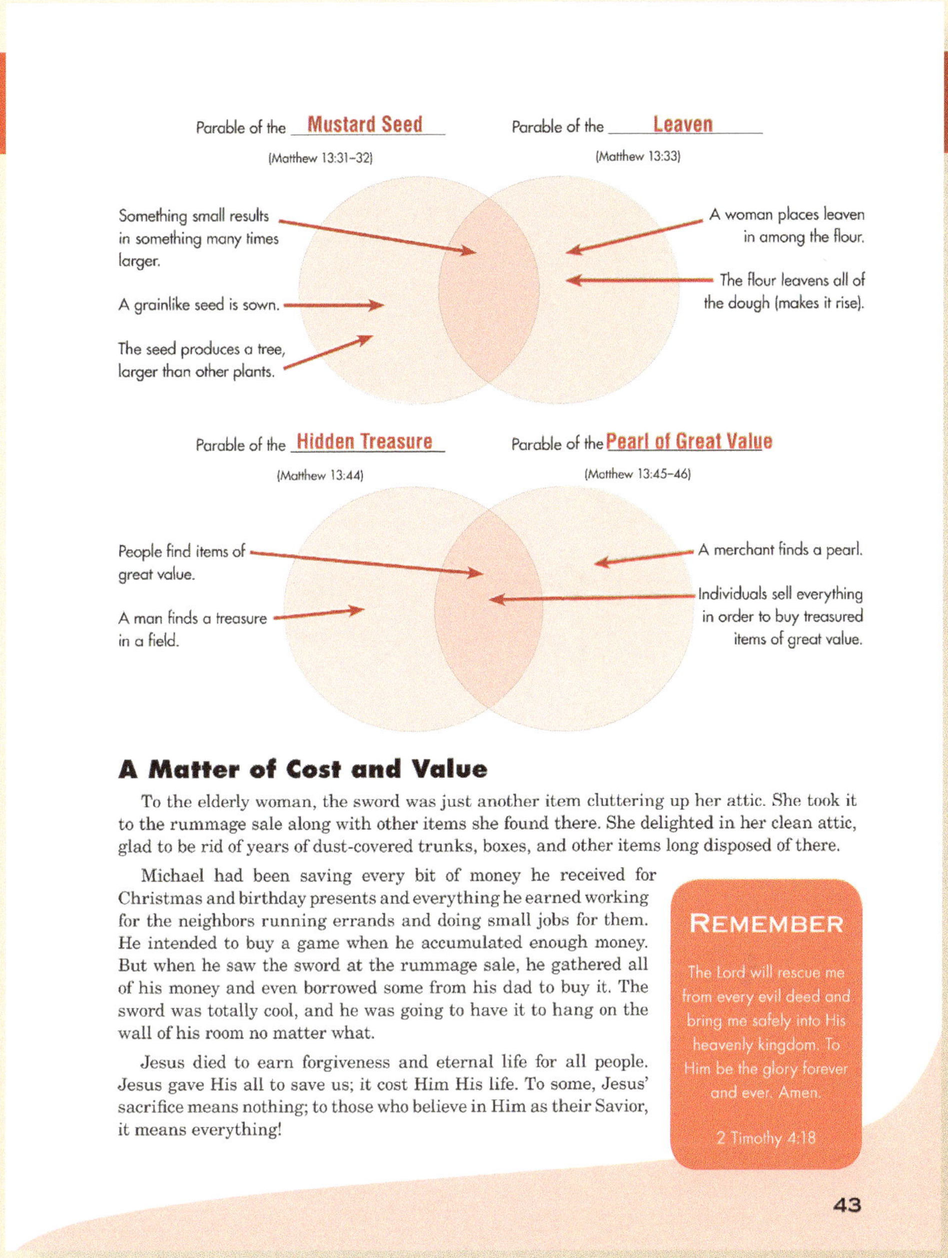
Parable of the **Mustard Seed**

(Matthew 13:31–32)

Parable of the **Leaven**

(Matthew 13:33)



Parable of the **Hidden Treasure**

(Matthew 13:44)

Parable of the **Pearl of Great Value**

(Matthew 13:45–46)



**A Matter of Cost and Value**

To the elderly woman, the sword was just another item cluttering up her attic. She took it to the rummage sale along with other items she found there. She delighted in her clean attic, glad to be rid of years of dust-covered trunks, boxes, and other items long disposed of there.

Michael had been saving every bit of money he received for Christmas and birthday presents and everything he earned working for the neighbors running errands and doing small jobs for them. He intended to buy a game when he accumulated enough money. But when he saw the sword at the rummage sale, he gathered all of his money and even borrowed some from his dad to buy it. The sword was totally cool, and he was going to have it to hang on the wall of his room no matter what.

Jesus died to earn forgiveness and eternal life for all people. Jesus gave His all to save us; it cost Him His life. To some, Jesus' sacrifice means nothing; to those who believe in Him as their Savior, it means everything!

**Remember**

The Lord will rescue me from every evil deed and bring me safely into His heavenly kingdom. To Him be the glory forever and ever. Amen.

2 Timothy 4:18

43

ber of Jesus' first followers as they shared the Good News, spreading into the world of their day—and into subsequent decades, centuries, millennia. In this case, the leaven was "hidden" in the flour. This could mean that though the crowds did not understand Jesus' reign at the time, it would be revealed to them in the future or even when Christ returns.

Compare the parable of the hidden treasure and parable of the pearl of great value. Ask, **The idea of buying and selling is prevalent in both, but who is doing the buying—and what is the treasured possession?**

The man in these parables is most likely **Christ, who gave up everything, even His life, for His treasures, the disciples**. Christ has purchased them at the price of everything He is and owns. We, too, can take confidence in this parable. Christ's grace covers us, and we are His followers. Review these six parables.

## Review

Allow time for students to define these terms. Comment on the ready application *leaven* (yeast) and *harvest* would have had for the men and women of Jesus' day.

Distribute copies of **Reproducible 20** for students to complete.

# Into our lives

## A Matter of Cost and Value

Stress that the parables of the hidden treasure and the pearl can be applied to remind us that we are valuable members of God's kingdom. Applied in another way, these parables remind us of the great treasure we have by faith in Christ Jesus. Eternal life and salvation are ours in His name!

## Remember

As you review this memory verse with your class, stress the confidence we have as followers of Jesus. We have a great treasure—forgiveness of sin and eternal salvation in Him. We, like the good seed among the weeds, will be kept safely in His care and grace until "the harvest."

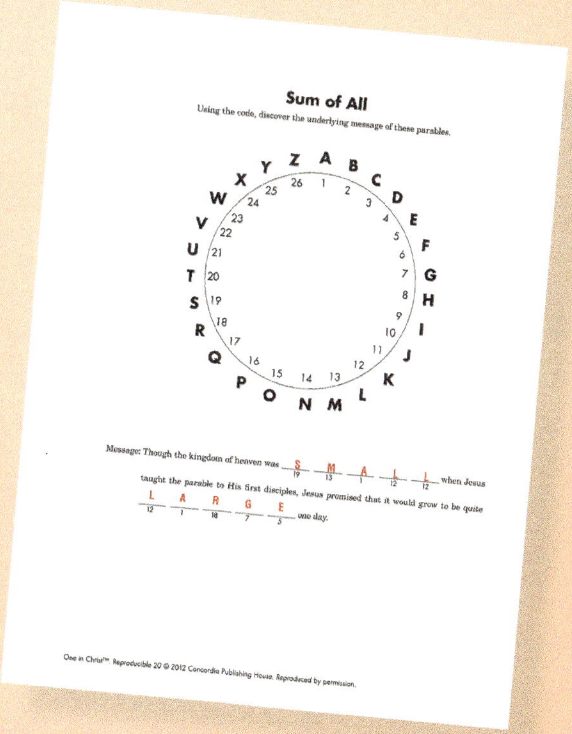
**Sum of All**

Using the code, discover the underlying message of these parables.



Message: Though the kingdom of heaven was S M A L L (19 13 1 12 12) when Jesus taught the parable to His first disciples, Jesus promised that it would grow to be quite L A R G E (12 1 18 7 5) one day.

# Sum of All

Using the code, discover the underlying message of these parables.

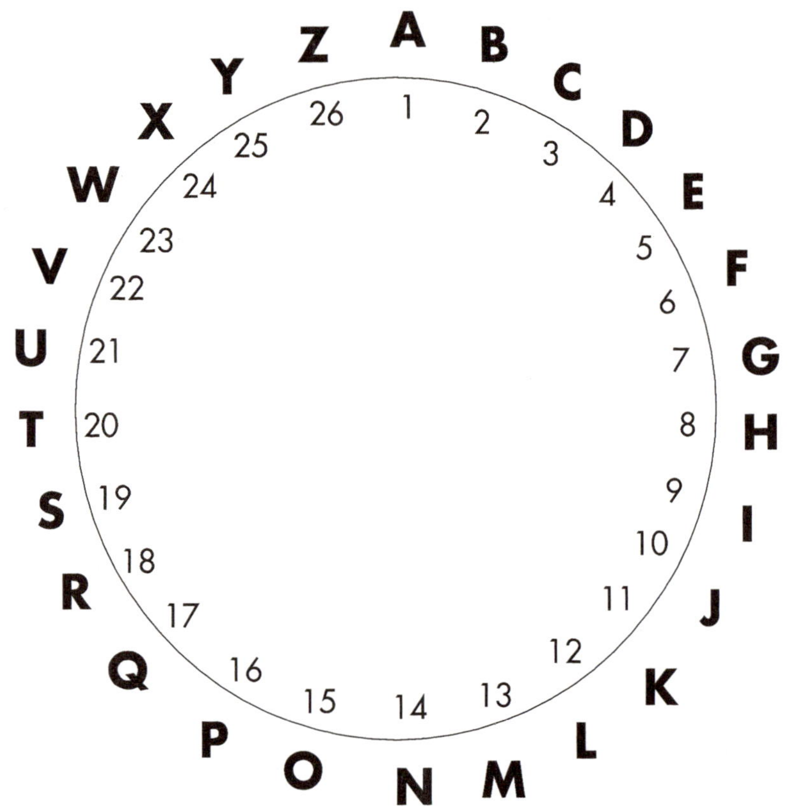


Message: Though the kingdom of heaven was ____ ____ ____ ____ ____ when Jesus
19 13 1 12 12

taught the parable to His first disciples, Jesus promised that it would grow to be quite

____ ____ ____ ____ ____ one day.
12 1 18 7 5

# Jesus and the Miraculous Catch of Fish

LUKE 5:1–11

## Central Truth

Although we in no way deserve God's love and grace, for Jesus' sake, He calls us to repentance and to be His disciples.

## Objectives

- Tell how Jesus called His disciples and how they responded to His call.
- Identify themselves with Peter and his confession.
- Rejoice that in Jesus they, too, are called to confess their faith to others.

## Materials

- The Basics
- Reproducible 21

## Bible Prep

Post in advance so students can bookmark references before class time.

- Luke 5:1–11
- Jeremiah 16:15–17

## Background

The lesson of Jesus' calling of disciples follows shortly after His rejection in Nazareth by the people with whom He had grown up. After leaving His hometown, Jesus traveled through the region, teaching and performing miracles. In this way, He established Himself as an authority, a teacher, and a healer. In this story, Jesus has such a large following eager for His word that He cannot easily speak to them from the land. Spying the empty fishing boats belonging to Peter and Andrew, James and John, all of whom have just spent a fruitless night fishing, Jesus asks Peter to take Him out just a short distance into the Sea of Galilee.

By speaking to the people from the water, Jesus sets Himself as the focus for all eyes, and when He teaches the people, they drink up His words. Peter does as well. Scripture indicates that Peter had heard Jesus speak before and followed Him for a while, but then he left to go back to his fishing. In this story, Jesus firmly calls Peter to follow Him, and Peter answers without hesitation. The immediacy of Peter's response challenges all of us to follow God's plan with similar enthusiasm and commitment.

## Devotion

"Joel, it's time," Grandpa said, shaking Joel's shoulder gently.

"Grandpa! It's not even light out yet," he mumbled. "A few more minutes."

"Joel," he insisted, "the fish don't wait for the sun to come up. If you want to come with me, you need to get up!"

Joel tossed the covers back and sat up, yawning and stretching. Grandpa's rough hand smoothed his hair. "Get dressed," he said, "and grab a granola bar. I'll see you in the truck in ten minutes."

By the time they got to the lake, the sun had just begun to rise, creating a pale line on the horizon, but Joel still hadn't fully awakened. He slumped in the boat, watching as Grandpa did all the work: putting the boat into the water, setting up the rods, baiting the lines, casting them both out. As the sun rose higher, a ball of cold fire, Grandpa thrust the rod into Joel's hand.

"Here you go, son," he said. "See what you can catch today."

Time stretched out as Joel stared at the water, the only sound was the gentle lapping of the waves and Grandpa's tuneless humming. A few birds. That was it. He was lost in his thoughts until he felt his rod tremble and then bob.

"Grandpa," Joel exclaimed. "I've got one!"

Grandpa nodded. "Bring it in, Joel. You can do it."

As Joel drew in the fish, gleaming and slippery, he felt a rush of pride. Fishing was fun, and getting up early on a summer morning suddenly seemed worthwhile. Joel felt like a true fisherman, and he baited his line again eagerly, his sleepiness gone with the dark of early morning.

**PRAY: Dear Jesus, thank You for Your Word in our hearts and in our lives. As You called Peter to be Your fisherman, You have called us to do the same. Help us always to be attentive to Your call and to do Your work with eager and willing hearts. In Your name we pray. Amen.**

Sing: "Hark, the Voice of Jesus Calling" (*LSB* 826) or "Christ Be My Leader" (*LSB* 861).

# INTO the lesson

Say, **Catching a fish seems like a matter more of patience and probability than of skill. You need to gather the right equipment, and then you need to cast and retrieve your bait or just wait for a bite. List some of the tools you might need for successful fishing.**

Students may list items such as a fishing rod, fishing line, hook, bobber, bait, boat, fish finder.

Follow up with, **In Bible times, some people fished with lines, but they didn't really do it for a hobby. Fishing was work, and it was done to put food on the table. Fishers who wanted to catch a lot of fish used nets. The men in our Bible story today fished for a living, catching enough fish to feed themselves and to sell to others. Their nets were twenty to twenty-five feet in diameter and had sinkers around the edges. Draw a picture on a clean sheet of paper showing how you think a fisherman might catch fish with a net like this.**

Students' drawings may show a fisherman in a boat or on the shore, throwing the net or casting it out to catch fish.

Say, **As you consider the similarities and differences between the two types of fishing, think about which type of fishing you would prefer. Then turn to the person sitting next to you and discuss your answer.**

Students may realize that line fishing would be less strenuous and less labor intensive. Students may consider the difference between the number of fish caught at once by line fishing and net fishing.

It will likely not surprise students to learn that fishing has not always been a pastime but was once a career. It remains a career for some. Draw students' attention to the differences between modern and biblical fishers. When Peter cast his net, it would have been quite large and very heavy. He would have tossed it from land or a boat, wrapping part of the edge around his wrist and casting it out into the water. The weights around the edges of the net would sink, trapping fish within the net.

This was difficult work and quite different from the sort of fishing most of us picture.

## 21 Jesus and the Miraculous Catch of Fish

Luke 5:1–11

### A Lesson and a Miracle

In today's Bible story, Jesus gathered His first disciples, and He did it by giving them a fishing lesson. Peter and the others did what Jesus told them without hesitation. Jesus worked a miracle for them, and He taught them about much more than how to catch a heavy load of fish.

Read the story for yourself in Luke 5:1–11, and, as you read, take notes on what happens, filling in main events in the appropriate boxes below.

| The Lesson | The Miracle | The Decision |
|---|---|---|
| Fishermen were washing their nets. Jesus got into Simon's boat and began to teach the people from the boat. | Jesus told Simon to put out into the deep and let down his nets for a catch. They caught so many fish that they called for another boat and filled both boats to the point where they began to sink. | Simon Peter fell at Jesus' knees saying, "Depart from me, for I am a sinful man, O Lord." Jesus told Simon and his partners, "Do not be afraid; from now on you will be catching men." And they left everything and followed Jesus. |

### Review

Lake of Gennesaret— another name for the Sea of Galilee

disciple— one who believes in and spreads the Word of God

miracle— an act of God that cannot be accomplished by human means alone

44

# INTO the Word

## A Lesson and a Miracle

In this section, students will read Luke's account of the story, taking notes of main ideas in the space provided in their books. Students will have to make judgments as they read about the organization of the story, placing their notes in the appropriate boxes.

Once students have read the introductory paragraph silently, explain, **As you read the text, you will need to decide how the story is organized. In the first box, labeled "The Lesson," take notes on the parts of the story that have to do with the lesson Jesus is teaching. In the second box, labeled "The Miracle," take notes on the miracle in the story. In the third box, labeled "The Decision," take notes on the decision that is made.**

The boxes are not large, so students should be encouraged to take brief notes in bullet points. It may be helpful to remind students that these notes should highlight main ideas, not include every detail.

As they begin to read and take notes, it is appropriate to remind students, **We do not make a decision to believe in Jesus. In His life, death, and resurrection, Jesus has done everything to earn forgiveness and new and eternal life for us. The creation of faith in our hearts is purely the**

## How to Catch People

After Jesus worked His miracle, He spoke using a metaphor to tell Peter, Andrew, James, and John that they were to leave their nets behind and become fishers of men. In both the Old and New Testaments, God calls us to spread the Gospel message to those who are lost. When Jesus told Peter and the others that they would be fishers of men, He was making a comparison to the life's-work kind of fishing rather than the hobby kind.

The day he met Jesus was a life-changing day for Peter. He found a new calling as one of Jesus' disciples. Jesus has called us as well. Read Luke 5:1–11 again. Using the diagram below, work with a partner to fill in the actions Peter took as Jesus transformed him from a fisherman to a fisher of people.

Students should write something similar to the following: "Peter listened to Jesus"

↓

"Peter confessed his sins"

↓

"Peter obeyed immediately"

**REMEMBER**

And He said to them, "Follow Me, and I will make you fishers of men." Immediately they left their nets and followed Him.

Matthew 4:19–20

45

**work of God, not by any means our own effort. However, we do make a decision, once faith has been created, to follow God's plan for our lives. It is this "decision" that the lesson refers to.**

## Review

Allow time for students to look up the words in the glossary and fill in the definitions.

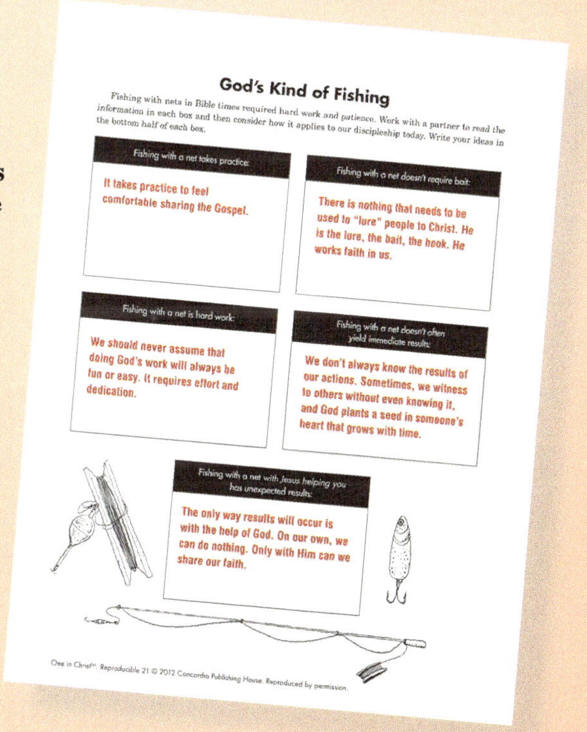

### God's Kind of Fishing

Fishing with nets in Bible times required hard work and patience. Work with a partner to read the information in each box and then consider how it applies to our discipleship today. Write your ideas in the bottom half of each box.

**Fishing with a net takes practice:**
It takes practice to feel comfortable sharing the Gospel.

**Fishing with a net doesn't require bait:**
There is nothing that needs to be used to "lure" people to Christ. He is the lure, the bait, the hook. He works faith in us.

**Fishing with a net is hard work:**
We should never assume that doing God's work will always be fun or easy. It requires effort and dedication.

**Fishing with a net doesn't often yield immediate results:**
We don't always know the results of our actions. Sometimes, we witness to others without even knowing it, and God plants a seed in someone's heart that grows with time.

**Fishing with a net with Jesus helping you has unexpected results:**
The only way results will occur is with the help of God. On our own, we can do nothing. Only with Him can we share our faith.



# INTO our lives

## How to Catch People

When Jesus told Peter that he was going to become a fisher of men, He was using the situation at hand to create a perfect image, but it was not a new idea. Jeremiah 16:15–17 says something very similar. If time permits, review and discuss this verse with your students. Reinforce the idea that God's concept of us as hunters and fishers of the lost is both appropriate and timeless. Fishing for people so they may be saved is the vital Christian mission.

Direct students back to the text from Luke's Gospel (5:1–11) to ponder Peter's response to Christ's call to discipleship. Ask students to read the text, looking for Peter's actions to the words of Jesus. They should fill in these three crucial actions in the diagram provided.

After students have completed their diagrams, remind them that these actions did not create Peter's faith. Faith is a gift from God (Ephesians 2:8–9), not a result of any action on our part. What Peter did is a natural result of the faith that Jesus had already created within Peter's heart.

The three key things Peter did are as follows: Peter listened to Jesus (v. 5), he confessed his sins "Depart from me, for I am a sinful man, O Lord" (v. 8), and he immediately obeyed Jesus' call (v. 11). Say, **You do realize that Jesus has been calling you, right? How have you answered Him? What level of commitment are you willing to make to follow Jesus? Write a prayer thanking Jesus for the opportunity to serve Him. Your prayer should include a confession of sins like Peter's and show your eagerness to share His Word with others.**

Student prayers should acknowledge the understanding of Christ's call to all of us to be His fishers, include a confession of sins, and show a willingness to share God's Word with others. Encourage them to pray this prayer silently. If any student would like to, encourage him or her to share and read aloud. This public confession of faith will acknowledge and affirm the power of Christ at work in their lives.

Use **Reproducible 21** to reinforce the concepts of the lesson. The sort of fishing the disciples understood is the type God implies when He calls us fishers of men. It is hard work, but yields miraculous results when He is involved.

## Remember

As you assign and review this verse with your class, remind them that as children of God through faith in Christ Jesus, this invitation applies also to them!

# God's Kind of Fishing

Fishing with nets in Bible times required hard work and patience. Work with a partner to read the information in each box and then consider how it applies to our discipleship today. Write your ideas in the bottom half of each box.

**Fishing with a net takes practice:**

**Fishing with a net doesn't require bait:**

**Fishing with a net is hard work:**

**Fishing with a net doesn't often yield immediate results:**

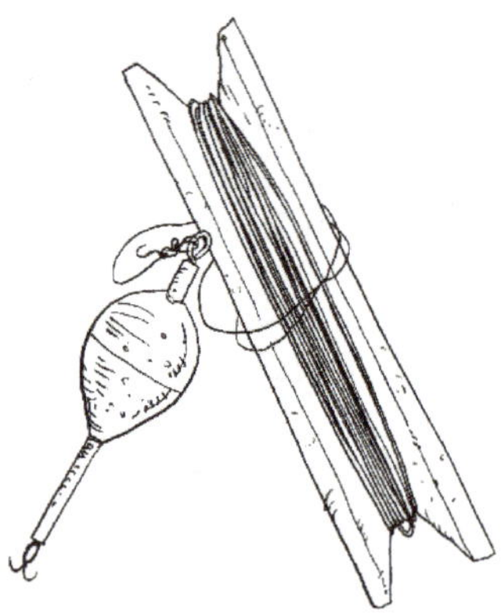

**Fishing with a net *with Jesus helping you* has unexpected results:**

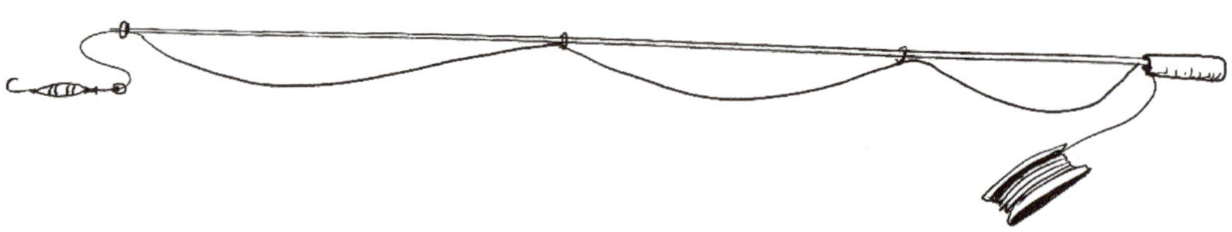

# The Good Samaritan

## LUKE 10:25–37

## Background

When the lawyer asks Jesus, "What must I do to be saved?" he was hoping to be assured that he was working out his own salvation. As a lawyer, he is an expert in Jewish law, and indeed, when Jesus replies to his question, asking what the law says about salvation, the lawyer knows the correct answer: Love God fully and love your neighbor as yourself. But the lawyer's pride is revealed fully in verse 29, when he asks Jesus the "wrong" question: "Who is my neighbor?" He is seeking to justify himself, hoping Jesus will define neighbor as the Jews typically did—friends and family.

His answer opens the door for Jesus to provide a broader definition of the word. Samaria lies between Judea and Galilee, a region populated by people of a mixed Jewish-Gentile race, despised by both Jews and Gentiles. For Jesus to say that a Samaritan had more compassion on the wounded man, showing more dignity and grace than a priest or Levite, would have been surprising and offensive to His listeners. Indeed, when Jesus asks the lawyer who showed more compassion, the lawyer can't even bring himself to say the word *Samaritan*, saying instead "the one who showed mercy."

In this fashion, Jesus reminds His listeners then and now that His practice of love is universal and utterly challenging. It is, in fact, beyond our human ability to act out this command of love for all. But this should not plunge us into despair; instead, it should inspire us to repent and to imitate our Lord while also reminding us of our need for Him.

## Central Truth

Because of sin we do not deserve eternal life; but like the Good Samaritan, Jesus gives us undeserved abundant care and blessings.

## Objectives

- Explain that because of sin we cannot please God or earn eternal life.
- Demonstrate a desire to receive from God forgiveness and salvation, just as the injured man received care from the Good Samaritan.
- Evidence the desire to serve God and others as empowered by the Holy Spirit.

## Materials

- The Basics
- Reproducible 22

## Bible Prep

Post in advance so students can bookmark references before class time.

- Matthew 16:13–20
- Luke 10:25–37
- Luke 18:18–27
- Acts 16:25–31
- James 4:17
- Matthew 25:35–40
- Romans 3:19–20
- Romans 5:6–8

## Devotion

Delaney strapped on her bike helmet and set off down the road, weaving back and forth in the empty street of her suburban neighborhood. As she rode, feeling the wind flutter against her jacket, she closed her eyes and thought about how many more days were left in the school year: not many, for spring had finally come and summer was creeping closer every day. A terrifying sound caught her attention then, and she opened her eyes.

What she saw brought her to a screeching halt, and she tossed her bike to the side of the road before she had even fully realized what she was looking at. Quickly, she knelt next to the boy lying on the road. His bike was in the ditch and his arm was twisted awkwardly out to the side. She touched his cheek; it was clammy and cool. "Help!" she cried, looking up and hoping someone was outside and nearby. The houses stared blankly at her. "Someone, help me!" she called again. Nothing.

Delaney tried to remember what she'd learned in school about first aid and what she'd seen on TV. She was pretty sure she shouldn't try to move the boy, but she didn't think she could leave him in the road. She knelt there, her heart and mind racing, pebbles biting her knees. Then, the boy groaned and stirred.

He rolled over and looked up at her. "Hey," Delaney said. "Are you okay? Do you think you can sit up?"

He nodded slowly and Delaney helped him sit and then slowly stand. He was shaking as he held his injured arm but seemed to get stronger with each step. "Thank you for helping me," the boy said. "If you hadn't stopped, I don't know how long I might have lain here."

**PRAY: Thank You, Savior, for showing us the true meaning of compassion. Help us to love and serve others as we share Your love. In Your name we pray. Amen.**

Sing: "Chief of Sinners Though I Be" (*LSB* 611) or "What a Friend We Have in Jesus" (*LSB* 770).

# INTO the lesson

## Good and Bad Questions

Distribute copies of **Reproducible 22**. Comment that people asked Jesus many questions, sometimes seeking clarification, sometimes wanting help, and sometimes hoping to trap Him. Ask students to share a time they hesitated to ask a question, soliciting the reason for their hesitation as well. Ask for examples of good questions and bad questions.

Then, appoint students to small groups of three or four. Assign each group one of the listed passages and give them time to read the passage and decide whether it shows an example of a good or bad question. When groups have done this, use the jigsaw method to have a member of each group work with members of each of the other groups to share their information. Each new group, therefore, should have representatives from each of the other groups. Alternatively, after the initial group work is done, groups can share with the whole class.

22 Luke 10:25–37

THE GOOD SAMARITAN

**Acting It Out**

Speaking part: NARRATOR

Actors: TRAVELER, ROBBER(S), PRIEST, LEVITE, SAMARITAN, INNKEEPER

Setting up the scene: ROBBERS should be hiding along a "road." TRAVELER should be prepared to walk along the road.

**NARRATOR:** A man was going down from Jerusalem to Jericho, (*TRAVELER walks along a "road."*)

**NARRATOR:** and he fell among robbers, (*ROBBERS leap from hiding place and assault TRAVELER.*)

**NARRATOR:** who stripped him and beat him (*ROBBERS pantomime beating TRAVELER.*)

**NARRATOR:** and departed, leaving him half dead. (*ROBBERS EXIT and TRAVELER lies on the floor.*)

**NARRATOR:** Now by chance a priest was going down that road, (*PRIEST starts walking down the road.*)

**NARRATOR:** and when he saw him he passed by on the other side. (*PRIEST sees TRAVELER and, in fear and disgust, crosses to the other side of the road, totally ignoring TRAVELER, then EXITS.*)

**NARRATOR:** So likewise a Levite, when he came to the place and saw him, (*LEVITE starts walking down the road.*)

**NARRATOR:** passed by on the other side. (*LEVITE, in fear and disgust, crosses to the other side of road, totally ignoring TRAVELER, then EXITS.*)

**NARRATOR:** But a Samaritan, as he journeyed, came to where he was, (*SAMARITAN starts walking down the path and notices TRAVELER.*)

**NARRATOR:** and when he saw him, he had compassion. (*SAMARITAN puts hands to face.*)

**NARRATOR:** He went to him and bound up his wounds, pouring on oil and wine. (*SAMARITAN crosses to TRAVELER, kneels, and pantomimes pouring liquid on his wounds.*)

**NARRATOR:** Then he set him on his own animal (*SAMARITAN lifts TRAVELER and helps him walk down road.*)

**NARRATOR:** and brought him to an inn and took care of him. (*SAMARITAN and TRAVELER meet INNKEEPER.*)

**NARRATOR:** And the next day he took out two denarii and gave them to the innkeeper, (*SAMARITAN pantomimes handing coins to INNKEEPER.*)

**NARRATOR:** saying, "Take care of him, and whatever more you spend, I will repay you when I come back." (*SAMARITAN walks away from INNKEEPER and sets out on the road again.*)

REVIEW

priest— a descendant of Aaron who served in the temple

Levite— member of the tribe of Levi who assisted the priests in the temple

Samaritan— a person of a group considered unclean and unworthy by Jews

46

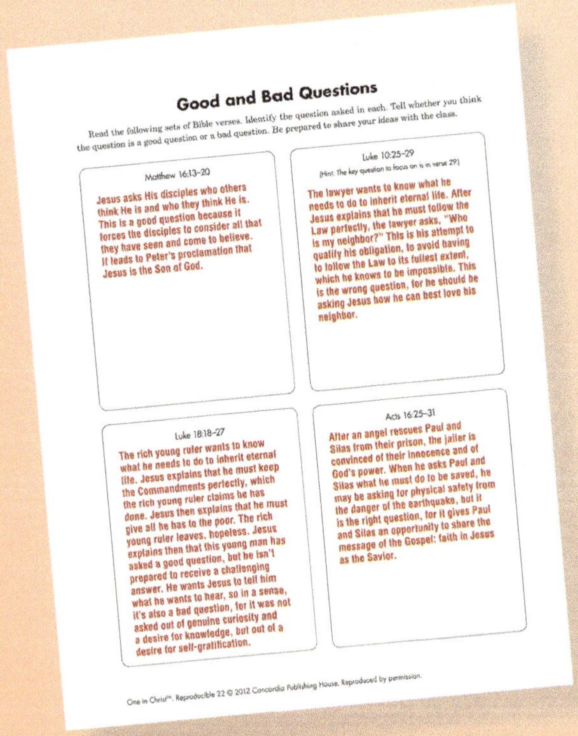

Good and Bad Questions

Read the following sets of Bible verses. Identify the question asked in each. Tell whether you think the question is a good question or a bad question. Be prepared to share your ideas with the class.

Matthew 16:13–20

Jesus asks His disciples who others think He is and who they think He is. This is a good question because it forces the disciples to consider all that they have seen and come to believe. It leads to Peter's proclamation that Jesus is the Son of God.

Luke 10:25–29

(Hint: The key question to focus on is in verse 29.)

The lawyer wants to know what he needs to do to inherit eternal life. After Jesus explains that he must follow the Law perfectly, the lawyer asks, "Who is my neighbor?" This is his attempt to qualify his obligation, to avoid having to follow the Law to its fullest extent, which he knows to be impossible. This is the wrong question, for he should be asking Jesus how he can best love his neighbor.

Luke 18:18–27

The rich young ruler wants to know what he needs to do to inherit eternal life. Jesus explains that he must keep the Commandments perfectly, which the rich young ruler claims he has done. Jesus then explains that he must give all he has to the poor. The rich young ruler leaves, hopeless. Jesus explains then that this young man has asked a good question, but he isn't prepared to receive a challenging answer. He wants Jesus to tell him what he wants to hear, so in a sense, it's also a bad question, for it was not asked out of genuine curiosity and a desire for knowledge, but out of a desire for self-gratification.

Acts 16:25–31

After an angel rescues Paul and Silas from their prison, the jailer is convinced of their innocence and of God's power. When he asks Paul and Silas what he must do to be saved, he may be asking for physical safety from the danger of the earthquake, but it is the right question, for it gives Paul and Silas an opportunity to share the message of the Gospel: faith in Jesus as the Savior.



# INTO the Word

## Acting It Out

Have students read Luke 10:30–35 to familiarize themselves with the basics of the story. Ask them to work in groups of at least seven to act out the skit. Alternatively, a group of students could perform the skit for the rest of the class. As student groups act out their role play or skit, circulate to make sure they stay on task.

## The Way of Blood

In Bible times, the road going down from Jerusalem to Jericho was often called "The Way of Blood." A rocky and desolate seventeen-mile stretch, it was attractive to robbers and vagabonds, and many were waylaid along its length.

Have students fill in the chart, reflecting on how the robbers, the priest, the Levite, and the Samaritan treated the man. Students may discuss their ideas for the chart with their groups.

Once all the groups have filled in their charts, ask students to share the information they supplied in the chart. Then, invite students to reflect on what they can learn from the parable. Ask them to look up James 4:17. Ask, **How does this verse apply to the parable?** James 4:17 serves as a reminder that sins of omission are just as much sins as those of commission. Call to mind the words of the Confession we speak in church: "We have sinned against You in thought, word, and deed, by what we have done and by what we have left undone" (*LSB*, p. 151) If we know what is right and do not do it, we are sinning.

## Review

Contrast these three types of individuals with their responses upon seeing the injured man by the side of the road. Note the irony in the responses.

### The Way of Blood

After you've performed the story of the Good Samaritan, fill in the diagram below. How did each of the following treat the traveler? What did they do to or for him?

| Robbers | Priest and Levite | Good Samaritan |
|---|---|---|
| beat him, stole his possessions, left him to die | ignored him, passed on the other side, refused to help him | cared for him, tended his wounds, paid for his care |

### Three Lessons

When He had finished telling the story of the Good Samaritan, Jesus asked the lawyer which of the three men was a neighbor, and the lawyer gave the correct answer: the one who showed mercy. Jesus replied, "Go and do likewise." Showing mercy—that sounds easy enough, right? But how easy is it to be merciful and compassionate all the time? Have you always done the compassionate thing? Do you always help those in need? Probably not. None of us do. We're all sinners, and none of us are perfect all the time.

There are three lessons we can learn from the parable of the Good Samaritan:

1. Demonstrating love to others, despite prejudice or hesitation, is not an option.
2. Neighbors can be anyone or everyone.
3. We can't possibly keep the Commandments all the time; therefore, we need a Savior.

Read Romans 3:19–20. What do these verses tell us about our ability to follow the Law? Then read Romans 5:6–8. What comfort can we find here?

**We are all sinners, and we cannot save ourselves. However, God has offered us justification through the death and resurrection of Christ.**

Now that you know what God has done for you, how can you be a Good Samaritan?

**Responses will vary.**

Something to think about: Were there any times when you were like the injured man? Who came to your rescue?

**Remember**

By this we know love, that He laid down His life for us, and we ought to lay down our lives for our brothers. But if anyone has the world's goods and sees his brother in need, yet closes his heart against him, how does God's love abide in him? Little children, let us not love in word or talk but in deed and in truth.

1 John 3:16–18

47

## INTO our lives

In Luke 10:27, the lawyer correctly sums up the Commandments by saying, "You shall love the Lord your God with all your heart and with all your soul and with all your strength and with all your mind, and your neighbor as yourself." Ask, **How did the Good Samaritan show this kind of love?** (The Good Samaritan did not think of cost or burden, but helped another in need.)

Review Matthew 25:35–40 with the class. Here, Jesus talks to His disciples about the final judgment, telling how He will know that we have truly followed His Commandments. Ask, **How is the theme of these verses similar to the story of the Good Samaritan?** Student responses should demonstrate understanding that by helping others, we are showing our obedience, love, and devotion to God.

Point out that the Good Samaritan did not stop to worry about whether the man was a Jew or Samaritan, whether he was alive or dead, whether the cost would be too great. He simply saw another in need and cared for him. In this parable, Jesus wanted His listeners to form higher level connections, so He told of a Samaritan, one who was despised by Jews and whose people were hated and considered enemies, yet who was the only one to show compassion.

Ask, **Are there people we know who are hated and considered enemies, people who need our compassion? How can we be Good Samaritans to them?** Students may talk about students who are targets of bullying, the poor and needy in the community, marginalized social groups. They should discuss ways to help such as defending those in need, giving time and talent to charitable groups, and learning more about cultural and social differences.

## Three Lessons

In this section, students will reflect on the lessons from this parable, focusing primarily on the idea that we are sinful creatures who cannot hope to keep the Commandments perfectly and thus desperately need a Savior.

After students have read the introductory paragraph, encourage them to reflect on moments when they have been given the opportunity to show compassion and failed to do so. Students may be uncomfortable sharing these examples, but provide the opportunity if it seems appropriate. Lead them to realize that we fail to act because we are sinful. Invite them to share possible reasons we do not do what we ought to do. Possible answers might be fear of getting hurt, distraction by other things, not realizing the need, or worry about what others might think.

Then, discuss the three lessons we can learn from the parable, asking students to share their thoughts and examples as appropriate.

To bring the lesson to a close, direct students to Romans 3:19–20 to remind them that all humans are, because of our sinful nature, incapable of fulfilling the Law. The Law convicts us of our sin and reminds us that we need a Savior. Continue with the reading of Romans 5:6–8. Emphasize that **our loving God knew we needed a Savior, and that is why He sent Jesus into the world.** Because we have Jesus' love and forgiveness, we reach out to share that love with others.

Talk with students about how they can put their faith into action by considering people they know who are in need and what they can do to help them. These examples should represent associations ranging from very personal (friends and family) to local (people in the community) and even to global (foreign mission work, perhaps).

## Remember

Something to think about: Encourage students to think about times when they needed help. Remind them that all sinners were like the injured man, and that Christ gave His life for them. How is Christ like the Good Samaritan to us?

# Good and Bad Questions

Read the following sets of Bible verses. Identify the question asked in each. Tell whether you think the question is a good question or a bad question. Be prepared to share your ideas with the class.

| Matthew 16:13–20 | Luke 10:25–29<br>(Hint: The key question to focus on is in verse 29.) |
|---|---|
| Luke 18:18–27 | Acts 16:25–31 |

# The Lost Son

LUKE 15:11–32

## Background

The lesson for today is familiar to many. Commonly known as the parable of the prodigal son—or someone who recklessly wastes his money, the story very directly spells out Jesus' unconditional love for sinners such as you and me. As with most parables, a good amount of symbolism is used to convey the "earthly story with a heavenly meaning." The father represents God, the prodigal son represents a sinner, and the older brother represents someone who feels "righteous" and in need of no repentance.

Help students realize just how negative the prodigal son's predicament was. First, he had the guilt of squandering his father's money, and then, of all times, a drought spread across the land, making it even harder to get food. Then, because he lost all of his friends, no one offered him any food—not even the pigs' food! All of these negative predicaments led to him being humbled enough to realize that repentance was necessary and that he would be better off going back to his father's house—even if it meant him being his father's servant. All of this is a fine illustration of Psalm 34:18, "The LORD is near to the brokenhearted and saves the crushed in spirit."

## Devotion

As Mom began preparing dinner, the phone rang. "Hello?" She listened intently. "Yes, Mr. Baker. I'll be sure to talk with him. Thank you so much for calling! Bye." Mom walked upstairs and knocked on Micah's door.

"Come in!" Micah was sitting on his bed.

"Micah, do you have something to show me?" Mom asked.

"Let me guess. That was Mr. Baker on the phone." Micah went and sat at his desk.

"Yes it was, and he told me you have an 'action note' to show me that says you were caught cheating on your math test."

Micah sighed, "Yeah. I thought if I could just see one answer, it would help me remember how to do the rest of the section on my own."

"Micah, I'm not concerned with your math abilities; you studied really hard, and even Mr. Baker said you did great on the other sections. I just don't want you to make getting a good grade more important than not cheating."

"I definitely know that now, Mom," Micah moved back to the bed. "I'm sorry."

"And," Mom continued, "I never want you to feel you can't tell me something like this!"

"I just thought you'd be all mad at me and think I was bad or something."

"I'm disappointed that it happened, but I will always forgive and love you—no matter what."

"Thanks, Mom!" Micah gave her a hug.

"Hey, how could I do anything else? Jesus has earned forgiveness for all of my mistakes too!"

**PRAY: Lord Jesus, thank You for forgiving and welcoming me, a sinner, back to You time and time again! In Your saving name we pray. Amen.**

Sing: "My Song Is Love Unknown" (*LSB* 430, recorded as the eighth grade Hymn of the Season).

## Central Truth

God forgives repentant sinners unconditionally because of the atoning work of Jesus Christ.

## Objectives

- Acknowledge and believe that God's grace in Christ is unconditional.
- Recognize that we are now children of God through faith in Christ Jesus.
- Express joy that Christ has made us children of God.

## Materials

- The Basics
- Reproducible 23

## Bible Prep

Post in advance so students can bookmark the reference before class time.

- Luke 15:11–32

## INTO the Word

Say, **The devotion today tells of a young boy, Micah, who was afraid to tell his mom about something he had done wrong. Why do you think he tried to hide his sin of cheating on the test?** (He did that because he was afraid his mom wouldn't love him anymore.) **Why did the boy have nothing to worry about?** (His mom loved him unconditionally.) **What is the best thing to do when you realize you have done something wrong?** (Repent and tell the truth.) **Where can we find the best advice on how to handle a problem?** (God's Word, the Bible. God's Word guides us along the right path to eternal life; it is our map for a Christian life.)

23 Luke 15:11–32

### The Lost Son

**The Loving Parent**

Today's Bible story tells us of a young man who received unconditional love. Read Luke 11:15–32, the parable of the lost son. Then number the events of the story below to place them in proper sequence. Finally, write the large letters from items 1 to 17, in order in the spaces below to reveal an important Bible truth.

__1__ The younGer son wants his share of the father's property now.

__16__ The older broTher becomes angry and refuses to go to the party.

__11__ The father runs and Greets his lost son with a hug and kiss.

__6__ DroughT occurs.

__3__ The younger son leAves home.

__14__ The older brother hears a party from A distance.

__2__ The fatheR divides his property among his sons.

__5__ The younger son begins to be in nEed.

__7__ The younger son Hires out to work feeding pigs.

__4__ The younger son goes to a far Country and squanders his father's money.

__8__ The youngeR son is starving and wants pigs' food.

__10__ The yoUnger son goes home.

__15__ The older brother fInds out about the party in honor of the younger brother.

__9__ The younger sOn comes to his senses and decides to return home.

__13__ The father organizes a party in honor oF his son's return.

__12__ The younger son repents of his sin to His father.

__17__ The father talks with the older brotHer and tells him why he is rejoicing.

We are saved by __g__ __r__ __a__ __c__ __e__ __t__ __h__ __r__ __o__ __u__ __g__ __h__ __f__ __a__ __i__ __t__ __h__!

**Review**

squandered— to spend extravagantly or foolishly

compassion— sympathetic to the distress of others with a desire to alleviate it

48

## INTO the Word

### The Loving Parent

Have students read Luke 11:15–32 together in verse-by-verse fashion, going up and down the aisles. Next, have students work in pairs to complete the activity. Underscore the theme of this lesson. God welcomes us into His family by grace through faith in Jesus and His redeeming work for us. **Jesus lived, died, and rose again so that we might be forgiven and brought back to God.** In your review of the key point of the story, stress the patient and loving attitude of the father. He recognizes and sees his returning son from far off and runs to meet him. Similarly, God comes to us and finds and reinstates us because of Jesus and His saving work for us, unconditionally, without any strings attached.

Say, **Think about how good it must feel to be poor and desperate and then to be reinstated as a son or daughter in a prosperous family. We, too, are rescued from our poor and condemned state because Christ has taken the burden of our sins upon Himself through His suffering and death on the cross. It is as if we were dead in our trespasses and sin and now we are alive in Christ! Praise God!**

### Welcome Home!

God sent His Son, Jesus, to pay the penalty of sin in our place. Jesus loves us unconditionally. He has forgiven our sins and removed them "as far as the east is from the west" (Psalm 103:12); His love for us is steadfast and unchangeable! Think about your life with Jesus in light of this parable. Match each of the following statements from the story with the connecting application on the right.

__b__ 1. The younger son misuses what his father has given him.

__d__ 2. The younger son reaches a hopeless state, but then remembers his father.

__g__ 3. The younger son plans to return to his father and appeal to him for mercy.

__e__ 4. The father welcomes the younger son back unconditionally.

__f__ 5. The father celebrates his son's return and honors him.

__c__ 6. The older brother resents the treatment of the wayward son.

__a__ 7. The younger son was dead and is alive again; he was lost and is found.

a. On our own, we are dead in trespasses and sin; lost eternally.

b. We take God's goodness for granted and follow our own wayward desires.

c. We sometimes criticize God's love and forgiveness for other sinners, telling ourselves we are somehow better than them.

d. When we are brought to a realization of our unworthiness and sin, God brings us to a remembrance of His love and grace.

e. God welcomes forgiven sinners back into His family, forgiving us for Jesus' sake.

f. With restoration and forgiveness, there is joy and celebration.

g. Realizing our sins, we ask God to forgive us for Jesus' sake.

**REMEMBER**

See what kind of love the Father has given to us, that we should be called children of God; and so we are.

1 John 3:1

49

# INTO our lives

## Welcome Home!

As a class, read the opening paragraph under this header. Allow time for students to work independently to complete this activity. Review responses.

If you choose to do so, distributes copies of **Reproducible 23** for students to complete as a class activity or assign it as homework. Comment that when we receive Jesus' forgiveness, it is as if God is welcoming us home once again. Because of Jesus, God always welcomes us back; He restores us and empowers and motivates us to live as His forgiven people, eager to serve Him. If time permits, allow some students to share their prayers with the class.

To close class, sing together, "Abide with Me" (*LSB* 878). Remind students that God's unconditional love is continually shown as He does "abide with" us forever—no matter what!

## Remember

Comment that in the words of today's memory verse, we marvel with the evangelist at the fact that in Christ Jesus we receive God's amazing love to the extent that we have become children of God—members of His family, with all the rights and privileges associated with that identity both now and evermore!

## Review

Comment that these two words illustrate well what happens in this parable as well as in our relationship with God. We squander His gifts to us. But God has compassion on us and forgives us for Jesus' sake.

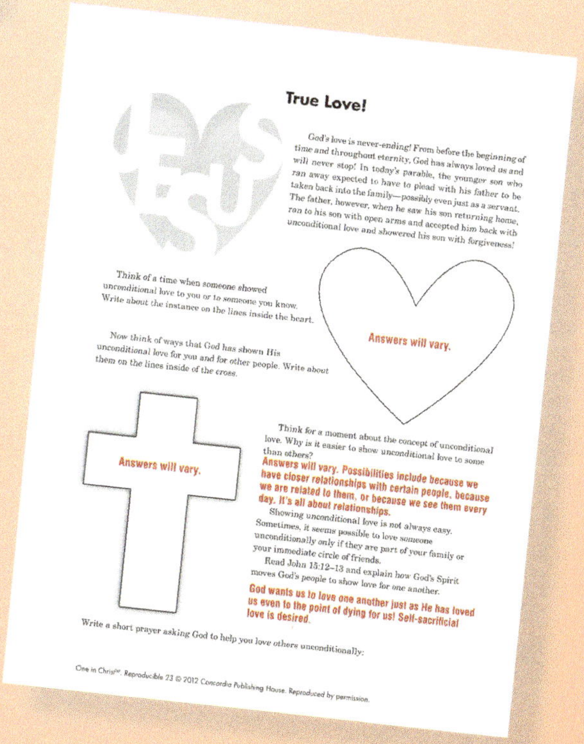

**True Love!**

God's love is never-ending! From before the beginning of time and throughout eternity, God has always loved us and will never stop! In today's parable, the younger son who ran away expected to have to plead with his father to be taken back into the family—possibly even just as a servant. The father, however, when he saw his son returning home, ran to his son with open arms and accepted him back with unconditional love and showered his son with forgiveness!

Think of a time when someone showed unconditional love to you or to someone you know. Write about the instance on the lines inside the heart.

Answers will vary.

Now think of ways that God has shown His unconditional love for you and for other people. Write about them on the lines inside of the cross.

Answers will vary.

Think for a moment about the concept of unconditional love. Why is it easier to show unconditional love to some than others?

Answers will vary. Possibilities include because we have closer relationships with certain people, because we are related to them, or because we see them every day. It's all about relationships.

Showing unconditional love is not always easy. Sometimes, it seems possible to love someone unconditionally only if they are part of your family or your immediate circle of friends.

Read John 15:12–13 and explain how God's Spirit moves God's people to show love for one another.

God wants us to love one another just as He has loved us even to the point of dying for us! Self-sacrificial love is desired.

Write a short prayer asking God to help you love others unconditionally:

# True Love!

God's love is never ending! From before the beginning of time and throughout eternity, God has always loved us and will never stop! In today's parable, the younger son who ran away expected to have to plead with his father to be taken back into the family—possibly even just as a servant. The father, however, when he saw his son returning home, ran to his son with open arms and accepted him back with unconditional love and showered his son with forgiveness!

Think of a time when someone showed unconditional love to you or to someone you know. Write about the instance on the lines inside the heart.

Now think of ways that God has shown His unconditional love for you and for other people. Write about them on the lines inside of the cross.

Think for a moment about the concept of unconditional love. Why is it easier to show unconditional love to some than others?

Showing unconditional love is not always easy. Sometimes, it seems possible to love someone unconditionally only if they are part of your family or your immediate circle of friends.

Read John 15:12–13 and explain how God's Spirit moves God's people to show love for one another.

Write a short prayer asking God to help you love others unconditionally:

# UNIT 4—JESUS SAVES— GOOD NEWS TO SHARE

## Overview

Unit 4 focuses on events associated with Jesus' death, resurrection, and ascension. These lessons, therefore, cover the portions of Holy Scripture upon which the chief doctrines of the Christian faith are built. Jesus Christ, God's only begotten Son, lived, died, and rose again to earn forgiveness of sins, new life, and eternal salvation for us and for all people. The final three lessons in the unit deal with the coming of the Holy Spirit at Pentecost and His life-changing work through the power of the Gospel in the life of an Ethiopian traveler and Saul, a notorious persecutor of early followers of Christ.

Before Jesus ascended in bodily form into heaven, He commissioned His followers with the task of bringing the Good News of His free gift of salvation for all people to those in our immediate surroundings and throughout the world. All who believe in Jesus as their Savior join in this vital and important work. You share in it when you witness and talk to your students about Jesus in natural, free-flowing conversation. You join in it significantly when you uphold the Good News of Jesus as central and foundational to all that you teach. You help to send it to the far corners of the world when you provide financial assistance and encouragement to missionaries and evangelists. Perhaps you have taken part in an overseas mission trip yourself. May Jesus, our Savior and Lord, continue to bless and encourage you in all that you do to share the saving message of Jesus and His love. May He grant success to your efforts!

### UNIT 4

24. The Last Supper
25. Jesus Dies and Is Buried
26. Jesus Rises from the Dead
27. The Ascension
28. Pentecost
29. Philip and the Ethiopian
30. Saul Comes to Faith

## Worship

Each lesson in this curriculum has a classroom devotion that teachers may read to students during the opening of the day or at the beginning of the religion lesson. (The devotions always have a direct connection to the day's Bible lesson. If you already have an established plan for opening devotions, you can still use the one suggested in the Teacher Guide as an introduction to the lesson.) It is suggested that throughout the teaching of this unit, you use the prayer titled For the Holy Spirit (*LSB*, p. 310). You will probably notice that, through frequent use, most students will know the prayer by memory by the end of the month. (Putting the prayer to use is a much more effective means for memorization than as an assignment.) Though you can feel free to choose a variety of hymns and songs, suggestions will be made mostly from the *LSB* and the songbook *All God's People Sing!* (*AGPS*). These hymns can be found on the recorded set of *Hymns of the Month* (*HOM*) or *Hymns of the Season* (*HOS*), available from Concordia Publishing House (CPH), which will give students a good background in Christian hymnody and will also help them to more readily participate in church worship services. Note that the CPH recording *Jesus' People Sing* (*JPS*) consists of fifty songs, all from *AGPS*.

## Extending Unit Concepts

### Community Building

*Keep on Moving.* Each player walks while carrying a beanbag on his or her head or shoulder while the leader keeps time. When a bean bag falls, the clock stops until someone places the beanbag back on the head or shoulder from which it fell. Compare to the restoring work of the Holy Spirit in the lives of God's forgiven people.

*According to Plan.* Have students stand in a circle. Challenge them to throw a ball around the circle so that no one throws a ball to a neighbor and no one touches the ball a second time before all have caught it. Talk about the value of planning. Relate to the value of planning when working with other Christians to share the Good News.

*We Are Letters.* Have students work together in pairs to spell their names, one letter at a time, by standing, sitting, or lying down to make a letter of the alphabet. Relate to 2 Corinthians 3:1–3, where Paul writes about a letter of another kind, commenting that each Christian is a letter from Christ.

### Tools for Witness

Bring to class or draw and construct symbols of Baptism. Use these to make a Baptism bulletin board. Refer to the Baptism accounts included in this unit. Talk about Baptism as one of the means through which God gives His good gifts to His people.

Have students each individually design and make a lamb, using various art and craft supplies. Talk about the uniqueness of each lamb. Read Revelation 5:6–7, where Jesus, the world's Redeemer, is pictured as a lamb that is both meek and majestic. Talk about these qualities as descriptive of Jesus. See also Isaiah 53 and Jeremiah 11:19.

## Service Projects

Acts 2:45 records that the early Christians gave to anyone who had a need. Assess needs in your community. Originate a class project to help meet one of these needs.

This unit deals with the Early Christian Church, which grew under persecution. List areas of the world in which Christians suffer persecution today. Organize and implement a prayer vigil for these brothers and sisters in Christ, asking the Holy Spirit to give them strength, courage, and joy in the face of adversity.

Refer students to 2 Corinthians 8:1–15. Talk about Jesus, the generous giver, who gave up everything for us and for our salvation.

## Reaching Every Individual

Develop a timeline to place the events from the life of Paul in chronological order.

Have students work in groups to generate a fact sheet on each of the books of the Bible studied in this unit. Encourage them to include pertinent information about the book, such as author, theme or themes, and information about the original audience.

Provide selected portions of each of the books of the Bible studied in this unit. Encourage students to keep these as representative of the book and its message.

# Integrating the Faith throughout the Curriculum

## Social Studies

- Draw a map of the Mediterranean world. Plot Rome, Corinth, Galatia, Ephesus, Philippi, Colossae, and Thessalonica on the map.
- Create travel brochures highlighting life in one of the cities to which Paul's epistles were addressed.
- Brainstorm together and list in chart form a collection of the unique positive qualities of each student in the class.

## Science

- Discuss the history of God's unfolding gifts of power. Include mechanical power, electronic power, nuclear power, and the spiritual power God gives freely through the Word and Sacraments.

## Mathematics

- Chart the crucifixion events, relating them to the third, sixth, and ninth hours (9:00 a.m., 12 noon, 3:00 p.m.).
- Ask what number might mathematically represent the number of cups of water in the ocean. Charles Spurgeon once laughed, "To think our little cups could exhaust the ocean of His grace." Relate this statement to Paul's words in 2 Corinthians 12:9.

## Technology

- Use a computer program to design birth announcements for the Christian Church, born at Pentecost.
- Talk about the use Paul is likely to have made of modern technology if it had been available to him.
- Study Romans 6. Then e-mail reflective thoughts to a partner and discuss.
- For an even closer Pentecost experience, try this: devise a way in which multiple sound clips of various languages can be played at once. In other words, use a computer or CD player to play five or six different languages at once with the obvious result being utter confusion on the listener's part. Be sure to convey how this *would be* a moment of confusion without the aid of the Holy Spirit and how it *was* a moment of complete Gospel clarity with the Holy Spirit.

## Fine Arts

- Dramatize the events of Acts 9.
- Write and perform skits illustrating how contemporary Christians sometimes have experiences similar to that of Philip and the Ethiopian.
- Sing songs and hymns celebrating God's gift of heaven.
- Find and compare artwork depicting the events of Pentecost.

## Language Arts

- Challenge students to learn a Bible verse in another language.
- Have students investigate and write a detailed description of the events associated with their Baptism.
- Write "help wanted" newspaper-style ads calling God's people for lives of service.
- Hand out hymnals, and allow students time to look through the words of the hymns sung during Lent and Holy Week. Have them write down meaningful phrases about God's sacrifice and our joyful response. Have them take the hymnals home and have parents and family members add phrases that they like to the list. Encourage students to add phrases from other praise songs that they may know. Give students an 8 × 10 piece of paper and markers, and have them create posters of those words and phrases, adding illustrations as desired. Purchase 8 × 10 frames at the dollar store and frame the posters. This can serve as a reminder to students and families of God's great gift to us.
- Together with their families, students can design a family coat of arms that depicts how his or her family lives in faith as disciples of Jesus. A template for a coat of arms can be found at edhelper.com. Write "graphic organizers" in the search bar, and click on "general - graphic organizers."

# The Last Supper

## MATTHEW 26:17–30

## Background

Today's Bible story contains the account of Jesus instituting the Last Supper. Because many eighth graders are confirmed in the faith during this school year, discussing the benefits of Holy Communion would be very timely as well as beneficial. Emphasize that, although we cannot fully grasp the miracle of the real presence of Christ's body and blood in, with, and under the bread and wine, we know that it is true because God's Word says it is! We cannot add or delete anything from God's Word, and His Word clearly says, "This is My body. . . . This is My blood" (Matthew 26:28). So we believe that all four elements (bread and wine, Christ's body and blood) are present in Holy Communion—thus, the term *Real Presence*.

The prediction of Judas' betrayal of Jesus also is highlighted in today's text. In spite of Judas knowing ahead of time that he would betray Jesus, we still marvel at how he could still go through with such a bold and callous plan. We must, however, remind our students that we daily betray Jesus through our sinful thoughts and actions, and we, too, must ask, "Is it I, Lord?" In your discussion with students, be sure to emphasize Christ's forgiveness!

Although the text tells of Judas' betrayal, it does not mention Judas' death by suicide. If the subject comes up, remind students that suicide is *never* necessary; there are other options for handling grief, guilt, remorse, anger, and other potentially destructive human emotions. As always, if you ever suspect that a student is thinking about suicide, make yourself available to that student but also be sure to work with the parents/guardians and refer him or her to get professional help.

## Central Truth

Jesus gave His body and shed His blood to earn our forgiveness and salvation.

## Objectives

- Explain that in the Lord's Supper, Jesus gives the gift of Himself.
- Anticipate receiving the Lord's Supper in faith.
- Thank and praise God for the gifts of forgiveness, life, and salvation that God offers to all through the Means of Grace.

## Materials

- The Basics
- Web Resource 23
- Newspapers; 1 per every 2 to 4 students)

## Bible Prep

Post in advance so students can bookmark the references before class time.

- Matthew 26:17–30
- Romans 3:23
- 2 Corinthians 5:15
- 1 Corinthians 10:16–17
- 2 Corinthians 13:5

## Devotion

"I'm pretty sure I know why I didn't make the team," Matthew told his mother. "Ben kept calling me a ball hog and a boss right in front of Coach!" Matthew paced the kitchen floor.

"Do you think any of that's true?" Mom asked thoughtfully.

"I don't know. Maybe. But he still shouldn't talk like that."

"You need to call Ben and talk with him; he's one of your best friends."

"It's still not going to get me on the team," Matthew snapped.

"I'm just trying to get you to think about what's more important," Mom asserted.

"You're right. I'll ask for forgiveness for being a boss and see what happens. Hopefully, he'll apologize too." Matthew walked upstairs. When he came down, Matthew asked, "Mom, can you drive Ben and me up to school? We want to shoot hoops at open gym time." Matthew had his shoes on and his ball ready to go.

"Is everything all worked out?" Mom asked cautiously.

"Yep. He apologized too, and we both forgave each other—it's all good! I figure if Jesus can forgive us for all of the things we do, I can forgive one person like Ben! Besides, at lunch today David told me he'll only be on the team for about three weeks and they'll need to replace him because his family is moving to Houston. I think I'm going to go and do a little apologizing to Coach too. No one wants a ball hog on his team!" Matt handed Mom her car keys.

Mom smiled.

**PRAY: Lord Jesus, thank You for the forgiveness that You offer through Your body and blood under the bread and wine of Holy Communion. When the time is right, may I receive Holy Communion in faithfulness and in gratitude toward You! Amen.**

Sing: "Lord, Be Glorified" (*AGPS* 165).

# INTO the lesson

Explain that in today's devotion Matthew and Ben experienced conflict because one wasn't acting the way he should and the other was talking behind his friend's back. In both cases, each boy needed to apologize, receive forgiveness, and give forgiveness. After Matthew cooled down from his anger, he remembered that **Jesus forgives all sins, including sins far greater than this.** So Matthew, too, was empowered to forgive more readily.

Ask students to share if they have ever been in a sticky situation like this one. Listen to and discuss students' responses. Introduce the lesson's Bible story by telling students that people were working behind Jesus' back to have Him crucified and their subsequent need for forgiveness as well. Unlike the story in our devotion today, however, Jesus did nothing wrong!

# INTO the Word

## Securing the Scene!

Read the opening paragraph and then read today's story as found in Matthew 26:17–30. Have students work in pairs to complete the Student Book activities in this section. Discuss the answers. Indicate that the disciples have now secured their place to celebrate the Feast of the Unleavened Bread, the drama begins.

## Review

Review student definitions, making connections with the Passover and Jesus' institution of the Lord's Supper. Stress that the Lord's Supper is the new Passover meal.

24 Matthew 26:17–30

### THE LAST SUPPER

**Securing the Scene!**

Celebrating the Feast of the Unleavened Bread would be somewhat more challenging for the disciples this year! Read Matthew 26:17–30. Jesus and His disciples appeared to be somewhat on the run; they had no permanent dwelling; the Pharisees and most everyone else were watching them for any false moves; not many trusted or respected Jesus. Very soon, Jesus would suffer and die for the sins of the world.

But against this backdrop, Jesus had a very clear plan for the disciples that would enable them to keep the Passover. Write *True* next to the statements in the righthand column that are true; correct each false statement to make it true.

1. Jesus told them to go and speak with a woman for a room. **They were to go to a "certain man."**
2. The disciples were told what to say. **True**
3. Jesus told them to call Him Son of God when asking for the room. **Not Son of God but Teacher**
4. The disciples quoted Jesus saying, "My time is at hand." **True**
5. The disciples did as directed. **True**
6. Jesus prepared for the Passover. **The disciples prepared for the Passover.**
7. In this room, Jesus instituted the Lord's Supper. **True**

**REVIEW**

unleavened bread— **bread in which the leaven, or rising agent, has been removed**

Passover— **a Jewish holiday commemorating the Hebrew's liberation from slavery in Egypt**

betray— **to deliver to an enemy by treachery**

covenant— **a formal, solemn, and binding agreement**

50

# INTO our lives

## Is It I, Lord?

Comment that when Jesus said to His disciples that one of them would betray Him, they all asked "Is it I, Lord?" And when Jesus told Judas it would have been better if he had not been born, He meant that the sin Judas was about to commit was going to cause him much grief and sorrow. Jesus knew Judas's suffering over his sin would eventually lead him to commit suicide.

Be sure all students understand the term *committing suicide.* Because Jesus knew that Judas was going to commit suicide because of his upcoming sin of betraying Jesus, it truly would have been better for him to not have been born. While it is often believed that those who commit suicide automatically go to hell, the Bible does not teach that. Remind students that God is the only one who knows each person's faith.

Conclude that we are all sinners and that we are all forgiven by Jesus, who not only died on the cross to redeem us from sin, death, and the devil, but who also freely gives us His body and blood in, with, and under the bread and wine in Holy Communion. What a wonderful gift—the gift of Himself—for such sinful people!

## Is It I, Lord?

Once in the room, Jesus reveals the fact that someone will betray Him. One by one, the disciples all asked, "Is it I, Lord?"

Write the name of the betrayer in the circle on the left; write your name in the circle on the right.

Then, look up the Bible passage written where the circles intersect.

What do you, the betrayer, and all other people have in common?

**We are all sinners!**

Read 2 Corinthians 5:15 and determine yet another common theme that is communicated.

**In spite of our sinfulness, God sent Jesus to forgive us!**

## For the Forgiveness of Sins

Read 1 Corinthians 10:16–17. What does this passage say we receive in Holy Communion?

**We receive Christ's body in, with, and under the bread, and we receive Christ's blood in, with, and under the wine.**

Draw arrows to show the relationship between Jesus' body and blood with the bread and the wine.

How do worthy recipients receive Holy Communion (2 Corinthians 13:5)?

**In faith**

Christ's body and blood, in, with, and under the bread and the wine convey the forgiveness of sins for those who take Holy Communion in all sincerity and with the knowledge of its benefits. Are we sometimes puzzled by how both the body and bread are present and how both the blood and wine are present? Yes. In spite of being puzzled, however, we can rest secure, knowing that God handles the "how" and works faith in our hearts to believe the "what" and, even more important, the "who" of this life-changing Sacrament! It's all God! He created us, His Son redeemed us, and His Holy Spirit sanctifies us!

**REMEMBER**

Now as they were eating, Jesus took bread, and after blessing it broke it and gave it to the disciples, and said, "Take, eat; this is My body." And He took a cup, and when He had given thanks He gave it to them, saying, "Drink of it, all of you, for this is My blood of the covenant, which is poured out for many for the forgiveness of sins."

Matthew 26:26–28

51

# For the Forgiveness of Sins

Just as Judas needed forgiveness, so also do we need forgiveness through Jesus. How wonderful it is to know that whenever we need Jesus' love and forgiveness, it is there! Every second, minute, hour, day, Jesus' forgiveness is there for us! Discuss the following questions with the class.

**What is the definition of a Sacrament?** (It is a sacred act, instituted by God, in which the Word of God is connected to a visible means and offers and conveys the forgiveness of sins.)

**What are the visible means in Holy Communion?** (The bread and the wine)

**Why are the words found in Matthew 26:26–28 and elsewhere in Scripture referred to as the Words of Institution?** (With these words, Jesus gave and established for us the Sacrament of the Lord's Supper.)

Be sure that students understand the doctrine of Real Presence. The Bible teaches that during Holy Communion the Word of God combined with the physical elements makes Communion "efficacious" or effective, able to forgive sins. The physical elements are the bread and the wine—they don't disappear so they are still present. However, the Bible says, "This is My body. . . . This is My blood" so we know that the body and blood are present too! God doesn't ever want us to take away from or add to Scripture. Therefore, we believe that the body and blood are in, with, and under the bread and wine. In other words, all of the elements are present and working together with the Word of God to bring the forgiveness of sins.

At this point, students may be confused. To encourage them in their faith walk, assure them that while we sometimes may have difficulty grasping the concept of Christ's body and blood being included with the bread and wine—after all, Jesus died about two thousand years ago—remember that God's ways are not our ways and His thoughts are higher than our thoughts (Isaiah 55:8). We accept Holy Communion in faith!

If time permits, lead students through the "Newspaper Scavenger Hunt" found on **Reproducible 24.** This may be carried out as a class on an interactive whiteboard or students can use regular newspapers and work in pairs to complete the hunt. Conclude with an emphasis on forgiveness. Say, **Forgiveness is a vital part of our spiritual life and is key to our relationship with God. The need for forgiveness is the whole reason Jesus came to die for us, and in response to God's love for us, we love (and forgive) too!**

Conclude class by singing, "Oh, That I Had a Thousand Voices" (*LSB* 811).

# Remember

Practice memorizing the verse by writing it on the board in its entirety and then reading it aloud several times in unison. As students become familiar with it, erase a few words and read it over and over again. Then erase more words, and so on. Keep doing this each day, and in a few days, the students will have the verse memorized.

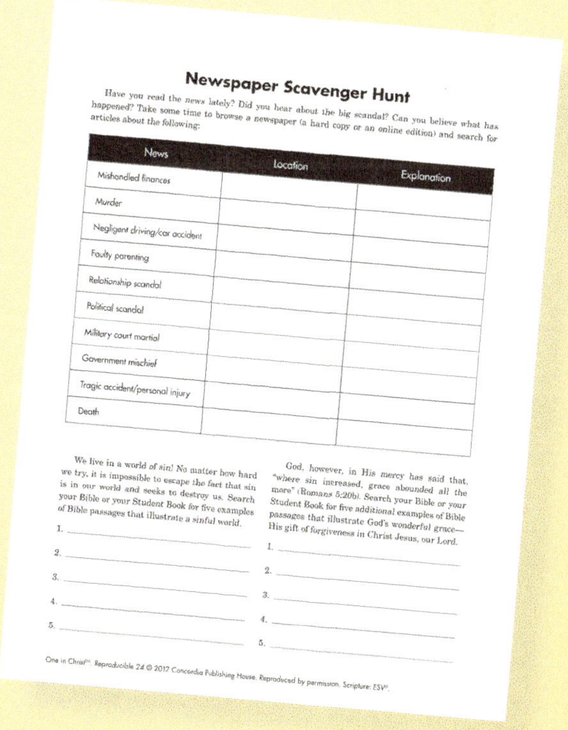

**Newspaper Scavenger Hunt**

Have you read the news lately? Did you hear about the big scandal? Can you believe what has happened? Take some time to browse a newspaper (a hard copy or an online edition) and search for articles about the following:

| News | Location | Explanation |
|---|---|---|
| Mishandled finances | | |
| Murder | | |
| Negligent driving/car accident | | |
| Faulty parenting | | |
| Relationship scandal | | |
| Political scandal | | |
| Military court martial | | |
| Government mischief | | |
| Tragic accident/personal injury | | |
| Death | | |

We live in a world of sin! No matter how hard we try, it is impossible to escape the fact that sin is in our world and seeks to destroy us. Search your Bible or your Student Book for five examples of Bible passages that illustrate a sinful world.

1. ______
2. ______
3. ______
4. ______
5. ______

God, however, in His mercy has said that, "where sin increased, grace abounded all the more" (Romans 5:20b). Search your Bible or your Student Book for five additional examples of Bible passages that illustrate God's wonderful grace—His gift of forgiveness in Christ Jesus, our Lord.

1. ______
2. ______
3. ______
4. ______
5. ______

# Newspaper Scavenger Hunt

Have you read the news lately? Did you hear about the big scandal? Can you believe what has happened? Take some time to browse a newspaper (a hard copy or an online edition) and search for articles about the following:

| News | Location | Explanation |
|---|---|---|
| Mishandled finances | | |
| Murder | | |
| Negligent driving/car accident | | |
| Faulty parenting | | |
| Relationship scandal | | |
| Political scandal | | |
| Military court martial | | |
| Government mischief | | |
| Tragic accident/personal injury | | |
| Death | | |

We live in a world of sin! No matter how hard we try, it is impossible to escape the fact that sin is in our world and seeks to destroy us. Search your Bible or your Student Book for five examples of Bible passages that illustrate a sinful world.

1. ______________________
2. ______________________
3. ______________________
4. ______________________
5. ______________________

God, however, in His mercy has said that, "where sin increased, grace abounded all the more" (Romans 5:20b). Search your Bible or your Student Book for five additional examples of Bible passages that illustrate God's wonderful grace—His gift of forgiveness in Christ Jesus, our Lord.

1. ______________________
2. ______________________
3. ______________________
4. ______________________
5. ______________________

# Jesus Dies and Is Buried

## MATTHEW 27:32–66

## Background

During Jesus' trial before the high priest and before Pontius Pilate, Jesus spoke only two times as recorded in Scripture. During His time on the cross, He spoke seven different times. Why didn't He speak during His trial? Why would He speak now? Words spoken during His trial may have taken Him off the path to save us from our sins. Words spoken from the cross teach us about His purpose for being on the cross. He spoke to His heavenly Father. He spoke to His mother who had been with Him since the beginning of His earthly life. He spoke to His disciple who had followed Him and trusted Him. He spoke to a criminal enduring the same punishment. And He spoke in a loud voice that all who were witnesses to the crucifixion could hear. This lesson focuses on what Jesus said as He willingly suffered and died in our place in order to redeem us. In His words spoken from the cross, we see the prophecies of ancient times being fulfilled. In His words spoken from the cross, we see God's plan of salvation being completed so that the eternal future of all believers is guaranteed by what Christ did. Christ died and arose again that we, too, might live. Thanks be to God!

## Devotion

Imagine the scene. On a road leading out of Jerusalem, a man, bloodied and beaten, is carrying His cross. People who love Him and care about Him follow at a distance, not believing what their eyes are seeing. He walks and stumbles, too tired to go on. A man standing nearby from a far away country is forced by the Roman soldiers to carry the man's cross. Why Simon? Why did the soldiers pick him instead of any other man standing nearby? Did he look strong? Did he look scared? Was he the man standing closest to Jesus? For whatever reason, the soldiers picked Simon. He was the one to accomplish the task of getting Jesus' cross to the hill of Golgotha—the Place of the Skull.

Simon was picked to accomplish this part of the journey, but He couldn't take Jesus' place in the next part of the story. Jesus, the only begotten Son of God, was the only one who could die on that cross to take away our sins. Only the death of the sinless Son of God could redeem us and remove the barrier between us and God that was put in place by sin.

Today's Bible story is very familiar to you. We, too, travel with Simon to the hill of Golgotha, knowing that Jesus is there because of our sins. May you see and experience God's love for you in this old, old glorious story. May you always know and remember that Jesus, the sinless Son of God, died that you may live in heaven eternally.

**PRAY: Dear Savior, thank You for loving me enough to go to the cross to suffer a horrible death in my place. Help me to live my life for You, forgiven and blessed eternally by Your holy name. Amen.**

Sing: "My Song Is Love Unknown" (*LSB* 430).

## Central Truth

Our sinless Savior willingly suffered and died in our place in order to redeem us.

## Objectives

- Describe Jesus' last words on the cross.
- Recognize that through His suffering and death Jesus earned the forgiveness of sins and eternal life for all people.
- Respond to God's love in joyful service of their Redeemer.

## Materials

- The Basics
- Reproducible 25

## Bible Prep

Post in advance so students can bookmark the reference before class time.

- Matthew 27:32–66

25 Matthew 27:32–66

## Jesus Dies and Is Buried

### Time to Speak Up

The time has come! The words of God spoken in Genesis 3:15 to the serpent are about to be completed—"I will put enmity between you and the woman, and between your offspring and her offspring; He shall bruise your head, and you shall bruise His heel."

Satan is rejoicing over the "bruising" of Jesus' heel. All things seem to be going in Satan's favor. However, we know the rest of the story. Jesus will not be silent as He "crushes" Satan's head.

### Jesus' Words

Jesus crushes Satan's head when He pays for the sins of the world by dying on a cruel wooden cross and then showing His victory by rising from the dead. Jesus spoke seven times while on the cross. Fill in the blanks below to complete three statements about the things Jesus said. Use the following three sets of words:

the extent of His suffering in our place
the completion of His work to save us
His love and concern for others

With the following words, Jesus shows **His love and concern for others.**

"Father, forgive them, for they know not what they do." (Luke 23:34)

"Truly, I say to you, today you will be with Me in Paradise." (Luke 23:43)

"Woman, behold, your son!" "Behold, your mother!" (John 19:26–27)

With the following words, Jesus shows **the extent of His suffering in our place.**

"My God, My God, why have You forsaken Me?" (Matthew 27:46/Mark 15:34)

"I thirst." (John 19:28)

With the following words, Jesus shows **the completion of His work to save us.**

"It is finished." (John 19:30)

"Father, into Your hands I commit My spirit!" (Luke 23:46)

### Review

Match the following words with their definitions

__a__ enmity — a. feelings of hatred and hostility

__c__ righteousness — b. bought back; recovered ownership of

__b__ redeemed — c. the state of being right, holy, and pure

52

# Into the Lesson

## Time to Speak Up

Read the paragraphs in the Student Book with the class. Remind students that God's plan of salvation was immediately put into effect when Adam and Eve first sinned. God immediately promised to send one who would "bruise" the head of Satan. Years have passed, and people have waited expectantly for the promised Messiah to come and accomplish God's plan of salvation. Now the time has come, but regretfully, not all recognize Jesus as the promised Savior. Still, the event promised eons before to our first parents reaches fulfillment when the promised Savior atones for human sin on the cross.

# Into the Word

## Jesus' Words

Say, **Jesus spoke seven times from the cross. In His loving mercy, three of those times were directed toward His care and concern for others.** Ask, **Why would that be? Who is He referring to when He speaks of those who "know not what they are doing"?** (Certainly, the crowd and the soldiers, but it could also extend to us because sometimes we do not know that we are sinning against God and/or our neighbor.) **What comfort comes in knowing that the thief on the cross would go to heaven?** (It reminds us that it is not because of what we have done, but because of what Christ has done for us.)

Holding the infant Jesus in his arms, Simeon told Mary that one day her heart would be pierced. Do you think Mary remembered those words as her Son hung on the cross? Both John and Mary were very close to Jesus. They could comfort each other. John 7:5 records at least one point at which Jesus' brothers did not believe in Him as the promised Messiah. Scripture does not record that any of them were present at the crucifixion. First Corinthians 15:7 and Acts 12:17 indicate that at least one of Jesus' brothers believed in Him after the resurrection. James, Jesus' half-brother, is believed to be the leader of the churches in Jerusalem.

Jesus also spoke to indicate the degree of His suffering.

Much of Psalm 22 is prophetic of Jesus' experience on the cross. **What other words from Psalm 22 reflect Jesus' suffering?** (vv. 6, 7, 8, 14, 15, 16, 17, 18) This psalm is often read during Maundy Thursday or Good Friday services. His cry of abandonment reflects what we should have experienced because of our sins.

Jesus would not lessen the pain of His suffering, and thus refused the wine mixed with gall as recorded in Matthew 27:34, but He spoke the words of Psalm 69:21 to fulfill the Scriptures.

Jesus' last two statements indicate the completion of the Father's plan of salvation.

**God's plan of salvation was completed once and for all through the suffering, death, and resurrection of Jesus Christ.** What comfort is there in knowing that Jesus' sacrifice on the cross completed our salvation for us? (We never have to wonder if we have done enough or if we are going to heaven. We are guaranteed heaven through faith in what Jesus did for us.)

Jesus gave up His spirit willingly as was prophesied in Psalm 31:5 and John 10:18. He willingly gave up His life that we may have eternal life. Note with students that He "cried out again with a loud voice" (Matthew 27:50). A person on the cross for three hours would not be expected to have the physical strength or breath to speak in a loud voice. Jesus did!

## Review

Have students match the words with their definitions. Discuss these definitions and why our righteousness and redemption are such blessings from God. Distribute copies of **Reproducible 25** for students to complete.

## The Centurion's Words

The centurion and soldiers at the foot of the cross participated in and witnessed a crucifixion like they had never seen before. Unlike other crimi-

### The Centurion's Words

Read Matthew 27:51–52. Fill in the blanks below to indicate amazing things that happened at the death of Christ.

And behold, the **curtain of the temple was torn in two, from top to bottom**. And **the earth shook**, and the **rocks were split**. The **tombs also were opened**. And **many bodies of the saints who had fallen asleep were raised**.

Read Matthew 27:54. What is amazing about the fact that the centurion recognized Jesus as the Son of God, but the high priest and temple leaders did not?

**He and his soldiers were Gentiles. The high priest and temple leaders were Jewish. They were looking for the Messiah to come, but failed to see Jesus as the Messiah. The Gentiles see this with their brief encounter with Jesus.**

### My Words . . . My Actions

Those at the foot of the cross on Good Friday probably wondered what the crucifixion of Jesus meant. They did not understand it at the time, but Jesus' sacrifice guaranteed their eternal life in heaven. We have the blessing of living after the cross and the joyful story of the Easter resurrection.

What words and actions in your life show that you know the enormity of Christ's gift on the cross—what it cost Him and what it gives to you?

**Answers will vary.**

**Remember**

Surely He has borne our griefs and carried our sorrows; yet we esteemed Him stricken, smitten by God, and afflicted. But He was wounded for our transgressions; He was crushed for our iniquities; upon Him was the chastisement that brought us peace, and with His stripes we are healed.

Isaiah 53:4–5

53

nals, who despised their crucifiers, Jesus loved and forgave His. Besides the loving spirit of Christ, they also heard the words of suffering and completion that Jesus spoke from the cross. His death was like none other.

Have students record the events and words after Jesus' death in their Student Books. The centurion and soldiers who witnessed Jesus' death saw that He truly was the Son of God, based on the marvelous events that accompanied His crucifixion. Ask students to think about what the centurion may have told his family or other soldiers. Review the details of the burial of Jesus. Joseph of Arimathea asked and was given permission to bury Jesus. Jesus was placed in Joseph's own tomb.

Review the words of Luther's explanation of the Second Article with the class. Luther lived after the cross and the Easter resurrection. He understood it because he could see the whole picture of God's plan of salvation as explained in the Bible. Ask students if they have ever seen home makeover TV shows—where they start with a run-down, dumpy home and then, through the hard work of many, transform it into an amazing home with all the best to offer.

We are living proof of "Extreme Makeover—Jesus Edition." But it did not take a whole team of architects and builders to make us over. It was accomplished on Good Friday by one man who hung on the cross. To borrow Luther's words from the explanation of the First Article, "For all this it is my duty to thank and praise, serve and obey Him." By the power of the Holy Spirit, our lives can be a joyful response to the gift God has given to us.

# INTO our lives

## My Words . . . My Actions

This is a part of the lesson that, as teachers, we can pray for and model for our students, but we cannot force their response to what Jesus did for them. Encourage your students to let God's gift of salvation make a difference in their everyday lives. We have a new life in Christ right now and are guaranteed eternal life in heaven through faith in Christ. Although we live after the cross and resurrection, many may still not understand or be willing to accept how it all applies to their lives.

It is our prayer that the Holy Spirit will use the words and the lessons that we teach to help Jesus be real for our students. We plant the seed each day, and God grants the increase. The increase may be evident today or tomorrow or twenty years from now. By God's grace, we keep planting the seeds of God's Word! We can trust in God to work His desired effect, even if we can't see it today.

## Remember

The words of this verse remind us of what Christ did for us. He endured the suffering and pain we deserved for our sins. Through His suffering, we receive peace and healing.

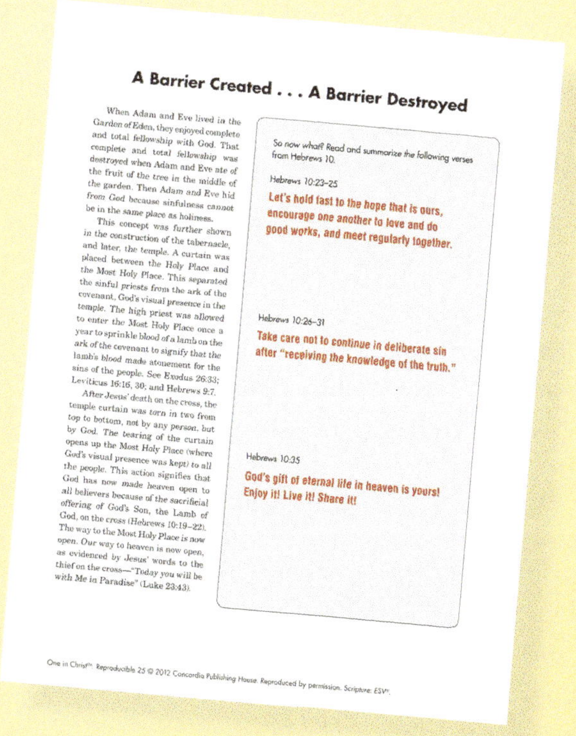

**A Barrier Created . . . A Barrier Destroyed**

When Adam and Eve lived in the Garden of Eden, they enjoyed complete and total fellowship with God. That complete and total fellowship was destroyed when Adam and Eve ate of the fruit of the tree in the middle of the garden. Then Adam and Eve hid from God because sinfulness cannot be in the same place as holiness.

This concept was further shown in the construction of the tabernacle, and later, the temple. A curtain was placed between the Holy Place and the Most Holy Place. This separated the sinful priests from the ark of the covenant, God's visual presence in the temple. The high priest was allowed to enter the Most Holy Place once a year to sprinkle blood of a lamb on the ark of the covenant to signify that the lamb's blood made atonement for the sins of the people. See Exodus 26:33; Leviticus 16:16, 30; and Hebrews 9:7.

After Jesus' death on the cross, the temple curtain was torn in two from top to bottom, not by any person, but by God. The tearing of the curtain opens up the Most Holy Place (where God's visual presence was kept) to all the people. This action signifies that God has now made heaven open to all believers because of the sacrificial offering of God's Son, the Lamb of God, on the cross (Hebrews 10:19–22). The way to the Most Holy Place is now open. Our way to heaven is now open, as evidenced by Jesus' words to the thief on the cross—"Today you will be with Me in Paradise" (Luke 23:43).

So now what? Read and summarize the following verses from Hebrews 10.

Hebrews 10:23–25

**Let's hold fast to the hope that is ours, encourage one another to love and do good works, and meet regularly together.**

Hebrews 10:26–31

**Take care not to continue in deliberate sin after "receiving the knowledge of the truth."**

Hebrews 10:35

**God's gift of eternal life in heaven is yours! Enjoy it! Live it! Share it!**

# A Barrier Created . . . A Barrier Destroyed

When Adam and Eve lived in the Garden of Eden, they enjoyed complete and total fellowship with God. That complete and total fellowship was destroyed when Adam and Eve ate of the fruit of the tree in the middle of the garden. Then Adam and Eve hid from God because sinfulness cannot be in the same place as holiness.

This concept was further shown in the construction of the tabernacle, and later, the temple. A curtain was placed between the Holy Place and the Most Holy Place. This separated the sinful priests from the ark of the covenant, God's visual presence in the temple. The high priest was allowed to enter the Most Holy Place once a year to sprinkle blood of a lamb on the ark of the covenant to signify that the lamb's blood made atonement for the sins of the people. See Exodus 26:33; Leviticus 16:16, 30; and Hebrews 9:7.

After Jesus' death on the cross, the temple curtain was torn in two from top to bottom, not by any person, but by God. The tearing of the curtain opens up the Most Holy Place (where God's visual presence was kept) to all the people. This action signifies that God has now made heaven open to all believers because of the sacrificial offering of God's Son, the Lamb of God, on the cross (Hebrews 10:19–22). The way to the Most Holy Place is now open. Our way to heaven is now open, as evidenced by Jesus' words to the thief on the cross—"Today you will be with Me in Paradise" (Luke 23:43).

So now what? Read and summarize the following verses from Hebrews 10.

Hebrews 10:23–25

Hebrews 10:26–31

Hebrews 10:35

# Jesus Rises from the Dead

MATTHEW 28:1–15

## Background

The Easter story, along with the story of the nativity, is found in nearly every religion book, every Sunday School and VBS curriculum your students have encountered. They've heard its message time and again. But this is a story that never gets old, and it is a story that we must emphasize because it is foundational to our Christian faith. Without the empty tomb, we have no hope.

The thread of the Gospel message—that we are dead to sin and alive in Christ—is no more clearly presented than in the story of Christ's death and resurrection. As Paul said in his Letter to the Corinthians: "One has died for all, therefore all have died; and He died for all, that those who live might no longer live for themselves but for Him who for their sake died and was raised" (2 Corinthians 5:14–15). Christ died for our sins, the final and atoning sacrifice for all; when He rose from the grave, He conquered sin, death, and the devil. Because of this, we have the assurance of salvation. What could be more wonderful? What could be more glorious?

## Devotion

She didn't think about it much, but if Sarah was going to be completely honest, she didn't really believe in Easter. Jesus rose from the dead? How could it possibly be true? Actually, she was pretty sure that most of the stories in the Bible were probably just stories, not really true. A giant fish swallowing a guy and then spitting him out after three days? Changing water into wine? Walking on water? The waters of the Red Sea parting to let a nation of people walk through? Hard to believe, indeed.

On Easter Sunday, as she pondered the important question of where her parents might have hidden her Easter basket, Sarah's ear was caught by the words of the pastor: "If there is no resurrection of the dead, then not even Christ has been raised. And if Christ has not been raised, then our preaching is in vain . . . your faith is futile and you are still in your sins. . . . If in Christ we have hope in this life only, we are of all people most to be pitied" (1 Corinthians 15:13–17).

All of her doubts were thrown into turmoil by the pastor's words. If Christ hadn't been raised, there was no point in being a good Christian—not even a good person. If He did not rise from the dead, then He wasn't really God. What was her purpose in life? Why did she pray at meals, sing in the choir, or put money in the offering plate? Why go to church at all? Sarah resolved to pay attention to the rest of the sermon, and at its end, she sat very still, praying a silent prayer of repentance.

If you have ever doubted the truth of God's Word, pray Sarah's prayer.

**PRAY: Dear God, forgive me for the times I have doubted Your Word. I believe that You are all powerful, God, and You can work miracles I can't even understand. Help my faith to become strong and firmly planted in my heart so that I may always confess my faith in You with my heart, mind, and soul. In Your most holy name. Amen.**

Sing: "I Know That My Redeemer Lives" (*LSB* 461) or "Jesus Lives! The Victory's Won" (*LSB* 490).

## Central Truth

Jesus demonstrated His power over death, freeing us from eternal death and giving us the hope of everlasting life with Him in heaven.

## Objectives

- Recognize that by His resurrection Jesus showed His victory over sin, death, and the power of the devil.
- Explain the comfort received in knowing that those who die in the faith will live forever in heaven.
- Demonstrate a desire to share the Good News of eternal life with others.

## Materials

- The Basics
- Reproducible 26

## Bible Prep

Post in advance so students can bookmark references before class time.

- Matthew 28:1–15
- Romans 1:4
- Hebrews 2:14–15
- 1 Corinthians 15:55–57
- Romans 5:15
- Romans 10:9

# INTO the lesson

Ask, **What sorts of Easter traditions do you have in your home? Jot down some ideas below and then turn to the person sitting next to you and describe what your family does to celebrate Easter.**

Say, **You probably could have anticipated that many of us share similar traditions. This is largely because our society has shaped the way we celebrate holidays. Aside from continuing the customs our families practice, we also tend to do what television, magazines, and stores tell us we should do. We buy candy and we fill baskets with delicious treats. We buy a new outfit in spring colors. We sit around a table and eat a feast. Of course, decorating eggs and hunting for candy or baskets are fun, but we must realize that without Christ, Easter would be completely meaningless.**

Emphasize that **Christ came to earth as a man, died for our sins, and then rose from the dead. Without this central truth, our holidays—and our lives—are without true meaning.**

26 Matthew 28:1–15

## Jesus Rises from the Dead

### Easter at the Empty Tomb

Every one of the Gospels tells the story of the resurrection, which is the most significant event in human history. We're going to focus on Matthew's Gospel. In your group, read Matthew 28:1–15 and answer the questions below.

1. Mary Magdalene and the other Mary go to the tomb at dawn after the Sabbath. Why might they choose this time to go?
   **The women were eager to care for Jesus' body, but they were forbidden to do so until the Sabbath was over. As soon as they were able, they went to tend to their Lord.**

2. What do they see as soon as they reach the tomb?
   **An earthquake has struck, the stone has been rolled away, and an angel is sitting on it.**

3. Why are the guards "like dead men"? Does their reaction surprise you? Explain.
   **The angel and the earthquake have frightened them badly. This is not surprising, as angels tend to have a similar effect on other people.**

4. The angel tells the women: "Do not be afraid." Where else have we heard an angel say these words?
   **We've heard them at the annunciation and when the angel appeared to the shepherds in the fields when Jesus was born.**

5. How do the women feel as they leave the tomb? Why might they feel this way?
   **The women are filled with fear and joy. They are excited about the angel's news and are also likely full of awe as well.**

6. What do both the angel and Jesus tell the women to do?
   **The women are to go back to the disciples (Jesus says "My brothers") and share the good news, telling them to meet Him in Galilee.**

7. What do the chief priests tell the guards to say? Why do you think they make up this story?
   **The chief priests tell the guards to lie and say that the disciples came in the night and stole Jesus' body. This lie will cast doubt on the story of His resurrection.**

#### Review

resurrection— **the act of rising from the dead or returning to life**

Sabbath— **a day of rest and worship for Jews**

54

# INTO the Word

## Easter at the Empty Tomb

Have students read the resurrection story as it is told in Matthew 28:1–15 and answer the questions in small groups of three or four. Or invite students to work individually.

Remind students that the Sabbath is a time of rest from labor, a solemn day of prayer and contemplation for the Jews. It was forbidden to do work on this day. Joseph of Arimathea convinced Pilate to let him bury Jesus' body quickly because the Sabbath started at sundown on Friday. Sabbath ends Saturday evening, so the women could gather materials to anoint Jesus' body then and set out as soon as possible in the morning to tend to His body.

The earthquake mentioned in verse 2 may have been caused by the angel's appearance, or it may have been sent by God to help the angel dislodge the stone. Whatever the cause, the stone has been rolled away, and an angel is sitting on it.

The soldiers guarding the tomb were probably accustomed to strange sights and battle scenes, but the appearance of the angel would have been completely incomprehensible. Because of their shock and because of the fear angels generally inspire, the soldiers fall to the ground insensible.

When the angel of the Lord appears to people, he usually begins with these words: "Do not be afraid." These words were also spoken at the annunciation and when the angel appeared to the shepherds in the fields when Jesus was born.

The women are filled with joy and excitement over the angel's news and are likely full of awe as well, for they have witnessed a stunning miracle, one which will change the course of history. There is no doubt now that Jesus is truly God.

The chief priests cannot let the guards go about telling people what they've seen. It would chip away at their authority and cast doubt on their motive for the crucifixion. They go back to the rumor they suggested in Matthew 27:62–66, bribing the guards for their silence with the promise that they will keep them from getting into trouble with Pilate.

### Why Easter Matters

Why do you think Easter is the most important day of the year for Christians? The Bible has a lot to say about the powerful meaning of Christ's resurrection. Read the following passages and answer the questions.

| | Easter matters because . . . |
|---|---|
| Romans 1:4 | **By dying and rising from the dead, Jesus proved that He truly was the Son of God.** |
| Hebrews 2:14–15 | **Christ took our sins upon Himself and defeated the devil through His death and resurrection.** |
| 1 Corinthians 15:55–57 | **We do not need to fear death, for Christ defeated it by His death and resurrection.** |
| Romans 5:15 | **As one man, Adam, brought sin into the world, so one man, Jesus Christ, brought salvation to all with His death and resurrection.** |
| Romans 10:9 | **If you confess that Jesus is Lord and believe that God raised Jesus from the dead, you will be saved.** |

Go back to your answer to the question at the beginning of this section. Do you have anything to add to it?

### Easter for the World

In Matthew 28:7 and then again in verse 10, the women who first witnessed the resurrection were told to "Go and tell." The angel told them, and then Jesus told them. The women were told to go quickly, and although they went with fear and trembling, the Bible tells us they ran. How then can we do any differently? The last words Jesus spoke before He ascended are words encouraging His disciples—and us as well—to share the Good News.

Easter is not a message we should hide. It is not a gift we should be ashamed of. It is the most glorious day in the history of the world, and we must share it with others.

In the space below, write a prayer expressing what you've learned in the lesson today about Easter and its importance on the day Christ rose from the dead as well as its importance in our lives.

**Students' prayers should thank Jesus for His death and resurrection and for the gift of eternal life that He won for us. Prayers should also include a resolution to share the Gospel message with others.**

**Remember**

For Christ also suffered once for sins, the righteous for the unrighteous, that He might bring us to God, being put to death in the flesh but made alive in the spirit.

1 Peter 3:18

55

# INTO our lives

## Why Easter Matters

In this section, students will examine various Scripture references to discern why Easter is the single most important day in history. First, students are asked to consider the issue individually. Ask students to write their answers on separate pieces of paper. Do not invite discussion at this point. After they have read the Bible passages, they will be asked to go back and reflect on their answer. Students may work on this section individually or in small groups. When students have finished answering the questions, encourage discussion. **Why is Easter the most important event in history?**

## Easter for the World

In this account of the resurrection, the women are charged by both the angel and by the resurrected Christ to share the good news with others. At this point, invite students to work individually to write a short prayer, thanking Jesus for His death and resurrection and for the gift of eternal life He brought. The prayer may also include evidence of students' understanding of the necessity of sharing the Good News of Easter with others. Ask for a volunteer or two to share their prayers.

## Remember

In your review of this memory verse, emphasize once again the centrality of the historical Easter event to the Christian faith and life. Distribute copies of **Reproducible 26** for students to complete.

## Review

Comment that most Christians worldwide have designated Sunday as their day of worship and rest since Jesus rose from the dead on Sunday.

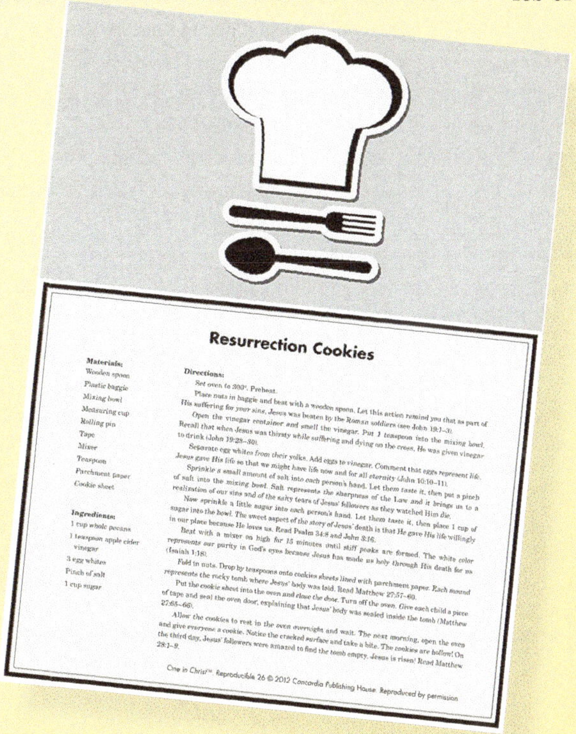

# Resurrection Cookies

**Materials:**

- Wooden spoon
- Plastic baggie
- Mixing bowl
- Measuring cup
- Rolling pin
- Tape
- Mixer
- Teaspoon
- Parchment paper
- Cookie sheet

**Ingredients:**

- 1 cup whole pecans
- 1 teaspoon apple cider vinegar
- 3 egg whites
- Pinch of salt
- 1 cup sugar

**Directions:**

Set oven to 300°. Preheat.

Place nuts in baggie and beat with a wooden spoon. Let this action remind you that as part of His suffering for your sins, Jesus was beaten by the Roman soldiers (see John 19:1–3).

Open the vinegar container and smell the vinegar. Put 1 teaspoon into the mixing bowl. Recall that when Jesus was thirsty while suffering and dying on the cross, He was given vinegar to drink (John 19:28–30).

Separate egg whites from their yolks. Add eggs to vinegar. Comment that eggs represent life. Jesus gave His life so that we might have life now and for all eternity (John 10:10–11).

Sprinkle a small amount of salt into each person's hand. Let them taste it, then put a pinch of salt into the mixing bowl. Salt represents the sharpness of the Law and it brings us to a realization of our sins and of the salty tears of Jesus' followers as they watched Him die.

Now sprinkle a little sugar into each person's hand. Let them taste it, then place 1 cup of sugar into the bowl. The sweet aspect of the story of Jesus' death is that He gave His life willingly in our place because He loves us. Read Psalm 34:8 and John 3:16.

Beat with a mixer on high for 15 minutes until stiff peaks are formed. The white color represents our purity in God's eyes because Jesus has made us holy through His death for us (Isaiah 1:18).

Fold in nuts. Drop by teaspoons onto cookies sheets lined with parchment paper. Each mound represents the rocky tomb where Jesus' body was laid. Read Matthew 27:57–60.

Put the cookie sheet into the oven and close the door. Turn off the oven. Give each child a piece of tape and seal the oven door, explaining that Jesus' body was sealed inside the tomb (Matthew 27:65–66).

Allow the cookies to rest in the oven overnight and wait. The next morning, open the oven and give everyone a cookie. Notice the cracked surface and take a bite. The cookies are hollow! On the third day, Jesus' followers were amazed to find the tomb empty. Jesus is risen! Read Matthew 28:1–9.

# The Ascension

## ACTS 1:1–11

## Background

David spoke prophetically of the ascension in Psalm 68:18, when he said, "You ascended on high, leading a host of captives in your train and receiving gifts among men." This verse refers both to the completion of Jesus' earthly mission and the coming of the Holy Spirit. By His redemptive work, Jesus conquered sin, death, and hell—foes holding sinners captive. At the ascension, Jesus rose bodily from earth to heaven where He remains at the Father's right hand until the Judgment.

Jesus' departure from earth was not the end. Rather, it ushered in the next phase, the promised Holy Spirit "receiving gifts among men." The Holy Spirit, the Helper, brings us to faith and keeps us in faith. Through Him in the waters of Baptism, we are washed clean of sin and continually renewed in Him. It is only through the Holy Spirit that we are able to witness faith or do anything good. This work of the Helper is joined to the ascension because Jesus told the disciples the Holy Spirit could not come until His departure. Before ascending into heaven, Jesus gave His followers the Great Commission, "Go and make disciples of all nations." Beginning with Acts and continuing throughout the New Testament, the focus of God's Word becomes Christian living, spreading the Gospel, and building the Church on earth. After Jesus ascended, the angels asked His disciples, "Why do you stand here? Jesus is coming back." In other words, don't just stand there. Get busy. Jesus will return and there will be no time after He reappears. Now is the time. Spreading the Gospel is a pressing issue. God desires that all may know the saving love of Jesus.

## Central Truth

Only by the Holy Spirit's power can we carry out the Lord's command to proclaim the Gospel to all people.

## Objectives

- Describe the events associated with Christ's visible ascension into heaven.
- Confront and confess our reluctance to witness and our need for the power of the Spirit.
- Rejoice in the presence of the Holy Spirit in our life, empowering and guiding us to share the Good News.

## Materials

- The Basics
- Reproducible 27

## Bible Prep

Post in advance so students can bookmark references before class time.

- Titus 2:11–14
- John 16:13
- 1 Corinthians 3:5–8
- Acts 1:1–11

## Devotion

Because Jason wanted to play clarinet, he decided to join the school band. "This will be a snap," he thought. His plan was to walk into the class on the first day and start performing toe-tapping songs. Instead, he found that he had a lot to learn. Just getting the clarinet out of the box and putting it together was a challenge. Then, he had to practice holding the instrument and placing his fingers in the right place. When it was time to learn how to place his mouth over the reed, he wondered if it was even possible to play the clarinet. He hadn't yet gotten to the part about reading music when his teacher gave him more instructions. "Jason, now you have to blow into the clarinet." To make the smallest sound, he had to exhale the breath from his lungs into the instrument. Regardless of all the other things he had to do, without his own breath, Jason's clarinet was just another instrument in a box.

In a way, Jason's experience is like our Christian life. Without the life-giving breath of the Holy Spirit, we would just be instruments in a box, unable to do anything good. But instead, the Spirit has breathed on us through Word and Sacrament, equipping us with gifts to share the Gospel with others. Now, we are instruments of the Holy Spirit, using the abilities and opportunities He provides for His important work of spreading the Good News that salvation is God's free gift through Jesus.

**PRAY: Dear Father, through Your mercy, Jesus has set me free of hell and opened the gates of heaven. Forgive my reluctance to share the Gospel. Thank You for the Holy Spirit's life-giving breath that makes me alive for Jesus. Give me the courage and joy of heart always to speak Your truths. In the name of the Savior I pray. Amen.**

Sing: "Lord, Be Glorified" (*AGPS* 165) or "Stand Up, Stand Up for Jesus" (*LSB* 660).

# INTO the lesson

The world is starving for the message of Jesus Christ, something that can only come from Christians. Through our actions and words, inspired and taught by the Holy Spirit, famished souls can know and believe in their Savior.

## He Came Down; He Ascended

This section ties together Jesus' purpose in coming to earth with His ascension into heaven. **Jesus came to earth to earn forgiveness, new life, and eternal salvation for us and for all people.**

On Maundy Thursday, before the events in the Garden of Gethsemane, Jesus spoke to the disciples about His imminent departure. He promised they would not be left as orphans, but that the Father would send another Helper, the Spirit of Truth (John 14:15–18). Say, **Jesus invites all people to know His redeeming love. Before going back to heaven, He commissioned His followers to teach the world about Jesus. What is the role of the Holy Spirit in fulfilling the Great Commission?** See 1 Corinthians 3:5–8. The Christian's role is merely to plant and water. Only the Holy Spirit gives the increase.

## Review

Sanctification is the work of the Holy Spirit. The Holy Spirit comes to us in Baptism, washing us clean from sin, vesting the saving faith in us. This "setting apart" is one aspect of sanctification. Each day of the Christian life is about baptismal renewal, as God's Word explains, drowning the old self and starting over again. The other facet of sanctification is actively performing the tasks the Holy Spirit brings, good works that show the love of Jesus. The Helper visits our fallen condition and makes us holy so that we might live holy lives, showing forth holiness to proclaim the glories of our God (1 Peter 2:9). Say, **In sanctification, you have been set apart and given the privileged task of sharing the Good News of Jesus with others.**

27 Acts 1:1–11

### THE ASCENSION

**He Came Down; He Ascended**

Jesus came to earth for specific reasons. Write the reasons you find recorded in Titus 2:11–14.

**Responses include salvation for all, training in righteousness, redeeming us from lawlessness, and purifying for Himself a people zealous for good works.**

Just because Jesus ascended and is gone from sight doesn't mean He abandoned you. When Jesus went to sit at the right hand of His heavenly Father, He sent us the Helper, the Holy Spirit. What is the Helper's job? Read John 16:13.

**The Holy Spirit guides in all truth and speaks for the Father.**

REVIEW

sanctification— **to make holy**

56

# INTO our lives

## Gazing Upward

Comment that Luke is the author of Acts. His "first book" (Acts 1:1) is his Gospel account that he describes through the end of verse 3. Luke is an observer to the events, so the "them" refers to the disciples. The disciples' inquiry of restoring Israel is, perhaps, a political question, regarding the earthly governance of Israel. Acts opens with the ascension, followed shortly by the promised coming of the Holy Spirit, the Helper.

This section is intended as a cooperative group activity. Divide students into groups to read the ascension account and fill in the graphic organizer according to the listed categories. After students have had time to complete the activity, ask for a retelling of the account. Then ask, **What does this story teach us about God?** The discussion should include observations about Jesus' love, forgiveness, and salvation for all people, His plan for sharing the Good News of His saving grace, His blessing of the disciples with the gift of the Holy Spirit.

Say, **Before ascending into heaven, Jesus claimed His kingship and told the disciples, "All authority in heaven and on earth has been given to Me." He said this in Matthew 28:18. He has power and rule over everything.** Ask, **How is it important to your life, faith, and**

### Gazing Upward

Read Acts 1:1–11. Then record the basic facts from the story as appropriate in each frame below.

| Commands | Promises | Questions |
| --- | --- | --- |
| Stay in Jerusalem and witness. | The Holy Spirit will come and Jesus will come back. | When will Israel be restored? Why are you standing here? |

| Answers Given | Actions |
| --- | --- |
| Jesus answered His disciples' question and told them to be His witnesses. | Jesus was lifted up in a cloud that took Him out of sight. |

| What's Next? |
| --- |
| Answers will vary, but they will reflect ideas about the Great Commission and living the Christian life. |

**Remember**

Therefore God has highly exalted Him and bestowed on Him the name that is above every name, so that at the name of Jesus every knee should bow, in heaven and on earth and under the earth, and every tongue confess that Jesus Christ is Lord, to the glory of God the Father.

Philippians 2:9–11

### Just the Beginning

Jesus ascended to heaven, but that wasn't the end. He left work to do. The Helper has come and put you on His team for sharing the Gospel. Don't just stand there! Jesus is coming back.

57

**discipleship that Jesus is all powerful and rules over everything?** This is a discussion question with no right or wrong answers. Encourage an honest discussion. Students may wish to talk about this in their cooperative groups before sharing with the entire class.

### Talk about it.

The Holy Spirit called you as a member of His team to share the Good News. How can you talk about Jesus in every part of your life? There's so much to say! And, remember, actions are a form of "talking." The Holy Spirit uses every seed you plant and water as you share God's Word.

Birthday Money ______

Homework ______

Social Media ______

Career Choice ______

Athletics ______

Leisure Activities ______

Phone Apps ______



# INTO the Word

## Talk about It

Even in the Old Testament, God insisted on His people keeping His Word and teaching His love and commands in all ways possible. Deuteronomy 6:5–9 teaches, "You shall love the Lord your God with all your heart and with all your soul and with all your might. And these words that I command you today shall be on your heart. You shall teach them diligently to your children, and shall talk of them when you sit in your house, and when you walk by the way, and when you lie down, and when you rise. You shall bind them as a sign on your hand, and they shall be as frontlets between your eyes. You shall write them on the doorposts of your house and on your gates." That means it's time to talk!

Say, **Beginning with the shepherds who couldn't keep quiet about the news of Jesus, the New Testament gives many examples of people talking about Him. It was through word of mouth that the people learned of the Savior's teachings and miracles. Matthew 4:23–25 reports, "His fame spread throughout all Syria." New Testament accounts tell of people coming to Jesus because they had "heard" about Him. That's right! People were talking. They are talking still!**

Pass out copies of **Reproducible 27**. Provide quiet time for student reflection and responses to each area mentioned. Discuss students' ideas and thoughts. Stress the privilege of sharing the Good News and that we are instruments of the Holy Spirit. We plant and water. The Holy Spirit brings the increase.

## Just the Beginning

Talk with students about Jesus' ascension serving as both an ending and a beginning. Jesus' physical ascension indicated that He completed His mission on earth. He would leave physically but promised to remain with His people through the power of His Holy Spirit. With the coming of the Holy Spirit, something new was beginning, the Christian Church! It was a church made up with people on a mission, a mission that continues to this day. The mission is to share the Good News and, through the working of the Holy Spirit, to extend God's kingdom, for the Gospel is for everyone.

## Remember

Say, **When Jesus came to earth, He set aside His glory and took on human form. As the conqueror of our foes, He now reigns in heaven as our King and Savior. Therefore, all of creation is to bow before Him in adoration and confess Jesus as Lord, in praise to the Father for our King.**

## Talk about it.

The Holy Spirit called you as a member of His team to share the Good News. How can you talk about Jesus in every part of your life? There's so much to say! And, remember, actions are a form of "talking." The Holy Spirit uses every seed you plant and water as you share God's Word.

Birthday Money ______________________________

______________________________

______________________________

Homework ______________________________

______________________________

______________________________

Social Media ______________________________

______________________________

______________________________

Career Choice ______________________________

______________________________

______________________________

Athletics ______________________________

______________________________

______________________________

Leisure Activities ______________________________

______________________________

______________________________

Phone Apps ______________________________

______________________________

______________________________

# Pentecost

## ACTS 2:1–41

## Background

Pentecost derives its name from a Greek word meaning "fiftieth day." Occurring fifty days after the Feast of Passover, the Feast of Pentecost (or "Shavuot") was a Jewish harvest feast commemorating the giving of the Ten Commandments to Israel. This day took on a new significance with the event recorded in Acts 2 and the imparting of the Holy Spirit.

In the moments following the inrushing of the Holy Spirit, Peter spoke to the gathering of peoples present. In his speech, he quoted the prophet Joel regarding the signs that would inaugurate the "last days." During the Old Testament period, God's people looked forward to the coming of the Messiah. The "last days," on the other hand, are the period from the time of Jesus onward. As the word of the prophet Joel indicates, the events of Pentecost ("pour out My Spirit") are proof that the last days are upon us.

Peter quotes three sections of Old Testament Scripture: Joel 2:28–32; Psalm 16:8–11; and Psalm 110:1. Certainly, these words from the Hebrew Bible resonated with those assembled at that Pentecost.

Peter announced that "everyone who calls upon the name of the Lord shall be saved" (Acts 2:21) and then ended his sermon with this final point: "God has made Him both Lord and Christ, this Jesus whom you crucified" (v. 36). Peter's sermon, spoken by the power of the Holy Spirit, illustrates well the role of the Spirit: to direct people to Jesus Christ. Rather than making His own presence known, the Holy Spirit works through means and points people to Christ.

## Central Truth

The Holy Spirit calls, restores, and empowers us to dedicate our lives to Him in response to all God in Christ has done for us.

## Objectives

- Describe the events of Pentecost and the reactions of the people who witnessed and experienced them.
- Identify the Means of Grace, through which the Holy Spirit continues to work today to create and strengthen faith.
- Thank God for gathering and equipping us as His people in Christ Jesus, our Lord.

## Materials

- The Basics
- Reproducible 28

## Bible Prep

Post in advance so students can bookmark the reference before class time.

- Acts 2:1–41

## Devotion

Jared's soccer team had worked incredibly hard to make it to the state championships. Everything was in place for them to win the final game—everything, that is, except for one thing: their coach could not be with them. Jared and his teammates understood that their coach could not make it because he had to attend a funeral three states away. Still, the team was afraid. Then, in the midst of their fears, their coach made a promise, saying, "I cannot be with you, but I will be sending someone in my place. Trust me; he will not let you down."

When the day of the championship finally arrived, the team learned that their coach had sent his brother! It was almost as if their coach was there with them! Their fears and worries were gone, and they knew there was nothing left to do but win the game.

Jared's soccer team felt much the same way as Jesus' disciples felt after Jesus ascended to heaven. The disciples knew that their Savior had taken on and defeated sin, death, and Satan's power on their behalf and had won. But now that He had left them, they were afraid to be without their leader. Still, Jesus had promised that He would send Someone He especially designated to lead the disciples. On Pentecost, the Holy Spirit arrived, and the Christian Church was born. Today is like that first Pentecost—the Holy Spirit is by our side, and God's people are never alone!

**PRAY: Holy Spirit, fill us with Your power. Help us to live as God's people and to share the Good News of Jesus every day with those we meet. We pray in Jesus' name. Amen.**

Sing: "Holy Spirit, Light Divine" (*LSB* 496).

# INTO the lesson

Talk with the class about times when they were fearful and apprehensive due to the absence of a trusted leader. Reflect with students about how life for the disciples in the presence of Jesus would have differed from life without the physical presence of Jesus after His ascension. Imagine the large crowds that came to hear Jesus. The disciples must have been excited to watch as their leader, Jesus, spoke to the crowds about the kingdom of God. Then they witnessed **Jesus' suffering, death, and resurrection to atone for the sins of the world**. They were with Him at His physical ascension into heaven. After Jesus' departure, they realized that the enormous task of communicating Jesus' words would fall upon them.

Like us, the disciples were never alone. At Pentecost, God's people received the Holy Spirit and the assurance that they would never be alone.

28 Acts 2:1–41

## Pentecost

### The Spirit Comes

The disciples knew what was coming: they knew Jesus was leaving and that He would ascend to heaven. Still, they were afraid of being without their leader and teacher. In the days leading up to Pentecost, the disciples were afraid and anxious. They begged Jesus: "Lord, show us the Father, and it is enough for us" (John 14:8). They were fearful about where Jesus was going: "Lord, we do not know where You are going. How can we know the way?" (John 14:5).

To calm their fears and anxieties, Jesus promised the disciples that He would not leave them alone as if they were orphans (John 14:18), and He promised that He would send a helper—the Holy Spirit.

On Pentecost, Jesus made good on His promises to the disciples. On that day, they very clearly and publicly received the gift of the Holy Spirit. There was no doubt in anyone's mind: Jesus had made good on His promises, and the disciples were certainly not alone.

Fill in each blank with the correct word(s) from the following list:

| | | | | |
|---|---|---|---|---|
| understand | baptized | Jerusalem | tongues | Holy Spirit |
| fifty | grave | three thousand | languages | primary languages |

Pentecost occurred **fifty** days after Christ's resurrection from the **grave**. People who spoke many different **languages** from many different countries had gathered in **Jerusalem**. The gift of the **Holy Spirit** allowed Jesus followers to speak in **tongues**. They spoke in **primary languages**, which they had never learned. As a result, everyone was able to hear and **understand** the same message. This allowed **three thousand** people to hear the Gospel, repent, and be **baptized**.

### Review

tongues—**languages; also refers to tonguelike shapes, as in tongues of fire**

witness—**to give an account of what has been seen, heard, or touched**

58

# INTO the Word

## The Spirit Comes

Review with students the meaning of Pentecost. Pentecost was a Jewish religious festival occurring fifty days after Passover and commemorating the giving of the Ten Commandments. It brought thousands of people to Jerusalem. Read Acts 2:1–41 together as a class. Allow time for students to write the missing words in the blanks to review the story events.

Talk about the Holy Spirit, the Third Person of the Holy Trinity. The Holy Spirit is God. He is also known as "the Comforter," "the Helper." He works through the Means of Grace to bring people to faith and to keep alive their saving faith in Jesus.

The gift God's people received at Pentecost is made that much greater when we realize that we have been given the gift of God Himself! The Holy Spirit is fully God, just as the Father and the Son are both fully God. He is not some lifeless force or "thing"; He is a person who does things you would expect a person to do. Distribute copies of **Reproducible 28.** Allow students to work in pairs or teams to look up the passages and record what God's Word reveals to us about the person and work of the Holy Spirit. A physical body is not the only determination of personhood.

Comment that those assembled in Jerusalem at Pentecost were Jews from many different cultures, speaking many diverse languages. Point out that the ability of a message to successfully get from the sender to the receiver depends greatly on language. Both speaker and hearer must know and understand the language that conveys the message. Play for the students an audio or video clip of someone speaking in a foreign language. Clips can come from any number of Internet resources (YouTube is a good source) or any one of CPH's multilingual resources. Ideally, the language played will be one in which none of the students is proficient. Ask what the clip was about. Naturally, there will be confusion, and the language barrier will be obvious. On Pentecost, the Holy Spirit did the unexpected by letting everyone hear the Gospel in their own native language through miraculous means.

Have students offer examples of different customs practiced by people from different countries. These customs may seem strange, even bizarre to us, but they are perfectly natural to those who practice them. Then have students offer examples of what Christians have in common with one another. It will become evident that Christ is the ultimate source of community for all of God's people. Even though we may say our prayers in different languages, the one and only Jesus Christ is still the source of our forgiveness. And that truth is the same truth that was presented on the day of Pentecost!

## Review

Allow time for students to define these words. As you review definitions with the class, relate these words and their meanings to today's lesson.

### One Though Many

Language can be a massive barrier when trying to communicate with someone; trying to make sense of a foreign language is frustrating, if not impossible. To make things even worse, there are thousands of different languages spread out across the world, resulting in ample opportunities for communication breakdowns.

Communicating with one another was not always this frustrating. In Genesis 11, we are told there was a time when all people spoke the same language. Having only one language made communication so easy that the people worked together and plotted to build a tower to heaven! This gateway to heaven that the people tried to build is known as the tower of Babel. God saw the people's great pride in their arrogant plan to build the tower. So He confused their language, mixing up their speech and creating many new languages.

Notice how what happened at Pentecost is the exact opposite of what happened at the tower of Babel. At Babel, the world went from one language to many languages, and people could no longer understand one another; at Pentecost, people miraculously were all able to understand what was being said, despite the fact that they spoke many different languages. On this day after Christ's death and resurrection, creation was given a glimpse of what life was like before sin corrupted the world. Not only did Christ conquer sin and death on the cross, but He also restored life to the way it was before sin! Pentecost offered a glimpse of the restored language that God's people will enjoy when Christ returns.

On the arrow below, write the letters *a* through *f* to place the following events of human history in their correct order: (a) tower of Babel, many languages in the world; (b) the Last Day, when language will never again be a barrier; (c) God's creation has one language; (d) sin enters the world; (e) Christ's perfect life, death, and resurrection; (f) Pentecost, when language is no longer a barrier.

_c_ _d_ _a_ _e_ _f_ _b_

**REMEMBER**

"Repent and be baptized every one of you in the name of Jesus Christ for the forgiveness of your sins, and you will receive the gift of the Holy Spirit. For the promise is for you and for your children and for all who are far off, everyone whom the Lord our God calls to Himself."

Acts 2:38–39

59

## Remember

As you review the memory verse with your class, stress that Pentecost makes us realize that God's people never walk alone; we have the gift of the Holy Spirit. Working through the Means of Grace, the Holy Spirit is always actively leading, comforting, and helping us. The Holy Spirit helps us spread the Good News of Christ. Without the Holy Spirit, our words are dead and lifeless; with the Holy Spirit, words can "cut to the heart" (Acts 2:37) and effect change in people, now and for eternity.

This distinction—dead words versus living words—is similar to an electrical circuit. When the power source is not connected or is offline, the electrical circuit is open and the appliance will not work. All the visible pieces might be in place, but if the unseen power source is missing, nothing will be accomplished. However, when the power source is online and the circuit is closed, the appliance works. Show the class an electrical circuit. A photograph or drawing will suffice; however, an actual working circuit that the students can gather around is ideal. Connect and disconnect the power source from the circuit for the students to see. Explain how the Holy Spirit does this very same thing with us, bringing us from being offline to online, transforming our words from powerless to powerful!

# INTO our lives

## One Though Many

Contrasts are most apparent when objects are viewed side by side. Something black is seen better when it is held against a white backdrop. A beautiful sound is fully appreciated when performed amid an otherwise silent setting. Convey this to students by holding a shiny ring or wristwatch in front of different objects: a mirror, a piece of yellow paper, and a piece of black paper. In the same manner, Pentecost is best understood when it is viewed together with its contrasting Old Testament event, the tower of Babel. At Babel, one language multiplied into many different languages. At Pentecost, people of many different languages and backgrounds were brought together and united by one saving message: Jesus Christ is Savior and Lord!

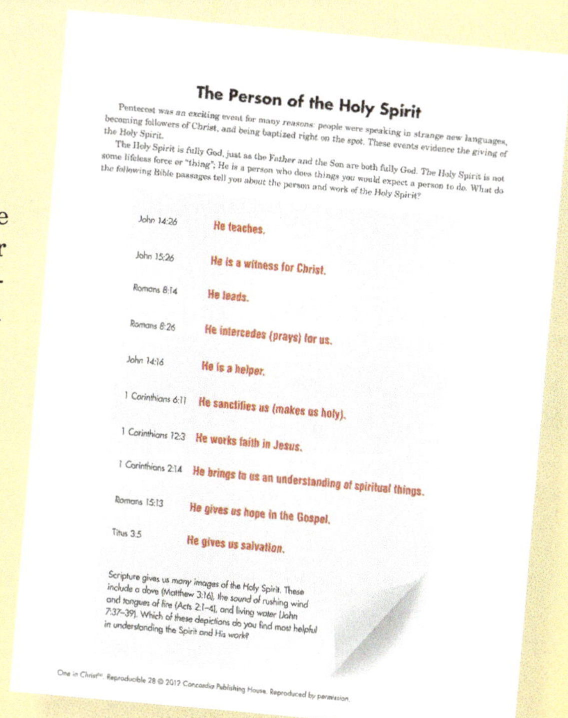

### The Person of the Holy Spirit

Pentecost was an exciting event for many reasons: people were speaking in strange new languages, becoming followers of Christ, and being baptized right on the spot. These events evidence the giving of the Holy Spirit.

The Holy Spirit is fully God, just as the Father and the Son are both fully God. The Holy Spirit is not some lifeless force or "thing"; He is a person who does things you would expect a person to do. What do the following Bible passages tell you about the person and work of the Holy Spirit?

John 14:26 He teaches.

John 15:26 He is a witness for Christ.

Romans 8:14 He leads.

Romans 8:26 He intercedes (prays) for us.

John 14:16 He is a helper.

1 Corinthians 6:11 He sanctifies us (makes us holy).

1 Corinthians 12:3 He works faith in Jesus.

1 Corinthians 2:14 He brings to us an understanding of spiritual things.

Romans 15:13 He gives us hope in the Gospel.

Titus 3:5 He gives us salvation.

Scripture gives us many images of the Holy Spirit. These include a dove (Matthew 3:16), the sound of rushing wind and tongues of fire (Acts 2:1–4), and living water (John 7:37–39). Which of these depictions do you find most helpful in understanding the Spirit and His work?

# The Person of the Holy Spirit

Pentecost was an exciting event for many reasons: people were speaking in strange new languages, becoming followers of Christ, and being baptized right on the spot. These events evidence the giving of the Holy Spirit.

The Holy Spirit is fully God, just as the Father and the Son are both fully God. The Holy Spirit is not some lifeless force or "thing"; He is a person who does things you would expect a person to do. What do the following Bible passages tell you about the person and work of the Holy Spirit?

John 14:26

John 15:26

Romans 8:14

Romans 8:26

John 14:16

1 Corinthians 6:11

1 Corinthians 12:3

1 Corinthians 2:14

Romans 15:13

Titus 3:5

Scripture gives us many images of the Holy Spirit. These include a dove (Matthew 3:16), the sound of rushing wind and tongues of fire (Acts 2:1–4), and living water (John 7:37–39). Which of these depictions do you find most helpful in understanding the Spirit and His work?

# Philip and the Ethiopian

ACTS 8:26–40

## Background

The Philip in this account is Philip the deacon, first mentioned in Acts 6, not Philip the apostle. Philip proclaimed Christ in Samaria, preaching, healing, and casting out demons. Once, God took him away from the crowds in Samaria to a lonely desert road, where he met up with an Ethiopian man riding in a chariot. The man, a eunuch, was a treasurer in the royal court of Candace of Ethiopia. The man was reading aloud from Isaiah when he encountered Philip.

In a hospitable manner, he invited Philip aboard the chariot. We don't know their exact conversation, though they may have discussed Baptism, which led to the Ethiopian's question: "What prevents me from being baptized?" Theologians name him the first Gentile to receive the Word from Philip. His conversion is the fulfillment of Psalm 68:31 (KJV): "Ethiopia shall soon stretch out her hands unto God." The Good News returned with him to Ethiopia, where, no doubt, he shared his joy and continued to study the Scriptures. After Philip ministered to the Ethiopian, God removed him to Azotus, and he preached the Gospel in other towns, possibly Emmaus, Lydda, and Joppa, before reaching Caesarea along the coast of the Mediterranean Sea. This account points out unusual events that display the power of the Holy Spirit, such as placing Philip in the exact location of the Ethiopian and then—after the Ethiopian's Baptism—removing Philip, who "found himself" in Azotus.

## Central Truth

God strengthens and guides us in our understanding of His Word and works faith in us through the power of the Holy Spirit.

## Objectives

- Acknowledge that the Holy Spirit works saving faith in human hearts.
- Express appreciation for the need to witness to all people, regardless of race, color, or nationality.
- Demonstrate a desire to share the Good News with others through words and actions as we have opportunity.

## Materials

- The Basics
- Reproducible 92

## Bible Prep

Post in advance so students can bookmark the reference before class time.

- Acts 8:26–40

## Devotion

Because of God's omnipresent quality, He is found everywhere, at all times. Wherever God is, there is also His love. He doesn't distinguish between people, regardless of nationality, location, gender, age, language, or frailty. His tender kindness belongs to everyone. "The LORD is good to all, and His mercy is over all that He has made" (Psalm 145:9). Because of His merciful goodness, He extends salvation to all people. God wants everyone to be saved and to know the truth of salvation (1 Timothy 2:4). Although Jesus was the promised Savior of Israel, He came to redeem *all* sinners, including Gentiles, not only those of Jewish heritage. In fact, the Wise Men, who were among some of the first people to worship Jesus, were Gentiles.

As part of His dispensation of mercy to the world, the Father sent the Helper, the Holy Spirit, to convert sinners. He hovers over the globe just as He hovered over the waters at the creation of the world. Through Word and Sacrament, the Spirit creates and sustains faith in human hearts. Before ascending, Jesus left His people with a task, namely, to make disciples of all nations (Matthew 28:19). Under the direction of the Holy Spirit, each Christian has the privilege of giving witness to the love of Jesus. Because we know and believe in Jesus as the Son of God and Savior of the world, we have the best news possible to share with others!

**PRAY: Heavenly Father, in love You created, redeemed, and sanctified me. I thank You for such tender mercy that surrounds and guides my life. I admit I don't always confess Your name. Sometimes, I am even ashamed to tell others I love You. Forgive my embarrassment over Your love. Nourish in me the desire and ability to witness to You in my life and to make known to everyone all You have done for me, an unworthy sinner. I pray expectantly in the name of Jesus. Amen.**

Sing: "Beautiful Savior" (*LSB* 537) or "Lift High the Cross" (*LSB* 837; *AGPS* 162).

# INTO the lesson

## Did Not Our Hearts Burn within Us?

As you begin to study and plan, pray for the Holy Spirit's guidance and wisdom to properly teach His truths. May He direct your actions and conversations as you involve students in discussions and activities that will vivify and make bold their witness of Jesus.

Ask students to recall the events on the road to Emmaus when Jesus, His identity as yet unknown to His fellow travelers, interpreted to them in all the Scriptures the things concerning Himself, beginning with Moses and the Prophets (Luke 24:27). Later, after Jesus had revealed Himself to them, they recalled, "Did not our hearts burn within us while He talked to us on the road, while He opened to us the Scriptures?" (v. 32). Comment that this "burning heart" may refer to the Holy Spirit's work of bringing joy, wonder, and appreciation to those who come to know and believe **God's great gift of salvation through Christ Jesus** and what it means, now and in eternity. In today's lesson, we will meet someone who comes to faith while on a desert road and goes on his way rejoicing over all that God has given him in Christ Jesus.

## The Source

Say, **Because we are sinners, we are unable to come to faith outside of the Holy Spirit's work. The explanation of the Third Article of the Apostles' Creed explains Scripture's teaching that the Holy Spirit calls, enlightens, sanctifies, and keeps us in faith. Match each of these workings of the Holy Spirit with the Bible verse that best matches or describes this work.** Or discuss and complete this section together.

## Review

Ask, **What makes you joyful?** Allow time for sharing and discussion. Engage students by inviting them to share why something brings them joy. Most likely, students will mention events and elements of their daily lives that are blessings from God's hand. Guide the discussion in a way that leads students to see that the purest and longest-lasting joy possible is the joy we have in Jesus. We receive this joy as a fruit of the Spirit (Galatians 5:22). Say, ***Rejoice* is a verb that comes from the noun *joy*.** Comment that Satan attempts to nudge away joy with temptations to doubt, worry, and be afraid. Still, by the power of the Holy Spirit, we can say with the psalmist, "I will greatly rejoice in the LORD; my soul shall exult in my God, for He has clothed me with the garments of salvation" (Isaiah 61:10).

---

**29** Acts 8:26–40

# PHILIP AND THE ETHIOPIAN

### Did Not Our Hearts Burn within Us?

On the first Easter, the disciples walking to Emmaus asked themselves this question after they realized that their walking companion had been Jesus. Their hearts were burning with joy and wonder as Jesus taught them from Scripture. You have the same blessing as the Holy Spirit empowers your faith with Word and Sacrament. He sets a burning joy in your heart with the Good News of Jesus and leads you to share that joy with others.

### The Source

The Holy Spirit brings you to faith, and His power is at work, keeping you in faith throughout your life. The Holy Spirit

a. calls us by the Gospel (He brings us to faith through the Means of Grace, Word and Sacrament.);

b. enlightens us with His gifts (He tends to our faith and lights our souls by bringing us the knowledge of God through the face of Jesus.);

c. sanctifies us (Working in the Word and Sacrament, through which He also calls us, the Holy Spirit gives us power for holy living and provides tools for good works.); and

d. keeps us in the one true faith (He faithfully preserves us in Jesus unto life everlasting.).

Write the letter of the statement of each working of the Spirit from the preceding list with the Bible verse below that best identifies or describes this work.

__d__ And I am sure of this, that He who began a good work in you will bring it to completion at the day of Jesus Christ. (Philippians 1:6)

__a__ To this He called you through our gospel, so that you may obtain the glory of our Lord Jesus Christ. (2 Thessalonians 2:14)

__c__ For He who sanctifies and those who are sanctified all have one source. (Hebrews 2:11)

__b__ For God, who said, "Let light shine out of darkness," has shone in our hearts to give the light of the knowledge of the glory of God in the face of Jesus Christ. (2 Corinthians 4:6)

How is the Holy Spirit at work in your life? How is His work important to you, both now and later in your life?

**Answers will vary.**

### REVIEW

rejoice— **to be joyful over and over again**

60

---

# INTO the Word

## The Spirit at Work

Say, **As we learned, the Holy Spirit calls, enlightens, sanctifies, and keeps each Christian in faith. When building the Christian Church on earth, He does those same actions plus one more. He gathers. He produces a harvest. In today's lesson, we will see how the Holy Spirit acted mightily in order to gather nations to faith in Jesus. You will read how God placed Philip in the pathway of an Ethiopian eunuch to share the Gospel.** You may choose to share with the students that a eunuch is a male person whose testicles have been removed. This procedure was often performed on those serving royalty so that they might be fully devoted to their work and to those they served. Say, **Look at the chart and see the categories in the left-hand column.** Choose a student to read the categories. **You are going to read the account found in Acts 8:26–40 and take notes regarding the various categories.** Divide students into groups to read the account of Philip and the Ethiopian and to complete the chart. When students have finished, reconvene the

### The Spirit at Work

Jesus came to save all people, regardless of nationality. The Holy Spirit gathers all lands and nations together in the Church. Acts 8:26–40 tells how the Holy Spirit sent Philip to a visitor from another country to explain the Word to him. Complete the following chart to tell how you see the Holy Spirit in His "gathering" function in the account of Philip and the Ethiopian.

| The Holy Spirit Gathers | |
|---|---|
| Questions | "Do you understand what you are reading?" "How can I unless someone guides me?" "Does the prophet speak about himself or of someone else?" "What prevents me from being baptized?" |
| Events | The angel sent Philip to the road from Jerusalem to Gaza. Philip came to the chariot where he heard the Ethiopian reading from Isaiah. Questions were exchanged, and Philip was invited to join him in the chariot. Philip taught Scripture from Isaiah forward. When they came to water, the Ethiopian asked to be baptized. After being baptized, he went on his way, rejoicing, and God took Philip to other places for preaching. |
| Attitudes | Asking for help, the Ethiopian was eager to learn Scripture. He had also traveled to Jerusalem to worship. He was humble by confessing he didn't understand. After being baptized, he went away, rejoicing. Philip was eager as he followed God's directives. He ran to the Ethiopian and gladly baptized him. He was kind to the Ethiopian. |
| Means of Grace | The Holy Spirit worked through Scripture and Philip's teaching as well as Baptism. |

### Rejoicing on Our Way

Why do you think the Ethiopian's heart was burning within him as he and Philip parted company? What makes you think as you do? What do you think the Ethiopian did when he got home? Why is it important in your life that the Holy Spirit keeps your heart burning?

Answers will vary. The Ethiopian was rejoicing for his Baptism and all he had learned. The Holy Spirit may have used him to spread the Gospel in Ethiopia. The Holy Spirit works through God's Word to keep our faith alive.

**REMEMBER**

For the kingdom of God is not a matter of eating and drinking but of righteousness and peace and joy in the Holy Spirit.

Romans 14:17

61

class and discuss the chart as a group.

Then ask, **How is it meaningful in your life that the Holy Spirit gathers all nations to Christ?** Allow students to reflect, and discuss their thoughts. Answers should acknowledge God's infinite mercy in choosing all sinners for salvation. He desires that no one should perish. Like the Ethiopian, we are Gentiles who have received God's grace. Also, like the Ethiopian, we rejoice.

### Reading the Word

Conduct a weekly time audit. What times during the week do you spend reading God's Word or talking to God in prayer? Where might you add time to read the Bible or to talk to God in prayer each day? Through God's Word, the Holy Spirit brings us great blessings. Referring to God's Word as His "testimonies," Psalm 119:111 reminds us, "Your testimonies are my heritage forever, for they are the joy of my heart."

| | Sunday | Monday | Tuesday | Wednesday | Thursday | Friday | Saturday |
|---|---|---|---|---|---|---|---|
| 4:00 AM | | | | | | | |
| 8:00 AM | | | | | | | |
| 12:00 PM | | | | | | | |
| 4:00 PM | | | | | | | |
| 8:00 PM | | | | | | | |
| 12:00 AM | | | | | | | |

What did you learn from your time audit?



# INTO our lives

## Rejoicing on Our Way

The questions listed in the Student Book under the chart are for discussion.

Say, **Go back to Acts 8. Who will read verse 35 for us?** Choose a student to read the passage. **We don't know what Philip said in the chariot that day. But he started with what was being read from Isaiah and continued from there. If you had been Philip, what would you have taught so the Ethiopian would learn what he needed to know for salvation?** A complete list of the important points would include Christ's birth, Passion, resurrection, ascension, the judgment to come, and Baptism. Conclude this section by pointing out that all who believe and have been baptized have received the same gifts as the Ethiopian did that day in the desert. Like the Ethiopian, we have ample reason to rejoice!

If you choose to do so, distribute copies of **Reproducible 29** at this point. Say, **The Ethiopian was reading aloud from Isaiah. He could have easily made excuses for ignoring God's Word, but he overcame the obstacles and kept at it. Given this pattern, what do you suppose the Ethiopian did during his discretionary time when he arrived home? Chances are, he continued in regular reading and studying of God's Word.** Say, **Like the Ethiopian, we can make Bible reading a regular part of our lives. God blesses us as we read His Word because through the Word, the Holy Spirit continues His faith-imparting work.** Ask, **What amount of time might you devote each day to reading the Bible?** Encourage students to do a time audit. Invite them to keep a record for one week of where they spend their time and when they might schedule daily Bible reading. To give students a pattern for Bible reading, point out the Daily Lectionary beginning on page 299 in *Lutheran Service Book*. The appointed readings for the dates in the time audit are a strong possibility for a reading pattern. If possible, allow for a silent reading time each day, when students may begin their individual Bible reading.

## Remember

Say, **Ephesians 3:6 says, "This mystery is that the Gentiles are fellow heirs, members of the same body, and partakers of the promise in Christ Jesus through the gospel." This passage indicates that the righteousness and peace described in Romans 14:17 are for all people. God desires to gather all people unto Himself. No one is to be excluded.**

# Reading the Word

Conduct a weekly time audit. What times during the week do you spend reading God's Word or talking to God in prayer? Where might you add time to read the Bible or to talk to God in prayer each day? Through God's Word, the Holy Spirit brings us great blessings. Referring to God's Word as His "testimonies," Psalm 119:111 reminds us, "Your testimonies are my heritage forever, for they are the joy of my heart."

| | Sunday | Monday | Tuesday | Wednesday | Thursday | Friday | Saturday |
|---|---|---|---|---|---|---|---|
| 4:00 AM | | | | | | | |
| 8:00 AM | | | | | | | |
| 12:00 PM | | | | | | | |
| 4:00 PM | | | | | | | |
| 8:00 PM | | | | | | | |
| 12:00 AM | | | | | | | |

What did you learn from your time audit?

________________________________________________

________________________________________________

________________________________________________

# Saul Comes to Faith

ACTS 9:1–31

## Background

In the post-Pentecost days, persecution rose against the Church. Pharisees and Jewish keepers of the Law fought against those who preached the Gospel, resulting in threats, arrest, and mistreatment of the apostles. Acts 6–7 records the seizure, final sermon, and stoning of Stephen, a man of God. As he was dying, Stephen asked God to forgive his enemies. One of the Pharisees on hand to hear Stephen's words was Saul, an active leader in the persecution. It was he who approved Stephen's execution (8:1). But God had plans for Saul; He had chosen Saul as His servant and had designated him for a special life of service.

Saul's conversion took place on the way to Damascus, where he intended to persecute followers of Christ. Saul, originally from Tarsus and first referred to as "Paul" in Acts 13:9, had quite a background in the Jewish traditions. Qualified as "good" according to Jewish law, he was circumcised, born of the tribe of Benjamin, "a Hebrew of Hebrews," a Pharisee, and zealous for persecuting the Christian Church (Philippians 3:4–6). Through his conversion, Saul lost confidence in his goodness according to the Law and instead by faith came to recognize his righteousness in Jesus' saving work. Paul's high-profile background in the Jewish traditions made his preaching more noticeable because his new life in Christ stood in stark contrast to his former behavior. In 1 Timothy 1:16, Paul discusses his conversion as an example of the "perfect patience" of Jesus Christ to those who believe on Him. The Hellenists mentioned in Acts 9:29 refer to a group of Jewish people who spoke Greek and practiced the Greek culture. This group quickly accepted the Gospel and were instrumental in converting Gentiles. When Paul called himself "a Hebrew of Hebrews," he meant he was not a Hellenist.

## Central Truth

As God calls us to repentance, He turns our lives around to a new life in Christ through the power of the Holy Spirit.

## Objectives

- Recognize that God gives us faith and a change of heart so that we may live as His children.
- Express the intent to live as faithful disciples and messengers of the Good News.
- Encourage others in their new life in Christ.

## Materials

- The Basics
- Reproducible 30

## Bible Prep

Post in advance so students can bookmark the reference before class time.

- Acts 9:1–31

## Devotion

Italian-born Simon Rodia came to America at a young age without benefit of training or formal education. He brought with him a fascination for Italian architecture and its elements of glass and steel. Once in America, he worked until he had earned enough to move to the West Coast. He settled on a triangular piece of property in an area of Los Angeles known as Watts, where he worked to replicate Italian architecture. Beginning in 1921 and working alone for more than thirty years without designs, scaffolding, or bolts, Simon completed works of art that came to be known as the Watts Towers. His ingenuity and determination created a collection of sculptural forms made of bent steel rebar covered with mortar and embedded with bits and pieces of ceramic tile, pottery shards, seashells, and broken glass. Most of the objects used to construct the towers had been discarded as trash. Simon used these items, considered ruined and useless, and turned them into works of art.

That's how it is with sinners. Once, we were worthless, like pieces of broken glass and rebar heaved onto a junk pile. Our sins condemned us. Death was our future. Our evil turned us to rubbish. Now, because of the Savior's mercy, we have been given a new life. Jesus' saving love has remade our trash-infected souls into His refurbished treasures. God's mercy retrieved us from the pit of gloom that was rightfully ours and remade us into something new. Now, through Baptism, we are new creatures in Christ, treasured and repurposed in Him.

**PRAY: Father of all mercy and consolation, I praise and thank You for retrieving my sin-infected heart from the depths of sin. I am unworthy of such mercy that made me a newborn creature. Teach me Your ways, and grant that I may walk in newness of life. Provide opportunities for me to share the riches of Your grace with all. Direct me according to Your will. In Jesus' name I pray. Amen.**

Sing: "Amazing Grace" (*LSB* 744) or "Lift High the Cross" (*LSB* 837; *AGPS* 162).

30

Acts 9:1–31

## Saul Comes to Faith

### An Unlikely Choice

Read the account of Saul becoming a Christian. In the spaces provided on the timeline below, summarize the details in each set of designated verses.

Acts 9:3–6
The light comes to Saul as he is traveling to Damascus. God and Saul have a conversation. God sends Saul to Damascus to wait for further instructions.

Acts 9:7–9
Saul is led to Damascus where he remains, blind, for three days, during which he neither eats nor drinks.

Acts 9:10–16
Ananias questions God when instructed to visit Saul. God declares Saul is His chosen instrument.

Acts 9:17–19a
Ananias visits Saul and restores his sight. Scales fall from Saul's eyes, and he is baptized.

Acts 9:19b–22
In Damascus, Saul proclaims Jesus as the Son of God. The Jews are confused by this because formerly, Saul had "made havoc in Jerusalem" by persecuting the Church.

Acts 9:23–25
The Jews plot to kill Saul. The disciples help him escape.

Acts 9:26–29
Barnabas introduces Saul in Jerusalem. Saul preaches boldly, but some try to kill Saul.

Acts 9:30–31
The brothers send Saul to Tarsus. The churches in Judea, Galilee, and Samaria experience peace and growth as the Christians walk in the Lord and are comforted by the Holy Spirit.

Why was Saul an unlikely choice as God's chosen instrument?
Saul had persecuted the Church and was known as an enemy to Jesus.

How are you an unlikely choice as God's chosen child?
We were once lost in sin, enemies of God.

How is God using you today?
Answers will vary, but would include newness of life through the power of the Holy Spirit in Baptism.

Notice that after the scales fell from Saul's eyes, the very first thing he did was to be baptized.

**Review**

adoption— being received into a family as a child and heir

conversion— changing from one belief or perspective to another; a turning around

62

# INTO the lesson

As a follow-up to the devotion, search for information about the Watts Towers on the Internet, and view together with your class images that show the intricacies and beauty of Rodia's work. The aerial view might also assist students in better understanding the setting of the Watts Towers. Ask students to suggest other examples of works in which something that has been discarded or deemed to be junk has been remade into something useful, such as an object of art and beauty. Comment that today's lesson will focus on how God does something similar every time He brings a person to faith.

# INTO the Word

## An Unlikely Choice

Say, **We're going to learn about Saul, someone who at first was God's enemy but later became God's servant. Let's get started by reading Acts 9:1–2.** Choose someone to read these verses. Say, **Saul was a Pharisee and lived according to Jewish traditions. He fervently believed that salvation was a matter of perfectly keeping the Law of Moses. He, along with other Jewish leaders, persecuted the Church after Pentecost. He was outspoken against the Gospel and personally approved the execution of Stephen.** Reiterate the first few words of verse 1 to underscore the drastic nature of Saul's actions. Say, **Saul was up to no good. He was "still breathing threats and murder against the disciples of the Lord."** Ask someone to retell the setting of the account, as explained in verse 2. Then, point out the timeline under the heading in the Student Book. Say, **You're going to read more about Saul and God's grace for him in Acts 9:1–31. The numbers above each cell in the timeline break the reading into segments. After you've read each part, stop for a minute, and draw the important points of the passages you read. When you have completed the last drawing, you'll have the full story of God's choice of Saul and his early life as God's new child.** This portion can be completed independently or in groups. When work is completed, ask for a retelling of the story using the "popcorn method": choose a student to start the retelling, who then calls on another student to resume the story where he or she left off.

Comment that Jesus appeared to Saul, accusing him of persecuting Him because Saul was persecuting His Church, a group of individual members, the members of Christ's Body, a living organism of which Christ Himself is the head.

Distribute copies of **Reproducible 30**. Use this activity to contrast Saul/Paul before Jesus came into his life with the new Saul/Paul after he became a believer. Stress that Jesus saved all people through His life, death, and resurrection. When we come to faith by the power of the Holy Spirit, we are remade into new people.

## Review

In your review of the concepts of adoption and conversion, stress that when we were converted, we were adopted into God's family with all the rights and privileges of belonging to God, including becoming full heirs of heaven. With complete assurance of our blood-bought heritage, we can nestle into the Father's arms, crying, "Abba!" Romans 8:15 reminds us, "For you did not receive the spirit of slavery to fall back into fear, but you have received the Spirit of adoption as sons, by whom we cry, 'Abba! Father!'"

## A Christian's Biography

Those who have come to faith have experienced a *conversion*, a changing from an old way of life—the natural condition into which we were born—to a new life in Christ Jesus. Draw arrows to indicate whether each of the following statements describes the old way of life according to our natural human condition or the new life we have received by grace through faith in Jesus.

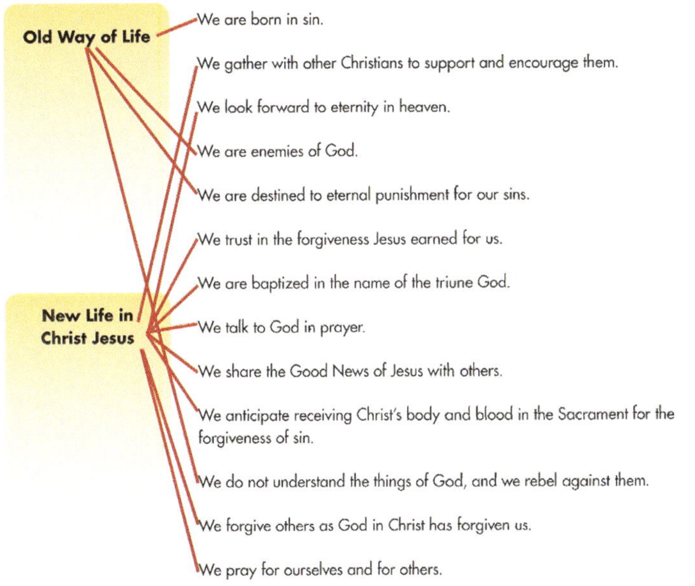


## Newness of Life

Before Baptism, you wore the old self. Now, since Baptism, the new self has come forth because you are wearing Christ. Now, through the Holy Spirit, the new self produces good works. Even though Saul persecuted the Church, many "brothers" were kind to him. Can an enemy become a friend? Yes! By God's grace and with His power, amazing, unlikely things happen!

**REMEMBER**

If Christ is in you, although the body is dead because of sin, the Spirit is life because of righteousness.

Romans 8:10

63

# INTO our lives

## A Christian's Biography

Comment that the story of any Christian coming to faith is, in a way, no less dramatic than the conversion of Saul. Once, each of us was dead in our trespasses and sins. Then God intervened. He shows us our sins (Law) and then shows us the Savior, who has paid the penalty for our sins (Gospel). **Without knowledge of sin, there is no need for a Savior. God's grace confronts and provides a remedy for sin and points to salvation.** Point out the headings and the statements that may be included in a Christian's biography. Once we were held under the Law. Because we were unable to obey God's Law, we stood condemned in our old way of life.

Make sure students recognize that the natural human condition is that of being lost in sin, a situation that is reversed only by God's grace. Washed clean in Baptism, sanctified Christians walk in newness of life. Comment that in the Small Catechism, in his explanation about Baptism titled "What does such baptism with water indicate?" Martin Luther writes, "The Old Adam in us should by daily contrition and repentance be drowned and die with all sins and evil desires, and . . . a new man should daily emerge and arise to live before God in righteousness and purity forever." Even though you are baptized, you are still a sinner. Because this is so, you need to constantly engage in this cycle of repentance, confessing your sins, receiving Christ's forgiveness, and—with the Holy Spirit's aid—amending your sinful ways. Then, renewed in forgiveness, we go forth again as God's new and forgiven people. This process will continue until heaven.

## Newness of Life

Say, **Ephesians 4:22–24 says we are to "Put off your old self, which belongs to your former manner of life and is corrupt through deceitful desires, and be renewed in the spirit of your minds, and to put on the new self, created after the likeness of God in true righteousness and holiness."** Point out the chart in the Student Book section "A Christian's Biography." Ask, **How can you live in newness of life with your family? friends? neighbors?** These are discussion questions, and answers will vary.

Say, **Saul was a well-spoken Jewish leader, well known as an enemy of the Gospel, and well educated in Jewish law. How did God use these qualities that were contradictory to Jesus for the growth of Christianity? How does God use even you and elements of your background and experiences for His purposes?** Accept and affirm responses.

## Remember

Ask, **How has God given you new life in His Spirit? When we were worthless and hopeless because of sin, God's grace sought and found us sinners, retrieving us from the trash heap and bringing us to new life in Jesus.** Once, we were enemies of God; in mercy, He has made us into His children.

### Paul's Biography

As God's chosen instrument, Saul/Paul was an active *evangelist* in the Early Church. However, that wasn't always the case. Construct his biography and learn how he is like *you*. Draw arrows to identify whether the following statements describe the old way of life, according to our natural human condition, or the new life Saul/Paul received by grace through faith in Jesus.

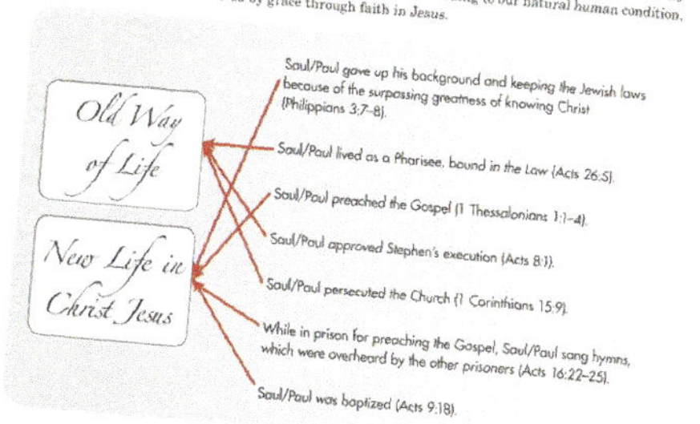


What does God's action in choosing such an outspoken critic and high-profile enemy of the Church as His chosen instrument tell us about God? See 1 Timothy 1:12–17.

**God's abundant mercy and unlimited patience are displayed in calling Saul/Paul, the "blasphemer, persecutor, and insolent opponent" of the Gospel (v. 12). If the grace of Jesus Christ is available to such a person, surely that love is in full supply for all sinners. The conversion of a Jew who was both a leader in the persecution and a knowledgeable Pharisee gained the attention of many for the purposes of the Gospel.**

How does Saul/Paul's biography make a difference for your life?

**Answers will vary, but should include that, just as with Saul/Paul, God's grace is displayed abundantly for each sinner, with a call to repentance and newness of life in Baptism. Encourage students to include personal examples of God at work in their lives.**

# Paul's Biography

As God's chosen instrument, Saul/Paul was an active evangelist in the Early Church. However, that wasn't always the case. Construct his biography and learn how he is like you. Draw arrows to identify whether the following statements describe the old way of life, according to our natural human condition, or the new life Saul/Paul received by grace through faith in Jesus.

*Old Way of Life*

*New Life in Christ Jesus*

Saul/Paul gave up his background and keeping the Jewish laws because of the surpassing greatness of knowing Christ (Philippians 3:7–8).

Saul/Paul lived as a Pharisee, bound in the Law (Acts 26:5).

Saul/Paul preached the Gospel (1 Thessalonians 1:1–4).

Saul/Paul approved Stephen's execution (Acts 8:1).

Saul/Paul persecuted the Church (1 Corinthians 15:9).

While in prison for preaching the Gospel, Saul/Paul sang hymns, which were overheard by the other prisoners (Acts 16:22–25).

Saul/Paul was baptized (Acts 9:18).

What does God's action in choosing such an outspoken critic and high-profile enemy of the Church as His chosen instrument tell us about God? See 1 Timothy 1:12–17.

How does Saul/Paul's biography make a difference for your life?

# UNIT 1—GOD'S GRACE TO HIS PEOPLE IN ANCIENT TIMES

## Multiple Choice

(1) b
(2) c
(3) a
4) d
(5) d
(6) c
(7) d
(8) d
(9) c
(10) d

## Short Answer/ Essay

Answers will vary. Suggested answers are given. (11) Wasting natural resources; polluting the air or water; taking of human lives through abortion or euthanasia. (12) Recycling; using public transportation; volunteering at a soup kitchen. (13) Sinful people were drowned in the flood; our old sinful selves were drowned in Baptism. God saved Noah by grace in the ark; God saves us by grace through the faith given at Baptism. Noah responded to God's grace with a sacrifice; we respond to God's baptismal grace with lives of service. God made a covenant to Noah after the flood; God makes a covenant with us at our Baptism. (14) Moses worked as a shepherd; Jesus is the Good Shepherd. Both Moses and Jesus performed miracles. Moses freed the Israelites from slavery; Jesus set us free from slavery to sin. Moses and Jesus were rejected by some of the people they came to help. Both Moses and Jesus interceded for their people. (Jesus still intercedes.) (15) Sample answer: (a) The Fifth Commandment—You shall not murder; (b) Jen tells her sister, "I hate you"; (c) Jill forgives her brother for reading her private journal. (16) Sin—God is a just God who demands payment for sin. He is also merciful in that He sent His Son to make payment for us. Examples: Adam and Eve, Noah. Faith—God counted the faith of those who trusted Him as righteousness. Examples: Abraham, Noah. Obedience—By God's power, those who trust in Him receive the desire and motivation to serve God in lives of obedience. Examples: Abraham, Noah. Leadership—God's Spirit enables His people to demonstrate bold and courageous acts of leadership. Examples: Abraham, Noah, Moses.

## Authentic Assessment

Provide students with the following directions and criteria. Award points, using the suggested scoring guide.

***Directions:*** In spite of their sinfulness and weakness of faith, God, in His grace and mercy, used the men and women of the Old Testament to accomplish great things. Write a description of a time in your own life or in the life of a close friend or family member when you or he or she experienced firsthand the undeserved love of God at work. Then share your story with your classmates, using one of the following suggestions or an idea of your own.

- Write a short skit and dramatize it for your classmates.
- Create a series of colorful illustrations or a cartoon strip of the event. Share it with your class.
- Write a hymn or song that describes God's grace in your life. Play or sing it for or with your classmates.
- Discuss an idea of your own with your teacher.

## Criteria—Each assignment should include the following components:

- The description is based on personal experience.
- The setting (time and place) is clear.
- The events are clearly described with appropriate details given.
- God's grace is evident.
- The presentation is appropriate for the audience.

## Suggested Scoring Guide

| | |
|---|---|
| 1—Unsatisfactory | Most criteria are missing. |
| 2—Developing | Some criteria are missing or incomplete. |
| 3—Satisfactory | All criteria have been met. |
| 4—Outstanding | All criteria have been met. The project has been thoughtfully designed and implemented. |
| 5—Exceptional | The project shows exceptional creativity, application, and/or development. |

## Multiple Choice

(1) b
(2) c
(3) b
(4) d
(5) a
(6) c
(7) d
(8) b
(9) d
(10) b

## Short Answer/ Essay

Answers will vary. Sample answers are given. (11) They continued to rebel against God and to serve idols. (12) God's love for us and forgiveness in Jesus is a free gift; we do not deserve it. We respond joyfully to God's love by worshiping God and serving others. (13) Specific types of idolatry may vary. Prayers should include confession and thanksgiving. (14) Thank You for forgiving us because of Jesus instead of punishing us as we deserve. Amen. (15) He has brought us to faith, punished Jesus in our place, forgiven our sins, and given us eternal life.

## Authentic Assessment

Provide students with the following directions and criteria. Award points, using the suggested scoring guide included in this section of Unit 1.

***Directions:*** Unit 2 tells the story of God's faithfulness to His people in spite of their unfaithfulness to Him. God used leaders such as Joshua, Gideon, and David and ordinary citizens in opportune positions to announce and carry out His plan for the preservation of His people. The tasks God gave these people were not easy, and they experienced a wide range of human emotions, including discouragement and fear. However, God guided and blessed their actions and efforts so that they could proclaim His message of sin and grace in the foretelling of the Savior who would redeem all people.

*God's people today have the same message to proclaim:* God keeps His promises. There is hope, forgiveness, and eternal life for all who trust in Jesus Christ. You also have been called to share that message with those around you. Keep your role as prophet in mind as you complete one of the following activities alone or within a small group.

- Write a realistic fiction (or nonfiction) story about your experiences as a teenage prophet in the twenty-first century. Illustrate your story.
- Write a skit or play about your experiences as a teenage prophet in the twenty-first century. Perform it for your class or another group.
- Create a videotape, slide presentation, or multimedia presentation about your experiences as a teenage prophet in the twenty-first century.

## Criteria—Each assignment should include the following components:

- The project includes *at least two* events or scenes where the main character is faced with a challenge or must take a stand because of the Word of God. *Note:* Just like Jonah, the character need not always do the right thing the first time.
- The conflict (challenge/problem) is clearly resolved.
- God's promises (to the prophet and the people) are evident.
- The final product is in "best-effort" form.
- For team projects, there is evidence of participation on the part of all team members.

# UNIT 3—JESUS COMES TO SERVE

## Multiple Choice

(1) a
(2) c
(3) b
(4) a
(5) b
(6) a
(7) b
(8) d
(9) a
(10) c

## Short Answer/ Essay

Answers will vary. Sample or suggested answers are given. (11) Through His death and resurrection for us, Jesus gives us forgiveness of sins and heals our broken relationship with God. He gives us the power to forgive others as He has forgiven us and to mend broken relationships with others as well. (12a) My favorite television show comes on while I'm in church. (b) Sunday School is so early that I sometimes would rather sleep in. (13) I can assist the pastor as an acolyte for a worship service. (14) Dear God, thank You for sending Jesus to die for me so I can have forgiveness and eternal life. Please forgive me for keeping this message to myself. Please send Your Holy Spirit to help me to share the Good News with my friends and family. (15) When I think about death and dying, I still think it's sad and a little frightening. I know, however, that Jesus died and rose again for me. When I die and when those I love die trusting in Jesus as their Savior, we will live forever in heaven with Jesus. When I think about what it means to follow Jesus, I know that it won't be easy. I'm sometimes afraid and sometimes want to "follow the leader" just like the disciples. I know that Jesus forgives my sin. I know also that Jesus is with me and always will be. I want to tell others what He has done for them and for me.

## Authentic Assessment

Provide students with the following directions and criteria. Award points, using the suggested scoring guide.

***Directions:*** Complete one of the projects below or use an idea of your own with your teacher's approval. *Answer the question below within your project.*

### *Question*

How did the events of Jesus' life, death, and resurrection show that Jesus was the promised Messiah, true God and true man?

### *Project Ideas*

1. Write journal entries (one per lesson) from the point of view of a disciple who was with Jesus during His ministry. Include a description of what that disciple was thinking and feeling as well as what he observed.
2. Write a series of at least five short skit scenes illustrating one of Jesus' teachings or miracles. Include the thoughts and feelings of the disciples as well as what they said. You can use the dramatic technique of an *aside* (where one character turns to talk directly to the audience) to express the disciples' thoughts and feelings.

## Criteria—Each assignment should include the following components:

- Using the events of Jesus' life and ministry, the project illustrates that Jesus is the Messiah, true God and true man.
- The project describes the human feelings of the disciples as they experienced Jesus teachings or miracles.
- The project is the original work of the student.
- The events are clearly described with appropriate details given.
- God's grace is evident.
- The presentation is appropriate for the audience.

## Suggested Scoring Guide

| | |
|---|---|
| 1—Unsatisfactory | Most criteria are missing. |
| 2—Developing | Some criteria are missing or incomplete. |
| 3—Satisfactory | All criteria have been met. |
| 4—Outstanding | All criteria have been met. The project has been thoughtfully designed and implemented. |
| 5—Exceptional | The project shows exceptional creativity, application, and development. |

# UNIT 4—JESUS SAVES—GOOD NEWS TO SHARE

## Multiple Choice

(1) d
(2) c
(3) b
(4) c
(5) d
(6) d
(7) c
(8) b
(9) b
(10) c

## Short Answer/ Essay

(11) The Holy Spirit called me to faith at Baptism (or through hearing/reading the Word of God), and He strengthens me in that faith each time I hear or study God's Word and each time I receive Christ's body and blood in Holy Communion. (12) The Holy Spirit gives us power and confidence to tell others about Jesus. He helps us to forgive one another and live lives of service to God and others. (13) Two sample answers are given: Philip shared Jesus with an Ethiopian man, who believed and was baptized. God used Saul/Paul, who had persecuted Christians, to be His missionary. (14) Dear Jesus, forgive me for keeping quiet about what You have done for me and the whole world. Please send the Holy Spirit to make me strong in my faith and eager to tell others about Your love and forgiveness. (15) Answers will vary but should include a personal anecdote describing a situation or event where the opportunity to share the Gospel was present.

## Authentic Assessment

Provide students with the following directions and criteria. Award points, using the suggested scoring guide.

***Directions:*** Using one of the project ideas below or another of your own with your teacher's approval, *compare and contrast* the Early Christian Church with the Church of today. Show at least three ways that they are the same and at least three ways that they are different. The word list may help you to get started.

### *Project Ideas*

1. Write an essay titled "The Christian Church: The Early Years and Today."
2. Draw a series of cartoons depicting the Early Christian Church and the Church of today.
3. Make a mural showing the Church during the time of the apostles and the Church today, or create two murals, one for each time period.

### *Word List*

apostles
Holy Spirit
persecution
God's Word
growth
healing
miracles
lying
sin
fellowship
conversion
obstacles
teamwork
places
false gods
controversies
missionaries
transformation
government leaders
methods of communication

## Criteria—Each assignment should include the following components:

- The project contains at least three similarities and at least three differences between the Early Christian Church and the Church of today.
- The events and concepts portrayed are accurate according to the Bible, history, and current events.
- The project is the original work of the student.

## Suggested Scoring Guide

| | |
|---|---|
| 1—Unsatisfactory | Most criteria are missing. |
| 2—Developing | Some criteria are missing or incomplete. |
| 3—Satisfactory | All criteria have been met. |
| 4—Outstanding | All criteria have been met. The project has been thoughtfully designed and implemented. |
| 5—Exceptional | The project shows exceptional creativity, application, and development. |

*To the teacher:* The mural project may work best as a small-group or whole-class activity. If the project is done as a group, the preceding criteria may also apply.

Name ______________________________



# UNIT 1—GOD'S GRACE TO HIS PEOPLE IN ANCIENT TIMES

## Multiple Choice

***Directions:*** Circle the letter of the best answer for each question.

1. Which of the following statements is *not* correct?
   a. God created the earth in six days and continues to preserve it.
   b. Because God made the earth for humans, we have the right to use it as we please.
   c. God's perfect earth has been corrupted and damaged by sin.
   d. Sin hurts plants and animals, as well as humans.

2. In tempting Eve to commit the first sin, Satan led Eve to doubt
   a. Adam.
   b. creation.
   c. God.
   d. herself.

3. When Satan deceived Adam and Eve, he used this lie:
   a. "You will not surely die."
   b. "You will become God."
   c. "You will see God."
   d. All of the above are correct.

4. The account of the flood in Genesis teaches us
   a. that God hates sin, including violence.
   b. that God is a just God.
   c. that God is a merciful God.
   d. All of the above are true.

5. God promised Abram that his offspring would be as numerous as the
   a. stones.
   b. lilies.
   c. sparrows.
   d. stars.

6. God credited Abraham with righteousness because of his
   a. children.
   b. wealth.
   c. faith.
   d. works.

7. The word *exodus* refers most directly to
   a. the shedding of blood.
   b. the assembling of a crowd or large group.
   c. the raising of hands by a leader.
   d. the act of leaving or departing.

8. God gave us His Law—the Ten Commandments—to serve as
   a. rod, staff, and gate.
   b. key, mirror, and path.
   c. gate, key, and path.
   d. mirror, curb, and guide.

9. Which commandment includes the word *testimony*?
   a. Seventh
   b. Third
   c. Eighth
   d. Tenth

10. Moses made a pole and placed a serpent on it
    a. for the people to worship.
    b. to remind the people of their sin.
    c. as a warning against committing evil.
    d. in obedience to God.

Name ______________________________

# Short Answer/Essay

***Directions:*** Answer each question as completely as possible. Some questions have more than one part.

11. Describe two specific ways that humans, by their sinfulness, have harmed God's perfect creation. (2 points)

12. Explain two ways that Christians can preserve and protect God's creation. (2 points)

13. Compare Baptism to the flood. Give at least two ways that they are similar. (2 points)

14. In what ways was Moses' work like the work of Jesus? Describe at least two ways that their work was alike. (2 points)

15. Choose one of the Ten Commandments. Write (a) the commandment; (b) a modern-day example of how that commandment is broken; and (c) an example of how, with the power of the Holy Spirit, the commandment is kept. (3 points)

16. After studying the Bible lessons in this unit, how would you describe God's attitude toward each of the following ideas? Give at least one example from the unit to support each answer. (4 points)

Sin:

Example:

Faith:

Example:

Obedience:

Example:

Leadership:

Example:

Name ____________________________________



# UNIT 2—GOD BLESSES A NATION

## Multiple Choice

***Directions:*** Circle the letter in front of the word or phrase that best completes each statement.

1. Which of the following is *not* a true statement about Joshua?
   a. He led the people of Israel across the Jordan River.
   b. He was the son of Moses.
   c. He directed the people in the building of a monument made of stones.
   d. He listened to the report of the spies whom Rahab had hidden.

2. After hearing the report about Canaan from the twelve spies, the people wanted to stone
   a. the Canaanite hostages.
   b. Aaron.
   c. Joshua and Caleb.
   d. Rahab.

3. Rahab
   a. returned with the spies.
   b. hid the spies on her roof.
   c. brought the spies to the Jordan River.
   d. held a banquet to honor the spies.

4. Gideon won the battle of Midian because
   a. of the large number of soldiers he recruited for battle.
   b. he asked God for a sign.
   c. he learned effective leadership strategies as he grew up in a prominent family.
   d. the Spirit of God came upon him.

5. David was a successful king because
   a. David was blessed by God.
   b. David was obedient to God.
   c. David was an ancestor of the Messiah.
   d. David was a strong warrior.

6. To show his love, honor, and thankfulness toward God, Solomon
   a. fought many battles.
   b. married many women.
   c. built a temple.
   d. All of the above are correct.

7. When Solomon turned from the true God to worship his wives' gods,
   a. God divided the kingdom and took Israel away from Solomon's son.
   b. God wanted Solomon to repent and return to Him.
   c. God was working through historical events.
   d. All of the above are correct.

8. Why did God rescue the captives from Israel?
   a. To reward them for their obedience
   b. To preserve them as His people
   c. Both A and B are correct
   d. Neither A nor B is correct

9. God allowed Jerusalem to be destroyed and His people led into captivity because ______ were unfaithful to God.
   a. the kings
   b. the scribes and religious leaders
   c. the people
   d. all of the above

10. God allowed the destruction of Jerusalem and captivity in Babylon
    a. because He wanted to wipe out His sinful people.
    b. because He wanted His people to repent of their sin and return to Him.
    c. Both answers are correct.
    d. Neither answer is correct.

Name ________________________________________

# Short Answer/Essay

***Directions:*** Answer each question as completely as possible. Some questions have more than one part. (2 points each)

11. How did Jeroboam and the kings of Israel and Judah carry on Solomon's legacy?

12. Even though they were sinful, God blessed David and Solomon—and all people—through their descendant Jesus. What does this mean for your life?

13. Today's idols are often not made of stone or metal. Think about your own life. What gets in the ways of worshiping the true God? Write a short prayer or song of confession. Conclude with words of thanksgiving for the forgiveness that is yours in Jesus.

14. God used the Assyrians to punish Israel for its rebellion. However, God also showed patience, love, and mercy to them and to us through the promised Savior. Write a sentence prayer thanking God for this gift.

15. God showed mercy to the people of Judah. How has He shown mercy to you?

Name ________________________________



# UNIT 3—JESUS COMES TO SERVE

## Multiple Choice

***Directions:*** Circle the letter in front of the answer that best completes each statement. Each question is worth one point.

1. The angel of the Lord announced the birth of Jesus to the shepherds beginning with the words
   a. "Fear not."
   b. "Peace be to you."
   c. "Blessed are you,"
   d. "The Lord be with you."

2. A disciple can best be thought of as one who
   a. preaches.
   b. teaches.
   c. learns.
   d. leads.

3. In the parable Jesus told about the sower, there are four different types of
   a. seeds.
   b. soil.
   c. seasons.
   d. sheaves.

4. Among the following parables of the Kingdom, the parable of the weeds compares most closely with the parable of the
   a. net.
   b. pearl.
   c. leaven.
   d. treasure.

5. When Jesus called Simon, Andrew, James, and John to follow and serve Him, they
   a. made arrangements for their replacements on the fishing boats.
   b. immediately followed Jesus.
   c. asked Jesus about the specific requirements of the new job.
   d. sought the advice of others before making a decision.

6. When Jesus performed the miracle of the abundant catch of fish, He got into Peter's boat and began to
   a. teach the people.
   b. admonish the disciples.
   c. extend the nets.
   d. rebuke Peter.

7. Samaria was
   a. a region of Palestine located north of Galilee.
   b. inhabited by people who were a mixture of cultures and religions.
   c. the location in which Jerusalem and Bethany could be found.
   d. home to many fishermen, including Peter, James, and John.

8. Jewish people in New Testament times tended to look down upon
   a. Levites.
   b. priests.
   c. merchants.
   d. Samaritans.

9. In the parable of the lost son, the father welcomes the son back because
   a. he loves him.
   b. he has no other choice.
   c. he needs his help.
   d. he believes his son has changed.

10. Which of the following best describes the attitude of the older brother in the parable of the lost son?
    a. Joyful
    b. Fearful
    c. Resentful
    d. Hopeful

Name ________________________________

# Short Answer/Essay

***Directions:*** Answer each question as completely as possible. Some questions may have more than one part. (2 points each)

11. Explain how Jesus heals human relationships as well as the relationship between God and humans.

12. List at least two specific factors or temptations that might keep you from following and serving Jesus.

13. Give an example of a specific way that you can serve Jesus in your congregation or community.

14. Write a prayer asking for God's forgiveness and help as you share His Gospel with others.

15. Think about what you have read about Jesus—His life, death, and resurrection. Now consider what that Gospel message means to you personally. Then finish each of the sentence starters below.

*When I think about death and dying . . .*

*When I think about what it means to follow Jesus . . .*

Name ________________________________________



# UNIT 4—JESUS SAVES—GOOD NEWS TO SHARE

## Multiple Choice

***Directions:*** Circle the letter in front of the word or phrase that best completes each statement. Each question is worth one point.

1. When Jesus gave His disciples instructions in preparation for the Passover meal, He referred to Himself as the
   a. Savior.
   b. Messiah.
   c. Son of God.
   d. Teacher.

2. In the Lord's Supper, Jesus gives us
   a. bread and wine only.
   b. His true body and blood only.
   c. His body and blood with the bread and wine.
   d. another sacrifice for our sins.

3. The crime of which the Jewish leaders accused Jesus was
   a. murder.
   b. blasphemy.
   c. insurrection.
   d. tyranny.

4. While on the cross, Jesus ________ His enemies.
   a. reprimanded
   b. encouraged
   c. forgave
   d. cursed

5. Right before Jesus ascended into heaven, He told the disciples that they would be His
   a. supporters.
   b. soldiers.
   c. guides.
   d. witnesses.

6. On the first Pentecost, after Jesus ascended into heaven,
   a. the Holy Spirit appeared to the disciples in a loud wind and tongues of fire.
   b. the apostles preached the Gospel in languages that they had never learned.
   c. many people heard God's Word in their own language, believed in Jesus, and were saved.
   d. All of the above.

7. At Pentecost, ______ preached to the multitude.
   a. James
   b. John
   c. Peter
   d. Andrew

8. After Philip told him about the meaning of a section of Isaiah, the Ethiopian asked Philip to
   a. go with him to Ethiopia.
   b. baptize him.
   c. give him the Lord's Supper.
   d. hear his confession.

9. After Jesus appeared to him, Saul
   a. remained in Jerusalem.
   b. became blind for three days.
   c. visited Ananias in prison.
   d. pretended to place Barnabas under arrest.

10. The phrase that best describes Paul is
    a. a lifelong Christian hater.
    b. a born missionary.
    c. a changed man.
    d. a self-made man.

Name ________________________________

# Short Answer/Essay

***Directions:*** Answer each question as completely as possible. Some questions may have more than one part. (2 points each)

11. Describe the Means of Grace through which the Holy Spirit called you to faith in Jesus and strengthens you in that faith.

12. How does the Holy Spirit use you and other believers to build up Christ's Church?

13. God wants us to witness to everyone about Jesus, including those whose skin color, language, or background is different from our own. Describe in your own words a Bible story from this unit that shows that God's gifts of forgiveness and eternal life in Jesus are for all people.

14. Write a prayer asking for God's help as you tell your friends, neighbors, family, and others what Jesus has done for them.

15. God provided many opportunities for witnessing through the circumstances of Paul's life. Describe a time when God used an event or a situation in your life as an opportunity for you to share the Gospel. Or write about a time when God used an event or a situation in your life as an opportunity for someone else to share the Gospel with you.

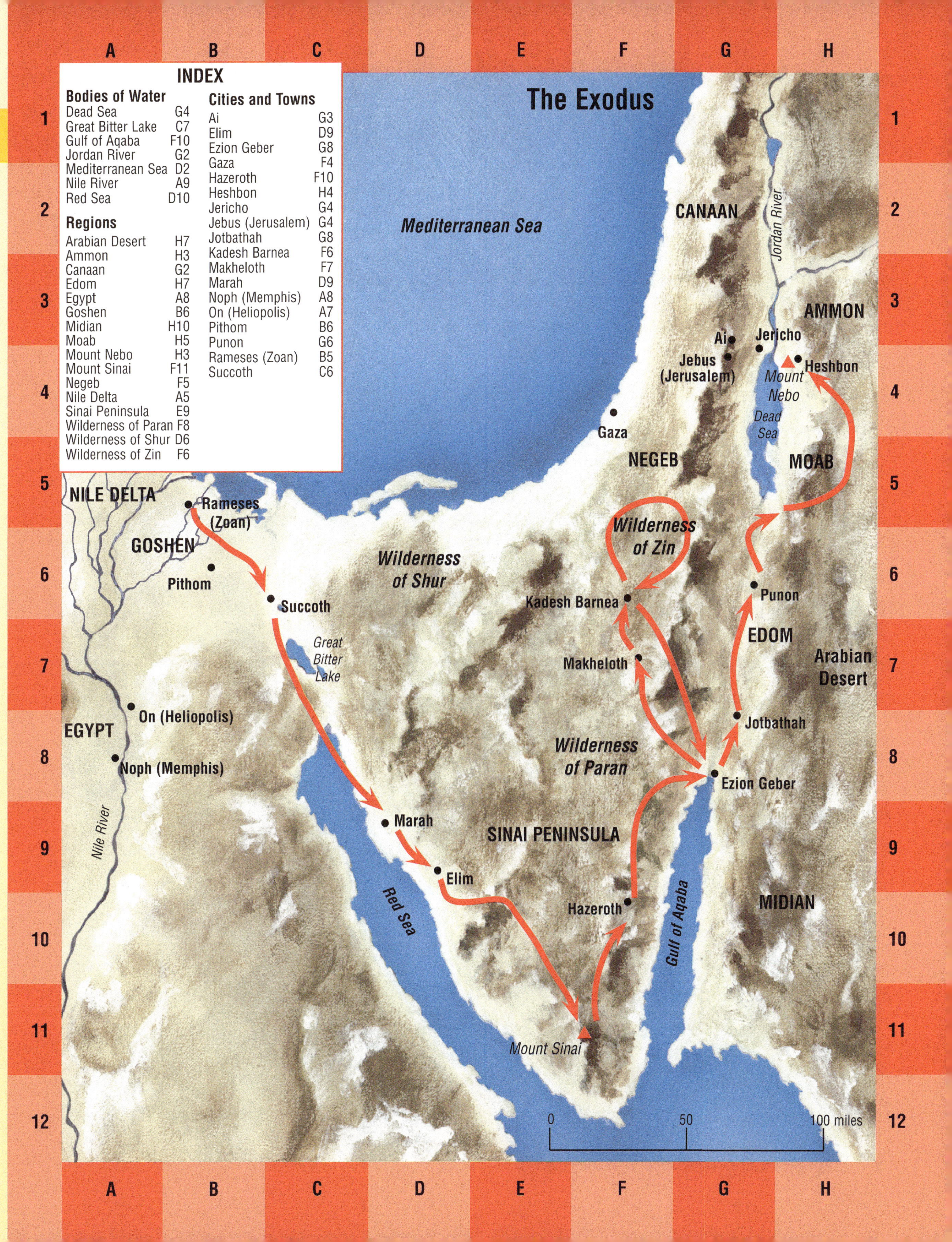
The Exodus
INDEX
Bodies of Water
Dead Sea G4
Great Bitter Lake C7
Gulf of Aqaba F10
Jordan River G2
Mediterranean Sea D2
Nile River A9
Red Sea D10
Regions
Arabian Desert H7
Ammon H3
Canaan G2
Edom H7
Egypt A8
Goshen B6
Midian H10
Moab H5
Mount Nebo H3
Mount Sinai F11
Negeb F5
Nile Delta A5
Sinai Peninsula E9
Wilderness of Paran F8
Wilderness of Shur D6
Wilderness of Zin F6
Cities and Towns
Ai G3
Elim D9
Ezion Geber G8
Gaza F4
Hazeroth F10
Heshbon H4
Jericho G4
Jebus (Jerusalem) G4
Jotbathah G8
Kadesh Barnea F6
Makheloth F7
Marah D9
Noph (Memphis) A8
On (Heliopolis) A7
Pithom B6
Punon G6
Rameses (Zoan) B5
Succoth C6
A B C D E F G H
1 2 3 4 5 6 7 8 9 10 11 12
Mediterranean Sea
CANAAN
Jordan River
AMMON
Ai
Jericho
Jebus (Jerusalem)
Heshbon
Mount Nebo
Dead Sea
Gaza
NEGEB
MOAB
NILE DELTA
Rameses (Zoan)
GOSHEN
Pithom
Succoth
Wilderness of Shur
Wilderness of Zin
Kadesh Barnea
Punon
EDOM
Great Bitter Lake
Makheloth
Arabian Desert
On (Heliopolis)
EGYPT
Jotbathah
Noph (Memphis)
Wilderness of Paran
Ezion Geber
Marah
SINAI PENINSULA
Nile River
Elim
Red Sea
Hazeroth
Gulf of Aqaba
MIDIAN
Mount Sinai
0 50 100 miles

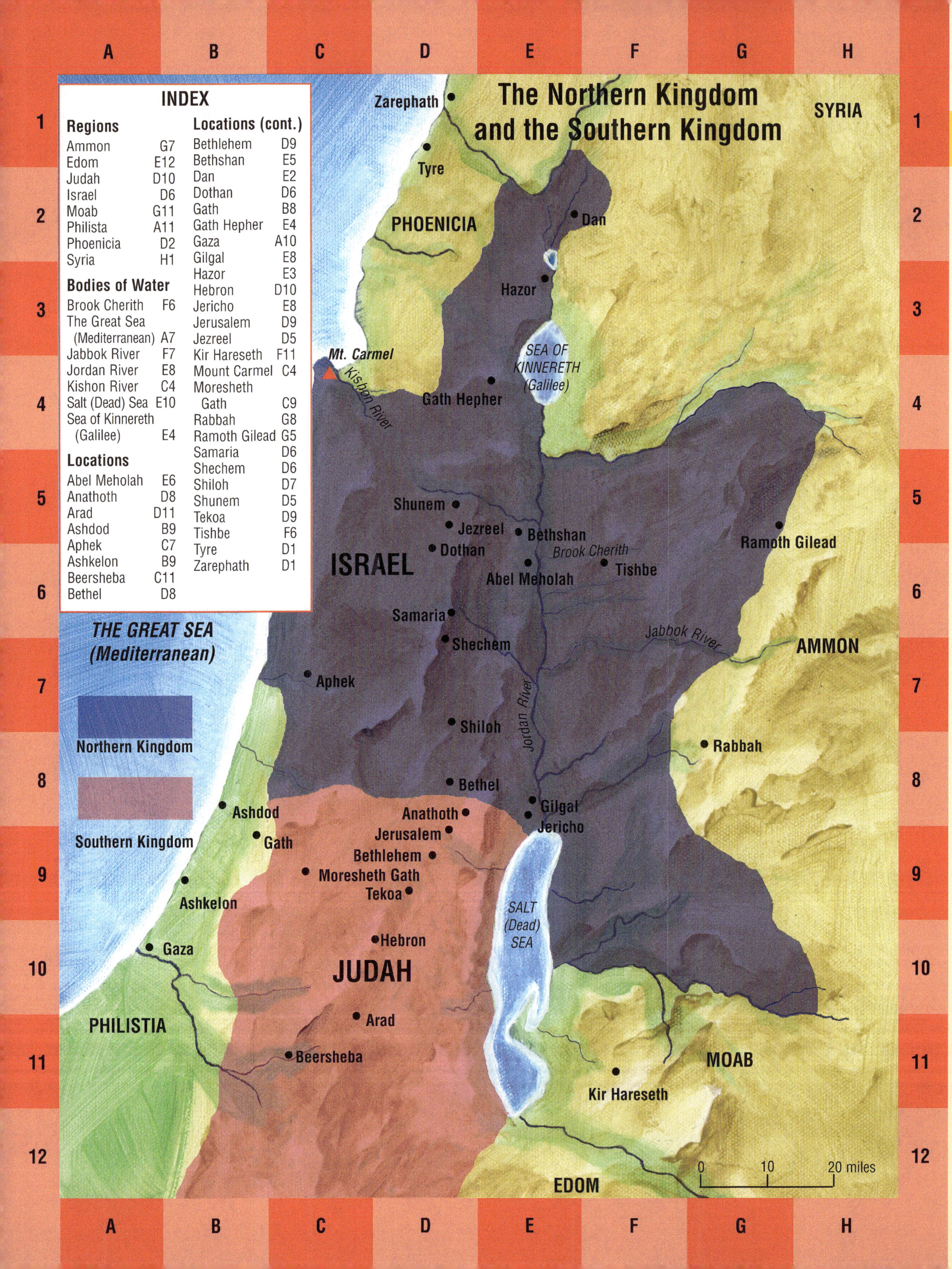
The Northern Kingdom and the Southern Kingdom
INDEX
Regions
Ammon G7
Edom E12
Judah D10
Israel D6
Moab G11
Philista A11
Phoenicia D2
Syria H1
Bodies of Water
Brook Cherith F6
The Great Sea (Mediterranean) A7
Jabbok River F7
Jordan River E8
Kishon River C4
Salt (Dead) Sea E10
Sea of Kinnereth (Galilee) E4
Locations
Abel Meholah E6
Anathoth D8
Arad D11
Ashdod B9
Aphek C7
Ashkelon B9
Beersheba C11
Bethel D8
Locations (cont.)
Bethlehem D9
Bethshan E5
Dan E2
Dothan D6
Gath B8
Gath Hepher E4
Gaza A10
Gilgal E8
Hazor E3
Hebron D10
Jericho E8
Jerusalem D9
Jezreel D5
Kir Hareseth F11
Mount Carmel C4
Moresheth Gath C9
Rabbah G8
Ramoth Gilead G5
Samaria D6
Shechem D6
Shiloh D7
Shunem D5
Tekoa D9
Tishbe F6
Tyre D1
Zarephath D1
A B C D E F G H
1 2 3 4 5 6 7 8 9 10 11 12
SYRIA
Zarephath
Tyre
PHOENICIA
Dan
Hazor
Mt. Carmel
Kishon River
SEA OF KINNERETH (Galilee)
Gath Hepher
Shunem
Jezreel
Bethshan
Dothan
Brook Cherith
Ramoth Gilead
ISRAEL
Abel Meholah
Tishbe
Samaria
Shechem
Jabbok River
AMMON
THE GREAT SEA (Mediterranean)
Aphek
Shiloh
Jordan River
Northern Kingdom
Rabbah
Bethel
Ashdod
Gilgal
Anathoth
Jericho
Southern Kingdom
Jerusalem
Gath
Bethlehem
Moresheth Gath
Ashkelon
Tekoa
SALT (Dead) SEA
Hebron
Gaza
JUDAH
PHILISTIA
Arad
Beersheba
MOAB
Kir Hareseth
0 10 20 miles
EDOM

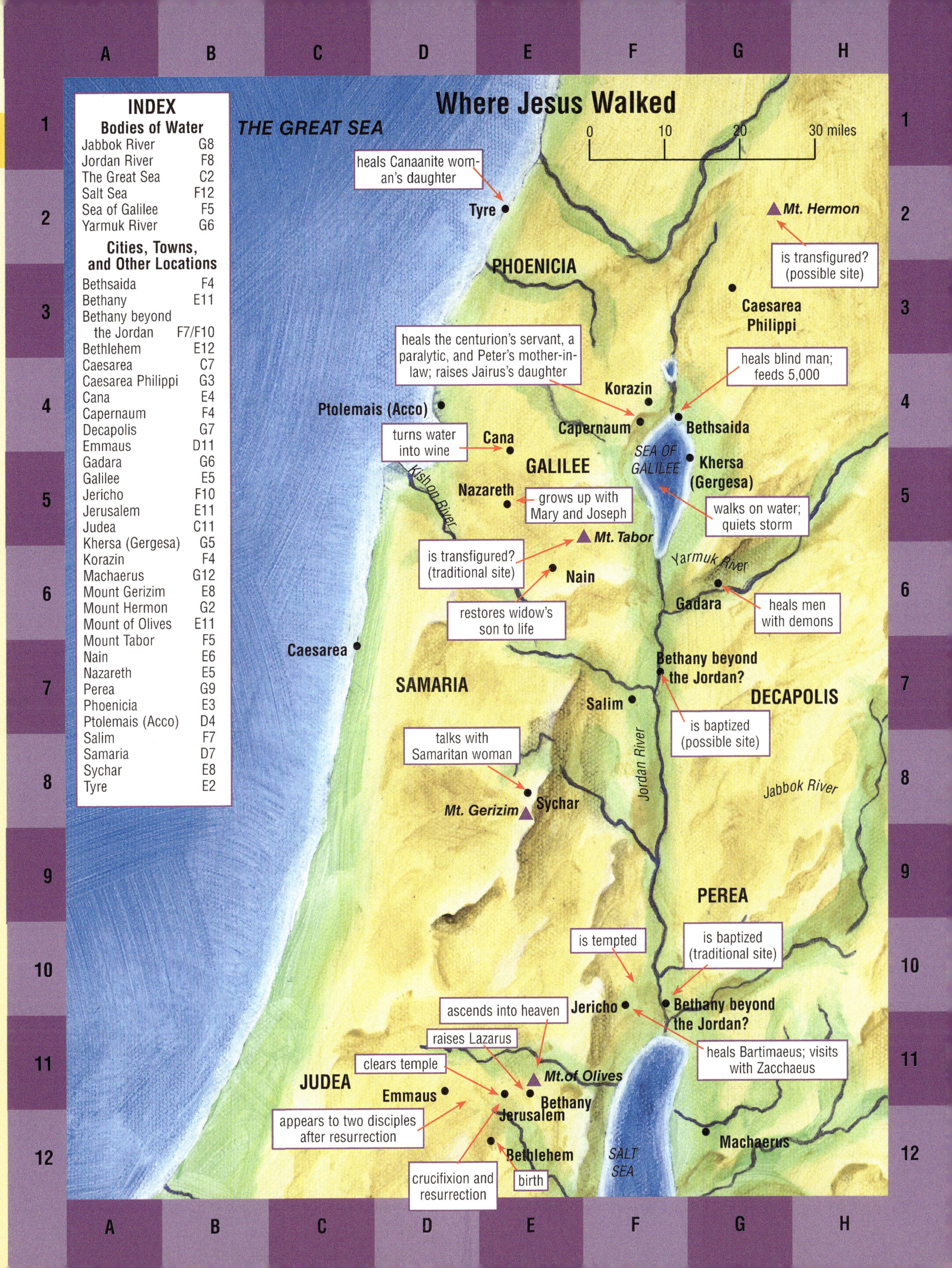
Where Jesus Walked
INDEX
Bodies of Water
Jabbok River G8
Jordan River F8
The Great Sea C2
Salt Sea F12
Sea of Galilee F5
Yarmuk River G6
Cities, Towns, and Other Locations
Bethsaida F4
Bethany E11
Bethany beyond the Jordan F7/F10
Bethlehem E12
Caesarea C7
Caesarea Philippi G3
Cana E4
Capernaum F4
Decapolis G7
Emmaus D11
Gadara G6
Galilee E5
Jericho F10
Jerusalem E11
Judea C11
Khersa (Gergesa) G5
Korazin F4
Machaerus G12
Mount Gerizim E8
Mount Hermon G2
Mount of Olives E11
Mount Tabor F5
Nain E6
Nazareth E5
Perea G9
Phoenicia E3
Ptolemais (Acco) D4
Salim F7
Samaria D7
Sychar E8
Tyre E2
THE GREAT SEA
0 10 20 30 miles
heals Canaanite woman's daughter
Tyre
Mt. Hermon
is transfigured? (possible site)
PHOENICIA
Caesarea Philippi
heals the centurion's servant, a paralytic, and Peter's mother-in-law; raises Jairus's daughter
heals blind man; feeds 5,000
Korazin
Ptolemais (Acco)
Capernaum
Bethsaida
turns water into wine
Cana
GALILEE
SEA OF GALILEE
Khersa (Gergesa)
Nazareth
grows up with Mary and Joseph
walks on water; quiets storm
Kishon River
Mt. Tabor
is transfigured? (traditional site)
Yarmuk River
Nain
Gadara
heals men with demons
restores widow's son to life
Caesarea
Bethany beyond the Jordan?
SAMARIA
Salim
DECAPOLIS
is baptized (possible site)
talks with Samaritan woman
Jordan River
Jabbok River
Sychar
Mt. Gerizim
PEREA
is tempted
is baptized (traditional site)
ascends into heaven
Jericho
Bethany beyond the Jordan?
raises Lazarus
heals Bartimaeus; visits with Zacchaeus
clears temple
Mt. of Olives
JUDEA
Emmaus
Bethany
Jerusalem
appears to two disciples after resurrection
Machaerus
Bethlehem
SALT SEA
crucifixion and resurrection
birth

# The World of First Century Christianity

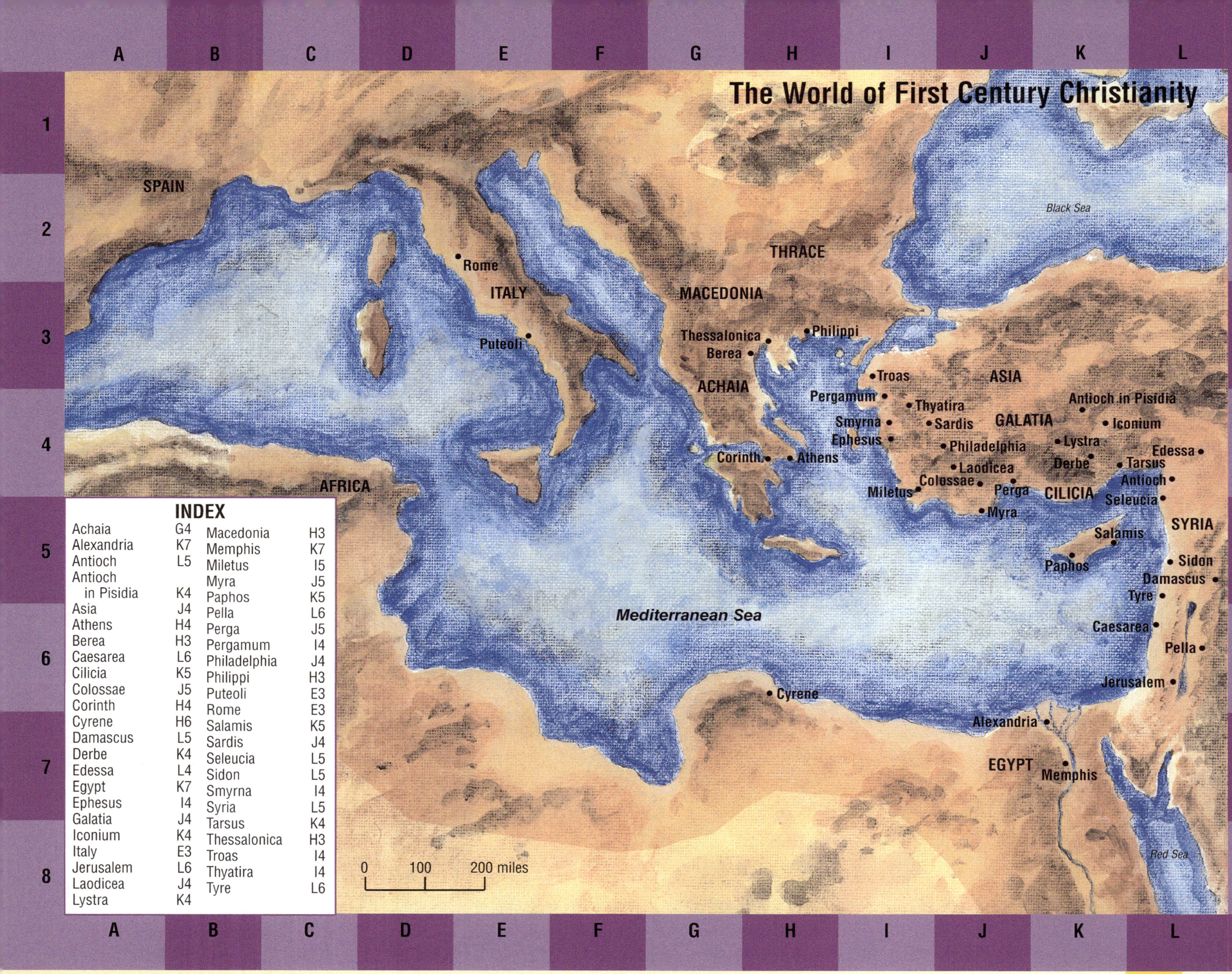


## INDEX

| | | | |
|---|---|---|---|
| Achaia | G4 | Macedonia | H3 |
| Alexandria | K7 | Memphis | K7 |
| Antioch | L5 | Miletus | I5 |
| Antioch in Pisidia | K4 | Myra | J5 |
| Asia | J4 | Paphos | K5 |
| Athens | H4 | Pella | L6 |
| Berea | H3 | Perga | J5 |
| Caesarea | L6 | Pergamum | I4 |
| Cilicia | K5 | Philadelphia | J4 |
| Colossae | J5 | Philippi | H3 |
| Corinth | H4 | Puteoli | E3 |
| Cyrene | H6 | Rome | E3 |
| Damascus | L5 | Salamis | K5 |
| Derbe | K4 | Sardis | J4 |
| Edessa | L4 | Seleucia | L5 |
| Egypt | K7 | Sidon | L5 |
| Ephesus | I4 | Smyrna | I4 |
| Galatia | J4 | Syria | L5 |
| Iconium | K4 | Tarsus | K4 |
| Italy | E3 | Thessalonica | H3 |
| Jerusalem | L6 | Troas | I4 |
| Laodicea | J4 | Thyatira | I4 |
| Lystra | K4 | Tyre | L6 |

# Glossary

## A

**absolution**—a remission (forgiveness) of sins

**adoption**—act or state of being received into a family as a child and heir

**adoration**—praising God for His qualities and His acts of grace and goodness

**adultery**—sexual relations between a married person and someone not his or her spouse; lust or any sexual act against God's will

**agnostic**—someone who argues we can't know whether or not God exists

**alliance**—a bond or union between individuals, groups, or states

**alms**—charitable donations; people who could not work lived off this; a lame man received the ability to walk instead of this

**anoint**—to apply oil in a sacred rite; to set aside for an office or sacred calling

**apologist**—someone who argues in defense of God or a person or cause

**apostasy**—the abandoning of previously held beliefs

**ark of the covenant**—special vault containing the Ten Commandments

**ark**—name for vessel in which Noah and his family as well as Moses were saved

**Artemis**—a Greek goddess; Ephesus was considered the central city for her worship

**Asherah**—Canaanite and Phoenician goddess associated with sexual love and fertility

**atheist**—someone who believes there is no God

**authorities**—those who have the right to tell us what to do and the responsibility to watch over us

## B

**Baal**—Canaanite and Phoenician local idol, sometimes cast in the form of a bull

**Baptism**—application of water by God's command and combined with God's Word

**betray**—to disappoint the hope or expectations of; to be disloyal to

**betrothal**—a contract to marry, usually arranged by the families of the bride and groom

**bind**—to secure or tie up

**birthright**—double portion of the inheritance, leadership of the family, and the blessing to carry on the covenant promise

**blasphemy**—claiming to be God; or showing irreverence toward God

**blessing**—a gift from God

**bullying**—taunting or humiliating those who are weak

## C

**call (or "a calling")**—summons; a vocation or an inclination

**called**—invited or summoned with a view to service

**captivity**—state of being confined or imprisoned

**censer**—an incense burner

**cherubim**—angels; especially in Old Testament, they appear with wings spread over the ark of the covenant

**Christ**—the Anointed One

**Christian**—literally, "little Christ," or someone belonging to or professing faith in Christ

**circumcision**—act performed on males; originally done to indicate identity as a follower of the true God

**command**—an order expected to be followed

**commitment**—dedication to a person or cause

**Communion**—another name for the Sacrament of the Altar; a joining or coming together

**conception**—the moment at which life begins

**concubine**—a woman to whom a man is legally bound in a form of marriage

**confess**—to acknowledge, reveal, or make known

**confession**—an acknowledgment of truth before God or others

**confirmation**—a rite designed to help a person identify with the life and mission of the Church; also an affirmation or verification

**contrition**—recognition of one's sin and the realization of one's inability to fix his or her brokenness

**conversion**—changing from one belief or perspective to another; a turning around

**covenant**—a binding promise or agreement

**covet**—a wrong and unhealthy desire to be, or to possess the things of, another

**cursed**—held under affliction

## D

**deliver**—to rescue or set free

**devoted**—designated

**disciple**—a student who learns from a master or teacher; a follower of Jesus

**divination**—to foretell the future through omens, oracles, or supernatural powers

**Divine Service**—weekly service that includes the celebration of the Lord's Supper

## E

**entice**—to coax or nudge away

**entreaty**—a plea or earnest request

**ephod**—an outer apron-like garment made of linen worn by Jewish priests in ancient times

**eternal death**—the unending separation from God of an unbelieving person's soul

**evolution**—theory that living things evolve from other living things

**exile**—a period of forced absence from one's country or home

**exodus**—a leaving or departing

**exorcist**—one who casts out demons

## F

**faith**—trust or reliance on God and His promises or on a person or concept

**faithful**—steadfast; loyal; resolute to a person or cause

**faithfulness**—quality of remaining true to a commitment

**famine**—duration of time in which little or no food grows over a large area

**festival**—time of celebration or special observances; the Life of Christ portion of the Church Year

**fisher of men**—someone who knows Jesus' love and wants others to know it too

**foreshadow**—to prefigure or indicate beforehand

**fornication**—voluntary sexual relationship outside of marriage

**funeral**—an observance or religious service held when someone has died

## G

**genealogy**—an account or list of one's ancestors

**Gospel**—the Good News that God sent Jesus to forgive and rescue us through His life, death, and resurrection

**grace**—to receive blessing not merited, earned, or deserved

**guilt**—feeling of responsibility for wrongs committed

## H

**heart**—organ responsible for circulating blood through the body; true self; the part of us that only God knows

**holy matrimony**—marriage; the union of a man and woman as husband and wife

**homage**—an expression of high regard or respect

**honor**—to highly regard in thought, speech, and action

**hosanna**—a Hebrew word meaning "save us now"

**humility**—state of lowliness; opposite of being proud or haughty

**hymn**—congregational song of prayer or praise, usually in stanza form

**hymnody**—the body of spiritual songs used in the Christian Church

## I

**idol**—an object of devotion other than God

**idolatry**—practice of worshiping a false god

**implore**—to call or pray for earnestly

**impudent**—disrespectful, rude words

**incarnation**—the act of taking on flesh

**inheritance**—possessions passed down to recipients by those who have gone before them

**iniquity**—sin and wickedness

**intercession**—petition or prayer offered on behalf of another

## J

**jealous**—unwilling to accept rivalry or unfaithfulness

**Jews**—those descended from Abraham through the line of Isaac and Jacob

**judge**—Old Testament deliverer; leader or official responsible for justice

**justice**—judgment involved in determining rights, rewards, and punishments

**justification**—righteousness that is ours in Christ Jesus; also, support for a position or condition

## K

**kinsman-redeemer**—a close relative who avenged wrongful deaths, helped poor family members claim their inheritances, and married the widow of a dead male relative so she would be protected and cared for

**knowledge**—an intellectual grasp of the facts; an understanding of a particular subject

## L

**Law**—God's decrees about how to live a holy life; it shows us our sin

**leadership**—effective guiding of others to achieve a goal

**Levite**—worker in the temple

**liturgical**—relating to an established procedure for worship

**loose**—to release or free (as in, to untie)

## M

**Magnificat**—Latin for "magnify, praise"—the song of Mary

**manna**—bread miraculously provided by God for His people in the wilderness

**marriage**—a legally binding commitment uniting a man and woman

**martyr**—witness; one killed for his or her beliefs, including faith in Christ

**Means of Grace**—the Word (Gospel) and the Sacraments (Baptism and Lord's Supper)

**meditate**—think carefully about

**mediums**—persons claiming to be able to bridge communication between earthly and spiritual realms

**mercy**—not getting the punishment that is deserved; the feeling that motivates compassion

**Messiah**—the promised Savior

**Midianites**—a group of people who lived south and east of Canaan

**missionary**—a person who takes up the task of sharing the truth, often in foreign lands

## N

**natural selection**—theory that states weaker species die out, while stronger species evolve into stronger, more complex species

**Nazirite**—a person dedicated to God for life or for a period of time during which he or she refrained from wine, grapes, and raisins, never cut his or her hair, and avoided being around dead bodies—even when family members died; Nazirites were signs to all Israel that they were called to stand out as God's people, witnessing God's love to the nations around them

**necromancers**—those who conjure up spirits of the dead to foretell the future or do supernatural acts

**neighbor**—any and every person

**nonfestival**—time outside of the celebration period; the Life of the Church portion of the Church Year

## O

**obedience**—act of fulfilling the will of another

**obstacle**—something that blocks your way or hinders your progress

**old Adam**—the corrupt and evil nature we inherit because of Adam's fall into sin

**omen**—occurrence used to predict or foretell future events

**omer**—a measure of about a quart or a liter

**omnipotent**—all powerful

**only-begotten son**—sole biological son

**oppressing**—an unfair use of power

**outward appearance**—what other people can see when they look at us and what they think about us based on what they see

## P

**parable**—story used to make a spiritual point or to teach a spiritual truth

**Passover**—annual festival held in remembrance of God's deliverance in Egypt when the angel of death spared the firstborn of those whose houses were marked with the blood of a lamb

**peace**—a calmness and sense of being at rest

**persecution**—subjecting others to cruelty because of their beliefs or identity

**Philistines**—a group of people living in Canaan during the time of the judges and kings; enemies of God's people

**pillar**—an upright shaft or column

**pilot**—the captain of a ship; also, the act of steering a boat or ship

**plunderers**—enemies who steal, loot, or take possessions by force

**prevail**—to prove more powerful than opposing forces

**Prince of Peace**—one of Isaiah's names for Jesus

**prophecy**—a divinely inspired prediction, instruction, or exhortation

**prophet**—one who speaks messages from God; one who foretells future events

**prototype**—something or someone that provides a type or model for something or someone else

**Purim**—Jewish holiday celebrating the deliverance of God's people at the time of Esther

**purity**—set apart from immoral behavior; chastity

## R

**reassure**—to remove doubts and fears

**rebellion**—to turn or act out against

**rebellious**—opposed to rules or authority

**redemption**—deliverance from sin; salvation

**reform**—to change and improve

**regeneration**—spiritual rebirth

**rejoice**—to be joyful

**relent**—to let up or back away from

**remembrance**—present manifestation of a past event or events

**remnant**—what is left when something else is removed

**repentance**—a change in direction; a gift of God that includes both sorrow for sin and a sincere desire to change

**reproof**—criticism for a fault (rebuke)

**reprove**—to scold or correct, usually gently or with kind intent

**respect**—to honor or hold in high regard

**restoration**—being brought back to a previous state, such as to a trust and belief in God

**rite**—a religious practice or ritual

## S

**Sabbath**—day of rest

**sacrament**—a sacred act instituted by God that joins a visible element (or elements) with His Word and conveys the forgiveness of sins

**sacrifice**—to give up something of value for a cause

**Sadducees**—the highest Jewish leaders of their time

**salvation**—deliverance from sin and its effects

**Samaritan**—member of a group commonly looked down on by Jewish people

**Sanhedrin**—Jewish religious leaders led by the high priest; composed of rich, upper-class men

**scheming**—attempts to direct the course of events

**Sheol**—realm of the dead; place where God's judgment overtakes evildoers; a grave

**signs/symbols**—shapes or actions that represent people or concepts

**sin**—transgressions; iniquities; wrongs; evil; corruption

**sinful nature**—innate inclination to disobey God

**slander**—a malicious, false, and defamatory statement

**sorcery**—attempt to use power received from evil spirits or spiritual forces

**spoil**—items of value captured or otherwise taken from an enemy

**sponsor**—one who assumes responsibility for a person or cause

**squandered**—spent extravagantly or foolishly

**steal**—to take the property of another wrongfully

**stiff-necked**—stubborn; unwilling to listen

**summon**—to call someone to take a specific action

**supplication**—request made of God or another

## T

**tabernacle**—the tent church built by Israelites, following God's commands, while living in the wilderness

**temporal death**—occurs at death when the soul leaves a person's body

**tenacious**—persistent; tending to hold fast; cling

**testimony**—authorization given of something as a fact

**thanksgiving**—expressing of gratitude to the giver for good things received

**tongues**—languages; also refers to tonguelike shapes, as in tongues of fire

**transformed**—changed in character or condition

**tribulation**—griefs, troubles, or sorrows

**tribute**—payment by one ruler of a nation to another as a sign of subjugation or price for protection

**trust**—reliance or expressed confidence; to rely on or to place hope in

**type of Christ**—a biblical person or object having similarities to Christ and foreshadowing, foretelling, or pointing to the coming of Christ and His purpose

## U

**unconventional**—unusual; eccentric

## V

**vessel**—a container, such as a bottle, bowl, or cup, for holding something

**victory**—win

**vocation**—a calling from God setting a baptized person apart for His service; also, a job or profession

## W

**wisdom**—good judgment; the ability to apply what one knows in everyday life and to make choices that lead to positive outcomes; to act in obedience to God and to express godly attributes in one's life

**witness**—to give an account of what has been seen, heard, and touched

**worthy**—qualified or acceptable

**wrath**—anger

## Z

**Zion**—the hill in Jerusalem; another name for Jerusalem; also a synonym for God's reign and His people